PENGUIN
COMPASS

MYTHS TO LIVE BY

Joseph Campbell became interested in mythology during his childhood in New York, when he read books about American Indians
and frequently visited the American Museum of Natural History,
where he was fascinated by the museum's collection of totem poles.
He earned his B.A. and M.A. degrees at Columbia in 1925 and 1927
and went on to study medieval French and Sanskrit at the universi-
ties of Paris and Munich. After a period in California, where he encountered John Steinbeck and the biologist Ed Ricketts, he taught at
the Canterbury School, then, in 1934, joined the literature department at Sarah Lawrence College, a post he retained for many years.
During the 1940s and '50s, he helped Swami Nikhilananda to translate
the Upanishads and *The Gospel of Sri Ramakrishna*. The many books
by Professor Campbell include *The Hero with a Thousand Faces*, *The
Flight of the Wild Gander*, *The Masks of God*, and *The Mythic Image*.
He edited *The Portable Arabian Nights*, *The Portable Jung*, and other
works. He died in 1987.

Joseph Campbell

MYTHS

Foreword by Johnson E. Fairchild

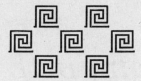

TO LIVE BY

PENGUIN COMPASS

COMPASS
Published by the Penguin Group
Penguin Putnam Inc.,
375 Hudson Street, New York, New York 10014, U.S.A.
Penguin Books Ltd, 80 Strand, London WC2R 0RL, England
Penguin Books Australia Ltd, 250 Camberwell Road, Camberwell,
Victoria 3124, Australia
Penguin Books Canada Ltd, 10 Alcorn Avenue, Toronto, Ontario, Canada M4V 3B2
Penguin Books India (P) Ltd, 11 Community Centre, Panchsheel Park,
New Delhi - 110 017, India
Penguin Books (N.Z.) Ltd, Cnr Rosedale and Airborne Roads, Albany,
Auckland, New Zealand
Penguin Books (South Africa) (Pty) Ltd, 24 Sturdee Avenue,
Rosebank, Johannesburg 2196, South Africa

Penguin Books Ltd, Registered Offices: Harmondsworth, Middlesex, England

First published in the United States of America by
The Viking Press, Inc. 1972
Published in Arkana 1993

24 23 22 21 20 19

ACKNOWLEDGEMENTS
The Clarendon Press: From *The Art of War* by Sun Tzu, translated by Samuel B. Griffith, 1963.
Harcourt Brace Jovanovich, Inc., and Faber and Faber Ltd.: From "Burnt Norton" by T. S. Eliot.
Harper & Row, Publishers, Inc., and Chatto and Windus Ltd.: From pp. 22–24 in *The Doors of Perception* by Aldous Huxley. Copyright 1954 by Aldous Huxley.Reprinted by permission of the publishers. The Macmillan Company, The Macmillan Company of Canada, and Mr. M. B. Yeats: From "The Second Coming" from *Collected Poems* by William Butler Yeats. Copyright 1924 by The Macmillan Company, renewed 1952 by Bertha Georgie Yeats.
Penguin Books Ltd: From *The Politics of Experience*, R. D. Laing. Copyright © R. D. Laing, 1967.
Random House, Inc.: From *Selected Poetry of Robinson Jeffers*. Copyright 1924and renewed 1952 by Robinson Jeffers.
University of Chicago Press: From "Fable of the Four Treasure-Seekers" from *Panchatantra*, translated by Arthur W. Ryder. Copyright 1925 by the University of Chicago.
I wish to thank Dr. Stanislav Grof for permission to adumbrate in my last chapter some of his findings, published in a work entitled *Agony and Ecstasy in Psychiatric Treatment* (Science and Behavior Books).

LIBRARY OF CONGRESS CATALOG CARD NUMBER:
78–181974
ISBN 0-670-50359-2 (hc.)
ISBN 0 14 019.461 4 (pbk.)

Printed in the United States of America

Foreword

The seminal mind of Peter Cooper (1791–1883)—the radical, free-thinking inventor, money-maker, and politician, the first real feminist of New York—conceived, among other great things, The Cooper Union for the Advancement of Science and Art. Cooper was disturbed by his own lack of education and by the knowledge that education was in his time conceived to be for the wealthy and for men alone. He changed both concepts, stimulated probably by the Chautauqua movement and the deeds of certain other philanthropists. His big and primary contribution was the idea of The Forum and adult education, which produced the first adult education college of this nation.

From the day of Abraham Lincoln's address to the present, more than five thousand speakers and artists have appeared on the Great Hall platform, and their ideas have reached an audience of millions: an average of over a thousand people a night, three nights a week. And today—thanks to Mr. Seymour Siegel's nudging and the help of Mr. Bernard Buck—the offerings are being broadcast by the New York City municipal radio station, WNYC, to hundreds of thousands more. This already is the

longest radio lecture series in history; and greatly to the credit
of The Cooper Union is the fact that the director programing the
lectures for The Forum—entrusted with the lonesome and awesome intellectual task of representing the past and looking into
the future—has never once been interrupted in his work, directed, or interfered with by The Cooper Union.

One of my precepts during my twenty-two years at The Cooper
Union has been that every one of the more than a thousand whom
I have invited to speak or to perform, and have presented on the
platform, should be my friend—as should also every member
both of the visible audience and of the millions of invisible radio
listeners. It would be difficult to select a single speaker; but Joseph
Campbell, the author of the present book, epitomizes the quality
of communication and intellectuality required for The Forum. He
never uses a note, speaks beautifully, and is brilliant; above all,
he transmits ideas that bridge the past and future and the worlds
of East and West. He has delivered at The Forum many great
lectures and lecture series, and they have always been a joy and
a pleasure. The present work, developed from those lectures,
synopsizes a lifetime of scholarship and the best principles of
The Cooper Union Forum. I am proud to be a part of this momentous book.

JOHNSON E. FAIRCHILD

New York City
October 15, 1971

Preface

From a series of some twenty-five talks on mythology delivered in The Great Hall of The Cooper Union Forum, New York City, between 1958 and 1971, I have here selected and arranged a baker's dozen—Number Four being put together of parts of two from the same year. The topics and titles I owe to the fertile mind of Dr. Johnson E. Fairchild, the Chairman of The Forum, whose wit, wisdom, and personal charm kept that blithesome institution running for the best part of a quarter of a century. My continuing pleasure in lecturing there derived in part, of course, from the old-fashioned, simple grandeur of the Great Hall itself and the knowledge that Abraham Lincoln once spoke from the very stage on which I stood (a certain secret sense of participation in the grand stream of the history of American eloquence); but also, more immediately, from the mood and character of the open-eyed, open-hearted audiences that Dr. Fairchild managed to attract to his numerous series of free lectures and discussions in that friendly place. The question hours following the lectures, when he would amble with a microphone up and down the aisles, letting anyone who raised a hand say what he would in comment, query, or prepared oration, contributed more to my appreciation of the sheer fun of talking to people of good will about the topics of my own concern in terms appropriate to their concerns than any other experience of my years. And I hope that even in the more formal cast of the written prose of this book, something of the freshness and ease of my delight in delivering these talks will have been retained.

I am happy indeed that Dr. Fairchild has very kindly agreed to introduce the volume, as he introduced from the platform every one of its talks; the last, March 1, 1971, delivered (by the way) on the last evening before retirement of his long career as both Chairman of The Forum and Director of the Department of Adult Education of The Cooper Union. I think of this collection as an appropriate token of my debt and gratitude to him for the encouragement, warm friendship, and always timely suggestions of themes and titles that taught me to bring my Buffalo-Gods, Quetzalcoatls, Buddhas, and Fairy Queens into mutually illuminating dialogue with those hundreds of members of his audiences—many of them faithful for years—who finally were the inspiration for these talks. My thanks go out to them all as well as to their chairman.

I would thank, also, the technicians and officers of radio station WNYC for the tape-recordings from which I have prepared these chapters; Miss Marcia Sherman for her faithful typing and retyping of the many drafts, not only of these, but also of the lectures not here included; and my wife, Jean Erdman, for the idea, in the first place, of turning these talks into the chapters of a book, and the criticism and suggestions, then, that brought the book into being.

J. C.

New York City
July 4, 1971

Contents

Myths to Live By

I

The Impact of Science on Myth

[1961]

I was sitting the other day at a lunch counter that I particularly enjoy, when a youngster about twelve years old, arriving with his school satchel, took the place at my left. Beside him came a younger little man, holding the hand of his mother, and those two took the next seats. All gave their orders, and, while waiting, the boy at my side said, turning his head slightly to the mother, "Jimmy wrote a paper today on the evolution of man, and Teacher said he was wrong, that Adam and Eve were our first parents."

My Lord! I thought. What a teacher!

The lady three seats away then said, "Well, Teacher was right. Our first parents *were* Adam and Eve."

What a mother for a twentieth-century child!

The youngster responded, "Yes, I know, but this was a *scientific* paper." And for that, I was ready to recommend him for a distinguished-service medal from the Smithsonian Institution.

The mother, however, came back with another. "Oh, those scientists!" she said angrily. "Those are only theories."

And he was up to that one too. "Yes, I know," was his cool

and calm reply; "but they have been factualized: they found the bones."

The milk and the sandwiches came, and that was that.

So let us now reflect for a moment on the sanctified cosmic image that has been destroyed by the facts and findings of irrepressible young truth-seekers of this kind.

At the height of the Middle Ages, say in the twelfth and thirteenth centuries, there were current two very different concepts of the earth. The more popular was of the earth as flat, like a dish surrounded by, and floating upon, a boundless cosmic sea, in which there were all kinds of monsters dangerous to man. This was an infinitely old notion, going back to the early Bronze Age. It appears in Sumerian cuneiform texts of about 2000 B.C. and is the image authorized in the Bible.

The more seriously considered medieval concept, however, was that of the ancient Greeks, according to whom the earth was not flat, but a solid stationary sphere in the center of a kind of Chinese box of seven transparent revolving spheres, in each of which there was a visible planet: the moon, Mercury, Venus, and the sun, Mars, Jupiter, and Saturn, the same seven after which our days of the week are named. The sounding tones of these seven, moreover, made a music, the "music of the spheres," to which the notes of our diatonic scale correspond. There was also a metal associated with each: silver, mercury, copper, gold, iron, tin, and lead, in that order. And the soul descending from heaven to be born on earth picked up, as it came down, the qualities of those metals; so that our souls and bodies are compounds of the very elements of the universe and sing, so to say, the same song.

Music and the arts, according to this early view, were to put us in mind of those harmonies, from which the general thoughts and affairs of this earth distract us. And in the Middle Ages the seven branches of learning were accordingly associated with those spheres: grammar, logic, and rhetoric (known as the *trivium*), arithmetic, music, geometry, and astronomy (the *quadrivium*). The crystalline spheres themselves, furthermore, were not, like glass, of inert matter, but living spiritual powers, presided over by angelic beings, or, as Plato had said, by sirens. And beyond all, there was that luminous celestial realm where God in majesty sat on his triune throne; so that when the soul, at death, returning to its maker, passed again through the seven spheres, it left off at each the accordant quality and arrived unclothed for the judgment. The emperor and the pope on earth governed, it was supposed, according to the laws and will of God, representing his power and authority at work in the ordained Christian commonalty. Thus in the total view of the medieval thinkers there was a perfect accord between the structure of the universe, the canons of the social order, and the good of the individual. Through unquestioning obedience, therefore, the Christian would put himself into accord not only with his society but also with both his own best inward interests and the outward order of nature. The Christian Empire was an earthly reflex of the order of the heavens, hieratically organized, with the vestments, thrones, and procedures of its stately courts inspired by celestial imagery, the bells of its cathedral spires and harmonies of its priestly choirs echoing in earthly tones the unearthly angelic hosts.

Dante in his *Divine Comedy* unfolded a vision of the universe that perfectly satisfied both the approved religious and the accepted scientific notions of his time. When Satan had been flung out of heaven for his pride and disobedience, he was supposed to have fallen like a flaming comet and, when he struck the earth, to have plowed right through to its center. The prodigious crater that he opened thereupon became the fiery pit of Hell; and the great mass of displaced earth pushed forth at the opposite pole became the Mountain of Purgatory, which is represented by Dante as lifting heavenward exactly at the South Pole. In his view, the entire southern hemisphere was of water, with this mighty mountain lifting out of it, on whose summit was the Earthly Paradise, from the center of which the four blessed rivers flowed of which Holy Scripture tells.

And now it appears that when Columbus set sail across that

"ocean blue" which many of his neighbors (and possibly also his sailors) believed was a terminal ocean surrounding a disklike earth, he himself had in mind an image more like that of Dante's world—of which we can read, in fact, in his journals. There we learn that in the course of his third voyage, when he reached for the first time the northern coast of South America, passing in his frail craft at great peril between Trinidad and the mainland, he remarked that the quantity of fresh water there mixing with the salt (pouring from the mouths of the Orinoco) was enormous. Knowing nothing of the continent beyond, but having in mind the medieval idea, he conjectured the fresh waters might be coming from one of the rivers of Paradise, pouring into the southern sea from the base of the great antipodal mountain. Moreover, when he then turned, sailing northward, and observed that his ships were faring more rapidly than when they had been sailing south, he took this to be evidence of their sailing now downhill, from the foot of the promontory of the mythic paradisial mountain.

I like to think of the year 1492 as marking the end—or at least the beginning of the end—of the authority of the old mythological systems by which the lives of men had been supported and inspired from time out of mind. Shortly after Columbus's epochal voyage, Magellan circumnavigated the globe. Shortly before, Vasco da Gama had sailed around Africa to India. The earth was beginning to be systematically explored, and the old, symbolic, mythological geographies discredited. In attempting to show that there was somewhere on earth a garden of Paradise, Saint Thomas Aquinas had declared, writing only two centuries and a half before Columbus sailed: "The situation of Paradise is shut off from the habitable world by mountains or seas, or by some torrid region, which cannot be crossed; and so people who have written about topography make no mention of it." Fifty years after the first voyage, Copernicus published his paper on the heliocentric universe (1543); and some sixty-odd years after that, Galileo's little telescope brought tangible confirmation to this Copernican view. In the year 1616 Galileo was condemned by the Office of the Inquisition—like the boy beside me at the lunch counter, by his mother—for holding and teaching a doctrine contrary to Holy Scripture. And today, of course, we have those very much larger telescopes on the summits, for example, of Mount Wilson in California, Mount Palomar in the same state, Kitt Peak in Arizona, and Haleakala, Hawaii; so that not only is the sun now well established at the center of our planetary system, but we know it to be but one of some two hundred billion suns in a galaxy of such blazing spheres: a galaxy shaped like a prodigious lens, many hundreds of quintillion miles in diameter. And not only that! but our telescopes now are disclosing to us, among those shining suns, certain other points of light that are themselves not suns but whole galaxies, each as large and great and inconceivable as our own— of which already many thousands upon thousands have been seen. So that, actually, the occasion for an experience of awe before the wonder of the universe that is being developed for us by our scientists surely is a far more marvelous, mind-blowing revelation than anything the prescientific world could ever have imagined. The little toy-room picture of the Bible is, in comparison, for children—or, in fact, not even for them any more, to judge from the words of that young scholar beside me at the counter, who, with his "Yes, I know, but this was a scientific paper," had already found a way to rescue his learning from the crumbling medieval architecture of his mother's Church.

For not only have all the old mythic notions of the nature of the cosmos gone to pieces, but also all those of the origins and history of mankind. Already in Shakespeare's day, when Sir Walter Raleigh arrived in America and saw here all the new animals unknown on the other side, he understood as a master mariner that it would have been absolutely impossible for Noah to have packed examples of every species on earth into any ark, no matter how large. The Bible legend of the Flood was untrue: a theory that could not be "factualized." And we today (to make matters worse) are dating the earliest appearances of manlike creatures on this earth over a million years earlier than the Biblical date for

God's creation of the world. The great paleolithic caves of Europe
are from circa 30,000 B.C.; the beginnings of agriculture, 10,000
B.C. or so, and the first substantial towns about 7000. Yet Cain,
the eldest son of Adam, the first man, is declared in Genesis 4:2
and 4:17 to have been "a tiller of the ground" and the builder of a
city known as Enoch in the land of Nod, east of Eden. The Biblical "theory" has again been proved false, and "they have found
the bones!"

They have found also the buildings—and these do not corrobo-
rate Scripture, either. For example, the period of Egyptian history
supposed to have been of the Exodus—of Ramses II (1301–1234
B.C.), or perhaps Merneptah (1234–1220) or Seti II (1220–
1200)—is richly represented in architectural and hieroglyphic
remains, yet there is no notice anywhere of anything like those famous Biblical plagues, no record anywhere of anything even comparable. Moreover, as other records tell, Bedouin Hebrews, the
"Habiru," were already invading Canaan during the reign of Ikh-
naton (1377–1358), a century earlier than the Ramses date.

The long and the short of it is simply that the Hebrew texts
from which all these popular Jewish legends of Creation, Exodus,
Forty Years in the Desert, and Conquest of Canaan are derived
were not composed by "God" or even by anyone named Moses,
but are of various dates and authors, all much later than was formerly supposed. The first five books of the Old Testament (Torah)
were assembled only after the period of Ezra (fourth century B.C.),
and the documents of which it was fashioned date all the way
from the ninth century B.C. (the so-called J and E texts) to the second or so (the P, or "priestly" writings). One notices, for example,
that there are two accounts of the Flood. From the first we learn
that Noah brought "two living things of every sort" into the Ark
(Genesis 6:19–20; P text, post-Ezra), and from the second, "seven
pairs of all clean animals, the male and his mate, and a pair of the
animals that are not clean" (Genesis 7:2–3; J text, ca. 800 B.C. ±
50). We also find two stories of Creation, the earlier in Genesis 2,
the later in Genesis 1. In 2, a garden has been planted and a man

created to tend it; next the animals are created, and finally (as in dream) Mother Eve is drawn from Adam's rib. In Genesis 1, on the other hand, God, alone with the cosmic waters, says, "Let there be light," etc., and, stage by stage, the universe comes into being: first, light; and the sun, three days later; then, vegetables, animals, and finally mankind, male and female together. Genesis 1 is of about the fourth century B.C. (the period of Aristotle), and 2, of the ninth or eighth (Hesiod's time).

Comparative cultural studies have now demonstrated beyond question that similar mythic tales are to be found in every quarter of this earth. When Cortes and his Catholic Spaniards arrived in Aztec Mexico, they immediately recognized in the local religion so many parallels to their own True Faith that they were hard put to explain the fact. There were towering pyramidal temples, representing, stage by stage, like Dante's Mountain of Purgatory, degrees of elevation of the spirit. There were thirteen heavens, each with its appropriate gods or angels; nine hells, of suffering souls. There was a High God above all, who was beyond all human thought and imaging. There was even an incarnate Savior, associated with a serpent, born of a virgin, who had died and was resurrected, one of whose symbols was a cross. The padres, to explain all this, invented two myths of their own. The first was that Saint Thomas, the Apostle to the Indies, had probably reached America and here preached the Gospel; but, these shores being so far removed from the influence of Rome, the doctrine had deteriorated, so that what they were seeing around them was simply a hideously degenerate form of their own revelation. And the second explanation, then, was that the devil was here deliberately throwing up parodies of the Christian faith, to frustrate the mission.

Modern scholarship, systematically comparing the myths and rites of mankind, has found just about everywhere legends of virgins giving birth to heroes who die and are resurrected. India is chock-full of such tales, and its towering temples, very like the Aztec ones, represent again our many-storied cosmic mountain, bearing Paradise on its summit and with horrible hells beneath. The Buddhists and the Jains have similar ideas. And, looking backward into the pre-Christian past, we discover in Egypt the mythology of the slain and resurrected Osiris; in Mesopotamia, Tammuz; in Syria, Adonis; and in Greece, Dionysos: all of which furnished models to the early Christians for their representations of Christ.

Now the peoples of all the great civilizations everywhere have been prone to interpret their own symbolic figures literally; and so to regard themselves as favored in a special way, in direct contact with the Absolute. Even the polytheistic Greeks and Romans, Hindus and Chinese, all of whom were able to view the gods and customs of others sympathetically, thought of their own as supreme or, at the very least, superior; and among the monotheistic Jews, Christians, and Mohammedans, of course, the gods of others are regarded as no gods at all, but devils, and their worshipers as godless. Mecca, Rome, Jerusalem, and (less emphatically) Benares and Peking have been for centuries, therefore, each in its own way, the navel of the universe, connected directly—as by a hot line—with the Kingdom of Light or of God.

However, today such claims can no longer be taken seriously by anyone with even a kindergarten education. And in this there is serious danger. For not only has it always been the way of multitudes to interpret their own symbols literally, but such literally read symbolic forms have always been—and still are, in fact—the supports of their civilizations, the supports of their moral orders, their cohesion, vitality, and creative powers. With the loss of them there follows uncertainty, and with uncertainty, disequilibrium, since life, as both Nietzsche and Ibsen knew, requires life-supporting illusions; and where these have been dispelled, there is nothing secure to hold on to, no moral law, nothing firm. We have seen what has happened, for example, to primitive communities unsettled by the white man's civilization. With their old taboos discredited, they immediately go to pieces, disintegrate, and become resorts of vice and disease.

Today the same thing is happening to us. With our old mythologically founded taboos unsettled by our own modern sciences, there is everywhere in the civilized world a rapidly rising incidence of vice and crime, mental disorders, suicides and dope addictions, shattered homes, impudent children, violence, murder, and despair. These are facts; I am not inventing them. They give point to the cries of the preachers for repentance, conversion, and return to the old religion. And they challenge, too, the modern educator with respect to his own faith and ultimate loyalty. Is the conscientious teacher— concerned for the moral character as well as for the book-learning of his students—to be loyal first to the supporting myths of our civilization or to the "factualized" truths of his science? Are the two, on every level, at odds? Or is there not some point of wisdom beyond the conflicts of illusion and truth by which lives can be put back together again?

That is a prime question, I would say, of this hour in the bringing up of children. That is the problem, indeed, that was sitting beside me that day at the lunch counter. In that case, both teacher and parent were on the side of an already outdated illusion; and generally—or so it looks to me—most guardians of society have a tendency in that direction, asserting their authority not for, but against the search for disturbing truths. Such a trend has even turned up recently among social scientists and anthropologists with regard to discussions of race. And one can readily understand, even share in some measure, their anxiety, since lies are what the world lives on, and those who can face the challenge of a truth and build their lives to accord are finally not many, but the very few.

It is my considered belief that the best answer to this critical problem will come from the findings of psychology, and specifically those findings having to do with the source and nature of myth. For since it has always been on myths that the moral orders of societies have been founded, the myths canonized as religion, and since the impact of science on myths results—apparently inevitably—in moral disequilibration, we must now ask whether it is not possible to arrive *scientifically* at such an understanding of the life-supporting nature of myths that, in criticizing their archaic features, we do not misrepresent and disqualify their necessity— throwing out, so to say, the baby (whole generations of babies) with the bath.

Traditionally, as I have already said, in the orthodoxies of popular faiths mythic beings and events are generally regarded and taught as facts; and this particularly in the Jewish and Christian spheres. There *was* an Exodus from Egypt; there *was* a Resurrection of Christ. Historically, however, such facts are now in question; hence, the moral orders, too, that they support.

When these stories are interpreted, though, not as reports of historic fact, but as merely imagined episodes projected onto history, and when they are recognized, then, as analogous to like projections produced elsewhere, in China, India, and Yucatán, the import becomes obvious; namely, that although false and to be rejected as accounts of physical history, such universally cherished figures of the mythic imagination must represent facts of the mind: "facts of the mind made manifest in a fiction of matter," as my friend the late Maya Deren once phrased the mystery. And whereas it must, of course, be the task of the historian, archaeologist, and prehistorian to show that the myths are as facts untrue —that there is no one Chosen People of God in this multiracial world, no Found Truth to which we all must bow, no One and Only True Church—it will be more and more, and with increasing urgency, the task of the psychologist and comparative mythologist not only to identify, analyze, and interpret the symbolized "facts of the mind," but also to evolve techniques for retaining these in health and, as the old traditions of the fading past dissolve, assist mankind to a knowledge and appreciation of our own inward, as well as the world's outward, orders of fact.

There has been among psychologists a considerable change of attitude in this regard during the past three-quarters of a century or so. When reading the great and justly celebrated *Golden Bough* of Sir James G. Frazer, the first edition of which appeared in

1890, we are engaged with a typically nineteenth-century author, whose belief it was that the superstitions of mythology would be finally refuted by science and left forever behind. He saw the basis of myth in magic, and of magic in psychology. His psychology, however, being of an essentially rational kind, insufficiently attentive to the more deeply based, irrational impulsions of our nature, he assumed that when a custom or belief was shown to be unreasonable, it would presently disappear. And how wrong he was can be shown simply by pointing to any professor of philosophy at play in a bowling alley: watch him twist and turn after the ball has left his hand, to bring it over to the standing pins. Frazer's explanation of magic was that because things are associated in the mind they are believed to be associated in fact. Shake a rattle that sounds like falling rain, and rain will presently fall. Celebrate a ritual of sexual intercourse, and the fertility of nature will be furthered. An image in the likeness of an enemy, and given the enemy's name, can be worked upon, stuck with pins, etc., and the enemy will die. Or a piece of his clothing, lock of hair, fingernail paring, or other element once in contact with his person can be treated with a like result. Frazer's first law of magic, then, is that "like produces like," an effect resembles its cause; and his second, that "things which once were in contact with each other continue to act on each other at a distance after the physical contact has been severed." Frazer thought of both magic and religion as addressed finally and essentially to the control of external nature; magic mechanically, by imitative acts, and religion by prayer and sacrifice addressed to the personified powers supposed to control natural forces. He seems to have had no sense at all of their relevance and importance to the inward life, and so was confident that, with the progress and development of science and technology, both magic and religion would ultimately fade away, the ends that they had been thought to serve being better and more surely served by science.

Simultaneously with these volumes of Frazer, however, there was appearing in Paris a no less important series of publications

by the distinguished neurologist Jean Martin Charcot, treating of
hysteria, aphasia, hypnotic states, and the like; demonstrating also
the relevance of these findings to iconography and to art. Sigmund
Freud spent a year with this master in 1885 and during the first
quarter of the present century carried the study of hysteria and of
dreams and myths to new depths. Myths, according to Freud's
view, are of the psychological order of dream. Myths, so to say,
are public dreams; dreams are private myths. Both, in his opinion,
are symptomatic of repressions of infantile incest wishes, the only
essential difference between a religion and neurosis being that the
former is the more public. The person with a neurosis feels
ashamed, alone and isolated in his illness, whereas the gods are
general projections onto a universal screen. They are equally man-
ifestations of unconscious, compulsive fears and delusions. Moreover, all the arts, and particularly religious arts, are, in Freud's
view, similarly pathological; likewise, all philosophies. Civilization itself, in fact, is a pathological surrogate for unconscious infantile disappointments. And thus Freud, like Frazer, judged the
worlds of myth, magic, and religion negatively, as errors to be refuted, surpassed, and supplanted finally by science.

An altogether different approach is represented by Carl G.
Jung, in whose view the imageries of mythology and religion serve
positive, life-furthering ends. According to his way of thinking, *all*
the organs of our bodies—not only those of sex and aggression—
have their purposes and motives, some being subject to conscious
control, others, however, not. Our outward-oriented consciousness,
addressed to the demands of the day, may lose touch with these
inward forces; and the myths, states Jung, when correctly read, are
the means to bring us back in touch. They are telling us in picture
language of powers of the psyche to be recognized and integrated
in our lives, powers that have been common to the human spirit
forever, and which represent that wisdom of the species by which
man has weathered the millenniums. Thus they have not been, and
can never be, displaced by the findings of science, which relate
rather to the outside world than to the depths that we enter in

sleep. Through a dialogue conducted with these inward forces through our dreams and through a study of myths, we can learn to know and come to terms with the greater horizon of our own deeper and wiser, inward self. And analogously, the society that cherishes and keeps its myths alive will be nourished from the soundest, richest strata of the human spirit.

However, there is a danger here as well; namely, of being drawn by one's dreams and inherited myths away from the world of modern consciousness, fixed in patterns of archaic feeling and thought inappropriate to contemporary life. What is required, states Jung therefore, is a dialogue, not a fixture at either pole; a dialogue by way of symbolic forms put forth from the unconscious mind and recognized by the conscious in continuous interaction.

And so what then happens to the children of a society that has refused to allow any such interplay to develop, but, clinging to its inherited dream as to a fixture of absolute truth, rejects the novelties of consciousness, of reason, science, and new facts? There is a well-known history that may serve as sufficient warning.

As every schoolboy knows, the beginnings of what we think of as science are to be attributed to the Greeks, and much of the knowledge that they assembled was carried and communicated to Asia, across Persia into India and onward even to China. But every one of those Oriental worlds was already committed to its own style of mythological thought, and the objective, realistic, inquisitive, and experimental attitudes and methods of the Greeks were let go. Compare the science of the Bible, for example—an Oriental scripture, assembled largely following the Maccabean rejection of Greek influence—with that, say, of Aristotle; not to mention Aristarchus (fl. 275 B.C.), for whom the earth was already a revolving sphere in orbit around the sun. Eratosthenes (fl. 250 B.C.) had already correctly calculated the circumference of the earth as 250,000 stadia (24,662 miles: correct equatorial figure, 24,902). Hipparchus (fl. 240 B.C.) had reckoned within a few miles both the moon's diameter and its mean distance from the earth. And now just try to imagine how much of blood, sweat, and real tears—people burned at the stake for heresy, and all that— would have been saved, if, instead of closing all the Greek pagan schools, A.D. 529, Justinian had encouraged them! In their place, we and our civilization have had Genesis 1 and 2 and a delay of well over a thousand years in the maturation not of science only but of our own and the world's civilization.

One of the most interesting histories of what comes of rejecting science we may see in Islam, which in the beginning received, accepted, and even developed the classical legacy. For some five or six rich centuries there is an impressive Islamic record of scientific thought, experiment, and research, particularly in medicine. But then, alas! the authority of the general community, the Sunna, the consensus—which Mohammed the Prophet had declared would always be right—cracked down. The Word of God in the Koran was the only source and vehicle of truth. Scientific thought led to "loss of belief in the origin of the world and in the Creator." And so it was that, just when the light of Greek learning was beginning to be carried from Islam to Europe—from circa 1100 onward—Islamic science and medicine came to a standstill and went dead; and with that, Islam itself went dead. The torch not only of science, but of history as well, passed on to the Christian West. And we can thereafter follow the marvelous development in detail, from the early twelfth century onward, through a history of bold and brilliant minds, unmatched for their discoveries in the whole long history of human life. Nor can the magnitude of our debt to these few minds be fully appreciated by anyone who has never set foot in any of the lands that lie beyond the bounds of this European spell. In those so-called "developing nations" all social transformation is the result today, as it has been for centuries, not of continuing processes, but of invasions and their aftermath. Every little group is fixed in its own long-established, petrified mythology, changes having occurred only as a consequence of collisions; such as when the warriors of Islam broke into India and for a time there were inevitable exchanges of ideas; or when the British arrived and another upsetting era dawned of startling, unanticipated innovations. In our modern Western world, on the other hand, as a result of the continuing open-hearted and open-minded quest of a few brave men for the bounds of boundless truth, there has been a self-consistent continuity of productive growth, in the nature almost of an organic flowering.

But now, finally, what would the meaning be of the word "truth" to a modern scientist? Surely not the meaning it would have for a mystic! For the really great and essential fact about the scientific revelation—the most wonderful and most challenging fact—is that science does not and cannot pretend to be "true" in any absolute sense. It does not and cannot pretend to be final. It is a tentative organization of mere "working hypotheses" ("Oh, those scientists!" "Yes, I know, but they found the bones") that for the present appear to take into account all the relevant facts now known.

And is there no implied intention, then, to rest satisfied with some final body or sufficient number of facts?

No indeed! There is to be only a continuing search for more— as of a mind eager to grow. And that growth, as long as it lasts, will be the measure of the life of modern Western man, and of the world with all its promise that he has brought and is still bringing into being: which is to say, a world of change, new thoughts, new things, new magnitudes, and continuing transformation, not of petrifaction, rigidity, and some canonized found "truth."

And so, my friends, we don't know a thing, and not even our science can tell us sooth; for it is no more than, so to say, an eagerness for truths, no matter where their allure may lead. And so it seems to me that here again we have a still greater, more alive, revelation than anything our old religions ever gave to us or even so much as suggested. The old texts comfort us with horizons. They tell us that a loving, kind, and just father is out there, looking down upon us, ready to receive us, and ever with our own dear lives on his mind. According to our sciences, on the other hand, nobody knows *what* is out there, or if there is any "out there" at all. All that can be said is that there appears to be a prodigious display of phenomena, which our senses and their instruments translate to our minds according to the nature of our minds. And there is a display of a quite different kind of imagery from within, which we experience best at night, in sleep, but which may also break into our daylight lives and even destroy us with madness. What the background of these forms, external and internal, may be, we can only surmise and possibly move toward through hypotheses. What they are, or where, or why (to ask all the usual questions) is an absolute mystery—the only absolute known, because absolutely unknown; and this we must all now have the magnitude to concede.

There is no "Thou shalt!" any more. There is nothing one *has* to believe, and there is nothing one *has* to do. On the other hand, one can of course, if one prefers, still choose to play at the old Middle Ages game, or some Oriental game, or even some sort of primitive game. We are living in a difficult time, and whatever defends us from the madhouse can be applauded as good enough— for those without nerve.

When I was in India in the winter of 1954, in conversation with an Indian gentleman of just about my own age, he asked with a certain air of distance, after we had exchanged formalities, "What are you Western scholars now saying about the dating of the Vedas?"

The Vedas, you must know, are the counterparts for the Hindu of the Torah for the Jew. They are his scriptures of the most ancient date and therefore of the highest revelation.

"Well," I answered, "the dating of the Vedas has lately been reduced and is being assigned, I believe, to something like, say, 1500 to 1000 B.C. As you probably know," I added, "there have been found in India itself the remains of an earlier civilization than the Vedic."

"Yes," said the Indian gentleman, not testily but firmly, with an air of untroubled assurance, "I know; but as an orthodox Hindu I cannot believe that there is anything in the universe earlier than the Vedas." And he meant that.

"Okay," said I. "Then why did you ask?"

To give old India, however, its due, let me conclude with the fragment of a Hindu myth that to me seems to have captured in a particularly apt image the whole sense of such a moment as we today are all facing at this critical juncture of our general human history. It tells of a time at the very start of the history of the universe when the gods and their chief enemies, the anti-gods, were engaged in one of their eternal wars. They decided this time to conclude a truce and in cooperation to churn the Milky Ocean— the Universal Sea—for its butter of immortality. They took for their churning-spindle the Cosmic Mountain (the Vedic counter-part of Dante's Mountain of Purgatory), and for a twirling-cord they wrapped the Cosmic Serpent around it. Then, with the gods all pulling at the head end and the anti-gods at the tail, they caused that Cosmic Mountain to whirl. And they had been churn-ing thus for a thousand years when a great black cloud of abso-lutely poisonous smoke came up out of the waters, and the churn-ing had to stop. They had broken through to an unprecedented source of power, and what they were experiencing first were its negative, lethal effects. If the work were to continue, some one of them was going to have to swallow and absorb that poisonous cloud, and, as all knew, there was but one who would be capable of such an act; namely, the archetypal god of yoga, Shiva, a fright-ening, daemonic figure. He just took that entire poison cloud into his begging bowl and at one gulp drank it down, holding it by yoga at the level of his throat, where it turned the whole throat blue; and he has been known as Blue Throat, Nilakantha, ever since. Then, when that wonderful deed had been accomplished, all the other gods and the anti-gods returned to their common labor. And they churned and they churned and they went right on tire-lessly churning, until lo! a number of wonderful benefits began coming up out of the Cosmic Sea: the moon, the sun, an elephant with eight trunks came up, a glorious steed, certain medicines, and yes, at last! a great radiant vessel filled with the ambrosial butter.

This old Indian myth I offer as a parable for our world today, as an exhortation to press on with the work, beyond fear.

II

The Emergence of Mankind

[1966]

🔲 Mythology is apparently coeval with mankind. As far back, that is to say, as we have been able to follow the broken, scattered, earliest evidences of the emergence of our species, signs have been found which indicate that mythological aims and concerns were already shaping the arts and world of Homo sapiens. Such evidences tell us something, furthermore, of the unity of our species; for the fundamental themes of mythological thought have remained constant and universal, not only throughout history, but also over the whole extent of mankind's occupation of the earth. Normally, when treating of the evolution of man, scientists concentrate on the physical traits, the anatomical features that distinguish us: erect posture, the great brain, the number and arrangement of our teeth, and the active apposable thumb, which enables our hands to manipulate tools. Professor L. S. B. Leakey, to whose discoveries in East Africa we owe most of what we now know about the earliest hominids, has named the most human of his earliest finds—from ca. 1,800,000 B.C.— Homo habilis, Able Man; and such a designation is undoubtedly appropriate, since the little fellow was perhaps the earliest fash-

ioner of crude tools. When we consider, however, instead of the
physical, the psychological character of our species, the most evident distinguishing sign is man's organization of his life according
primarily to mythic, and only secondarily economic, aims and
laws. Food and drink, reproduction and nest-building, it is true,
play formidable roles in the lives no less of men than of chimpan-
zees. But what of the economics of the Pyramids, the cathedrals of
the Middle Ages, Hindus starving to death with edible cattle
strolling all around them, or the history of Israel, from the time of
Saul to right now? If a *differentiating* feature is to be named, separating human from animal psychology, it is surely this of the sub-
ordination in the human sphere of even economics to mythology.
And if one should ask why or how any such unsubstantial impul-
sion ever should have become dominant in the ordering of physical life, the answer is that in this wonderful human brain of ours
there has dawned a realization unknown to the other primates. It
is that of the individual, conscious of himself as such, and aware
that he, and all that he cares for, will one day die.

This recognition of mortality and the requirement to transcend
it is the first great impulse to mythology. And along with this
there runs another realization; namely, that the social group into
which the individual has been born, which nourishes and protects
him and which, for the greater part of his life, he must himself
help to nourish and protect, was flourishing long before his own
birth and will remain when he is gone. That is to say, not only
does the individual member of our species, conscious of himself as
such, face death, but he confronts also the necessity to adapt himself to whatever order of life may happen to be that of the community into which he has been born, this being an order of life su-
perordinated to his own, a superorganism into which he must
allow himself to be absorbed, and through participation in which
he will come to know the life that transcends death. In every one
of the mythological systems that in the long course of history and
prehistory have been propagated in the various zones and quarters
of this earth, these two fundamental realizations—of the inevita-

bility of individual death and the endurance of the social order—
have been combined symbolically and constitute the nuclear structuring force of the rites and, thereby, the society.

The youngster growing up in a primitive hunting community,
however, will have to adapt himself to an altogether different social order from that, say, of a youth in such an industrial nation as
our own; and between these two extremes of enduring social life
there have been other types, innumerable. Consequently, in the
dual nuclear unit just named, there is to be recognized, not only a
factor representative of the *unity* of our species, but also one of
differentiation. Not only does all mankind face death, but the various peoples of the world face death in greatly differing ways. A
cross-cultural survey of the mythologies of mankind, consequently,
will have to note not only universals but also the transformations
of those common themes in the ranges of their occurrence.

And there is a third factor, furthermore, which has everywhere
exerted a pervasive influence on the shaping of mythologies, a
third range and context of specifically human experience, of which
the developing individual becomes inevitably aware as his powers
of thought and observation mature, the spectacle, namely, of the
universe, the natural world in which he finds himself, and the
enigma of its relation to his own existence: its magnitude, its
changing forms, and yet, through these, an appearance of regularity. Mankind's understanding of the universe has greatly altered in
the course of the millenniums—particularly most recently, as our
instruments of research have improved. But there were great
changes also in the past: for example, in the time of the rise of the
early Sumerian city-states, with their priestly observers of the
heavenly courses; or in that of the Alexandrian physicists and astronomers, with their concept of an earthly globe enclosed within
seven revolving celestial spheres.

We shall therefore have to recognize in our analysis of the
myths, legends, and associated rites of our general species, besides
certain constant themes and principles, certain variables also, according not only to the great variety of social systems that have

flourished on this planet, but also to the modes of nature-knowledge that in the course of the millenniums have shaped and reshaped man's image of his world.

Still further: It is apparent in the light of the findings of archaeology that during the first and primitive stages of the history of our species there was a general centrifugal movement of peoples into distance, to all sides, with the various populations becoming increasingly separated, each developing its own applications and associated interpretations of the shared universal motifs; whereas, since we are all now being brought together again in this mighty present period of world transport and communication, those differences are fading. The old differences separating one system from another now are becoming less and less important, less and less easy to define. And what, on the contrary, is becoming more and more important is that we should learn to see *through* all the differences to the common themes that have been there all the while, that came into being with the first emergence of ancestral man from the animal levels of existence, and are with us still.

One consideration more, before proceeding to our next concern: that of the fact that in our present day—at least in the leading modern centers of cultural creativity—people have begun to take the existence of their supporting social orders for granted, and instead of aiming to defend and maintain the integrity of the community have begun to place at the center of concern the development and protection of the individual—the individual, moreover, not as an organ of the state but as an end and entity in himself. This marks an extremely important, unprecedented shift of ground, the implications of which for future developments in mythology we shall have presently to consider.

Let us first consider, however, some of those outstanding differences in traditional points of view which in the past, in various parts of the world, have given rise to contrasting interpretations of shared myths.

2

In relation to the first books and chapters of the Bible, it used to be the custom of both Jews and Christians to take the narratives literally, as though they were dependable accounts of the origin of the universe and of actual prehistoric events. It was supposed and taught that there had been, quite concretely, a creation of the world in seven days by a god known only to the Jews; that somewhere on this broad new earth there had been a Garden of Eden containing a serpent that could talk; that the first woman, Eve, was formed from the first man's rib, and that the wicked serpent told her of the marvelous properties of the fruits of a certain tree of which God had forbidden the couple to eat; and that, as a consequence of their having eaten of that fruit, there followed a "Fall" of all mankind, death came into the world, and the couple was driven forth from the garden. For there was in the center of that garden a second tree, the fruit of which would have given them eternal life; and their creator, fearing lest they should now take and eat of that too, and so become as knowing and immortal as himself, cursed them, and having driven them out, placed at his garden gate "cherubim and a flaming sword which turned every way to guard the way to the tree of life."

It seems impossible today, but people actually believed all that until as recently as half a century or so ago: clergymen, philosophers, government officers, and all. Today we know—and know right well—that there was never anything of the kind: no Garden of Eden anywhere on this earth, no time when the serpent could talk, no prehistoric "Fall," no exclusion from the garden, no universal Flood, no Noah's Ark. The entire history on which our leading Occidental religions have been founded is an anthology of fictions. But these are fictions of a type that have had—curiously enough—a universal vogue as the founding legends of other religions, too. Their counterparts have turned up everywhere—and yet, there was never such a garden, serpent, tree, or deluge.

How account for such anomalies? Who invents these impossible tales? Where do their images come from? And why—though obviously absurd—are they everywhere so reverently believed?

What I would suggest is that by comparing a number from different parts of the world and differing traditions, one might arrive at an understanding of their force, their source and possible sense. For they are not historical. That much is clear. They speak, therefore, not of outside events but of themes of the imagination. And since they exhibit features that are actually universal, they must in some way represent features of our general racial imagination, permanent features of the human spirit—or, as we say today, of the psyche. They are telling us, therefore, of matters fundamental to ourselves, enduring essential principles about which it would be good for us to know; about which, in fact, it will be necessary for us to know if our conscious minds are to be kept in touch with our own most secret, motivating depths. In short, these holy tales and their images are messages to the conscious mind from quarters of the spirit unknown to normal daylight consciousness, and if read as referring to events in the field of space and time—whether of the future, present, or past—they will have been misread and their force deflected, some secondary thing outside then taking to itself the reference of the symbol, some sanctified stick, stone, or animal, person, event, city, or social group.

Let us regard a little more closely the Biblical image of the garden.

Its name, Eden, signifies in Hebrew "delight, a place of delight," and our own English word, Paradise, which is from the Persian, *pairi-*, "around," *daeza,* "a wall," means properly "a walled enclosure." Apparently, then, Eden is a walled garden of delight, and in its center stands the great tree; or rather, in its center stand two trees, the one of the knowledge of good and evil, the other of immortal life. Four rivers flow, furthermore, from within it as from an inexhaustible source, to refresh the world in the four directions. And when our first parents, having eaten the fruit, were driven forth, two cherubim were stationed (as we have heard) at its eastern gate, to guard the way of return.

Taken as referring not to any geographical scene, but to a land-scape of the soul, that Garden of Eden would have to be within us. Yet our conscious minds are unable to enter it and enjoy there the taste of eternal life, since we have already tasted of the knowl-edge of good and evil. That, in fact, must then be the knowledge that has thrown us out of the garden, pitched us away from our own center, so that we now judge things in those terms and expe-rience only good and evil instead of eternal life—which, since the enclosed garden is within us, must already be ours, even though unknown to our conscious personalities. That would seem to be the meaning of the myth when read, not as prehistory, but as re-ferring to man's inward spiritual state.

Let us turn now from this Bible legend, by which the West has been enchanted, to the Indian, of the Buddha, which has enspelled the entire East; for there too is the mythic image of a tree of im-mortal life defended by two terrifying guards. That tree is the one beneath which Siddhartha was sitting, facing east, when he wak-ened to the light of his own immortality in truth and was known thereafter as the Buddha, the Wakened One. There is a serpent in that legend also, but instead of being known as evil, it is thought of as symbolic of the immortal inhabiting energy of all life on earth. For the serpent shedding its skin, to be, as it were, born again, is likened in the Orient to the reincarnating spirit that as-sumes and throws off bodies as a man puts on and puts off clothes. There is in Indian mythology a great cobra imagined as balancing the tablelike earth on its head: its head being, of course, at the pivotal point, exactly beneath the world tree. And according to the Buddha legend, when the Blessed One, having attained om-niscience, continued to sit absorbed for a number of days in abso-lute meditation, he became endangered by a great storm that arose in the world around him, and this prodigious serpent, coming up from below, wrapped itself protectively around the Buddha, cover-ing his head with its cobra hood.

Thus, whereas in one of these two legends of the tree the service of the serpent is rejected and the animal itself cursed, in the other it is accepted. In both, the serpent is in some way associated with the tree and has apparently enjoyed its fruits, since it can slough its skin and live again; but in the Bible legend our first parents are expelled from the garden of that tree, whereas in the Buddhist tradition we are all invited in. The tree beneath which the Buddha sat corresponds, thus, to the second of the Garden of Eden, which, as already said, is to be thought of not as geographically situated but as a garden of the soul. And so, what then keeps us from returning to it and sitting like the Buddha beneath it? Who or what are those two cherubim? Do the Buddhists know of any such pair?

One of the most important Buddhist centers in the world today is the holy city of Nara, Japan, where there is a great temple sheltering a prodigious bronze image, 53½ feet high, of the Buddha seated cross-legged on a great lotus, holding his right hand lifted in the "fear not" posture; and as one approaches the precincts of this temple, one passes through a gate that is guarded, left and right, by two gigantic, marvelously threatening military figures flourishing swords. These are the Buddhist counterparts of the cherubim stationed by Yahweh at the garden gate. However, here we are not to be intimidated and held off. The fear of death and desire for life that these threatening guardsmen arouse in us are to be left behind as we pass between.

In the Buddhist view, that is to say, what is keeping us out of the garden is not the jealousy or wrath of any god, but our own instinctive attachment to what we take to be our lives. Our senses, outward-directed to the world of space and time, have attached us to that world and to our mortal bodies within it. We are loath to give up what we take to be the goods and pleasures of this physical life, and this attachment is the great fact, the great circumstance or barrier, that is keeping us out of the garden. This, and this alone, is preventing us from recognizing within ourselves that immortal and universal consciousness of which our physical senses, outward-turned, are but the agents.

According to this teaching, no actual cherub with a flaming sword is required to keep us out of our inward garden, since we are keeping ourselves out, through our avid interest in the outward, mortal aspects both of ourselves and of our world. What is symbolized in our passage of the guarded gate is our abandonment of both the world so known and ourselves so known within it: the phenomenal, mere appearance of things seen as born and dying, experienced either as good or as evil, and regarded, consequently, with desire and fear. Of the two big Buddhist cherubim, one has the mouth open, the other, the mouth closed—in token (I have been told) of the way we experience things in this temporal world, in terms always of pairs-of-opposites. Passing between, we are to leave such thinking behind.

But is that not the lesson, finally, of the Bible story as well? Eve and then Adam ate the fruit of the knowledge of good and evil, which is to say, of the pairs-of-opposites, and immediately experienced themselves as different from each other and felt shame. God, therefore, no more than confirmed what already had been accomplished when he drove them from the garden to experience the pains of death and birth and of toil for the goods of this world. Furthermore, they were experiencing God himself now as totally "other," wrathful and dangerous to their purposes, and the cherubim at the garden gate were representations of this way— now theirs—of experiencing both God and themselves. But as we are told also in the Bible legend, it would actually have been possible for Adam to "put forth his hand and take also of the tree of life, and eat, and live forever." And in the Christian image of the crucified redeemer that is exactly what we are being asked to do. The teaching here is that Christ restored to man immortality. His cross, throughout the Middle Ages, was equated with the tree of immortal life; and the fruit of that tree was the crucified Savior himself, who there offered up his flesh and his blood to be our "meat indeed" and our "drink indeed." He himself had boldly walked, so to say, right on through the guarded gate without fear of the cherubim and that flaming turning sword. And just as the

Buddha, five hundred years before, had left behind all ego-oriented desires and fears to come to know himself as the pure, immortal Void, so the Western Savior left his body nailed to the tree and passed in spirit to atonement—at-one-ment—with the Father: to be followed now by ourselves.

The symbolic images of the two traditions are thus formally equivalent, even though the points of view of the two may be difficult to reconcile. In that of the Old and New Testaments, God and man are not one, but opposites, and the reason man was expelled from the garden was that he had disobeyed his creator. The sacrifice on the cross, accordingly, was in the nature not so much of a realization of *at-one-ment* as of penitential *atonement*. On the Buddhist side, on the other hand, man's separation from the source of his being is to be read in psychological terms, as an effect of misdirected consciousness, ignorant of its seat and source, which attributes final reality to merely phenomenal apparitions. Whereas the level of instruction represented in the Bible story is that, pretty much, of a nursery tale of disobedience and its punishment, inculcating an attitude of dependency, fear, and respectful devotion, such as might be thought appropriate for a child in relation to a parent, the Buddhist teaching, in contrast, is for self-responsible adults. And yet the imagery shared by the two is finally older by far than either, older than the Old Testament, much older than Buddhism, older even than India. For we find the symbolism of the serpent, tree, and garden of immortality already in the earliest cuneiform texts, depicted on Old Sumerian cylinder seals, and represented even in the arts and rites of primitive village folk throughout the world.

Nor does it matter from the standpoint of a comparative study of symbolic forms whether Christ or the Buddha ever actually lived and performed the miracles associated with their teachings. The religious literatures of the world abound in counterparts of those two great lives. And what one may learn from them all, finally, is that the savior, the hero, the redeemed one, is the one who has learned to penetrate the protective wall of those fears within, which exclude the rest of us, generally, in our daylight and even our dreamnight thoughts, from all experience of our own and the world's divine ground. The mythologized biographies of such saviors communicate the messages of their world-transcending wisdom in word-transcending symbols—which, ironically, are then generally translated back into such verbalized thoughts as built the interior walls in the first place. I have heard good Christian clergymen admonish young couples at their marriage ceremonies so to live together in this life that in the world to come they may have life everlasting; and I have thought, Alas! The more appropriate mythic admonishment would be, so to live their marriages that in *this* world they may experience life everlasting. For there is indeed a life everlasting, a dimension of enduring human values that inheres in the very act of living itself, and in the simultaneous experience and expression of which men through all time have lived and died. We all embody these unknowingly, the great being simply those who have wakened to their knowledge—as suggested in a saying attributed to Christ in the Gnostic *Gospel According to Thomas:* "The Kingdom of the Father is spread upon the earth and men do not see it."

Mythologies might be defined in this light as poetic expressions of just such transcendental seeing; and if we may take as evidence the antiquity of certain basic mythic forms—the serpent god, for example, and the sacred tree—the beginnings of what we take today to be mystical revelation must have been known to at least a few, even of the primitive teachers of our race, from the very start.

3

What, then, are the earliest evidences of the mythological thinking of mankind?

As already remarked, among the earliest evidences we can cite today of emergent manlike creatures on this earth are the relics recently unearthed in the Olduvai Gorge of East Africa by

Dr. L. S. B. Leakey: distinctly humanoid jaws and skulls discovered in earth strata of about 1,800,000 years ago. That is a long, long drop into the past. And from that period on, until the rise in the Near East of the arts of grain agriculture and domestication of cattle, man was dependent absolutely for his food supply on foraging for roots and fruit and on hunting and fishing. In those earliest millenniums, furthermore, men dwelt and moved about in little groups as a minority on this earth. Today we are the great majority, and the enemies that we face are of our own species. Then, on the other hand, the great majority were the beasts, who, furthermore, were the "old-timers" on earth, fixed and certain in their ways, at home here, and many of them extremely dangerous. Only relatively rarely would one community of humans have to face and deal with another. Normally, it would be with animals that their encounters—desperate and otherwise—would occur. And as we today confront our human neighbors variously with fear, respect, revulsion, affection, or indifference, so also then—for all those millenniums of centuries—it was normally animal neighbors that were thus experienced. Moreover, as we today have understandings with our neighbors—or at least imagine that we have—so also those earliest ape-men seem to have imagined that there were certain mutual understandings which they shared with the animal world.

Our first tangible evidences of mythological thinking are from the period of Neanderthal Man, which endured from ca. 250,000 to ca. 50,000 B.C.; and these comprise, first, burials with food supplies, grave gear, tools, sacrificed animals, and the like; and second, a number of chapels in high-mountain caves, where cave-bear skulls, ceremonially disposed in symbolic settings, have been preserved. The burials suggest the idea, if not exactly of immortality, then at least of some kind of life to come; and the almost inaccessible high-mountain bear-skull sanctuaries surely represent a cult in honor of that great, upright, manlike, hairy personage, the bear. The bear is still revered by the hunting and fishing peoples of the far North, both in Europe and Siberia and among our North

American Indian tribes; and we have reports of a number among whom the heads and skulls of the honored beasts are preserved very much as in those early Neanderthal caves.

Particularly instructive and well reported is the instance of the bear cult of the Ainu of Japan, a Caucasoid race that entered and settled Japan centuries earlier than the Mongoloid Japanese, and are confined today to the northern islands, Hokkaido and Sakhalin —the latter now, of course, in Russian hands. These curious people have the sensible idea that *this* world is more attractive than the next, and that godly beings residing in that other, consequently, are inclined to come pay us visits. They arrive in the shapes of animals, but, once they have donned their animal uniforms, are unable to remove them. They therefore cannot return home without human help. And so the Ainu do help—by killing them, removing and eating the uniforms, and ceremonially bidding the released visitors *bon voyage*.

We have a number of detailed accounts of the ceremonials, and even now one may have the good fortune to witness such an occasion. The bears are taken when still cubs and are raised as pets of the captor's family, affectionately nursed by the womenfolk and allowed to tumble about with the youngsters. When they have become older and a little too rough, however, they are kept confined in a cage, and when the little guest is about four years old, the time arrives for him to be sent home. The head of the household in which he has been living will prepare him for the occasion by advising him that although he may find the festivities a bit harsh, they are unavoidably so and kindly intended. "Little divinity," the caged little fellow will be told in a public speech, "we are about to send you home, and in case you have never experienced one of these ceremonies before, you must know that it has to be this way. We want you to go home and tell your parents how well you have been treated here on earth. And if you have enjoyed your life among us and would like to do us the honor of coming to visit again, we in turn shall do you the honor of arranging for another bear ceremony of this kind." The little fellow is quickly and skillfully dispatched. His hide is removed with head and paws attached and arranged upon a rack to look alive. A banquet is then prepared, of which the main dish is a chunky stew of his own meat, a lavish bowl of which is placed beneath his snout for his own last supper on earth; after which, with a number of farewell presents to take along, he is supposed to go happily home.

Now a leading theme, to which I would call attention here, is that of the invitation to the bear to return to earth. This implies that in the Ainu view there is no such thing as death. And we find the same thought expressed in the final instructions delivered to the departed in the Ainu rites of burial. The dead are not to come back as haunts or possessing spirits, but only by the proper natural course, as babies. Moreover, since death alone would be no punishment for an Ainu, their extreme sentence for serious crimes is death by torture.

A second essential idea is that of the bear as a divine visitor whose animal body has to be "broken" (as they say) to release him for return to his other-world home. Many edible plants, as well as hunted beasts, are believed to be visitors of this kind; so that the Ainu, killing and eating them, are doing them no harm, but actually a favor. There is here an obvious psychological defense against the guilt feelings and fears of revenge of a primitive hunting and fishing folk whose whole existence hangs upon acts of continual merciless killing. The murdered beasts and consumed plants are thought of as willing victims; so that gratitude, not malice, must be the response of their liberated spirits to the "breaking and eating" of their merely provisional material bodies.

There is a legend of the Ainu of Kushiro (on the southeastern coast of Hokkaido) which purports to explain the high reverence in which the bear is held. It tells of a young wife who used to go every day with her baby to the mountains to search for lily roots and other edibles; and when she had gathered her fill, she would go to a stream to wash her roots, removing the baby from her back and leaving it wrapped in her clothes on the bank, while she went naked into the water. One day thus in the stream she began to sing a beautiful song, and when she had waded to shore, still singing, commenced dancing to its tune, altogether enchanted by her own dance and song and unaware of her surroundings, until, suddenly, she heard a frightening sound, and when she looked, there was the bear-god coming. Terrified, she ran off, just as she was. And when the bear-god saw the abandoned child by the stream, he thought: I came, attracted by that beautiful song, stepping quietly, not to be heard. But alas! Her music was so beautiful it moved me to rapture and inadvertently I made a noise.

The infant having begun to cry, the bear-god put his tongue into its mouth to nourish and to quiet it, and for a number of days, tenderly nursing it this way, never leaving its side, contrived to keep it alive. When, however, a band of hunters from the village approached, the bear took off, and the villagers, coming upon the abandoned child alive, understood that the bear had cared for it, and, marveling, said to one another, "He took care of this lost baby. The bear is good. He is a worthy deity, and surely deserving of our worship." So they pursued and shot him, brought him back to their village, held a bear festival, and, offering good food and wine to his soul, as well as loading it with fetishes, sent him homeward on his way in wealth and joy.[1] *

Since the bear, the leading figure of the Ainu pantheon, is regarded as a mountain god, a number of scholars have suggested that a like belief may account for the selection of lofty mountain caves to be the chapels of the old Neanderthal bear cult. The Ainu too preserve the skulls of the bears they sacrifice. Moreover, signs of fire hearths have been noted in the high Neanderthal chapels; and in the course of the Ainu rite the fire-goddess Fuji is invited to share with the sacrificed bear the banquet of his meat. The two, the fire-goddess and the mountain god, are supposed to be chatting together while their Ainu hosts and hostesses entertain them with song the night long, and with food and drink. We cannot be certain, of course, that the old Neanderthalers of some two hundred thousand years ago had any such ideas. A number of authoritative

* Numbered reference notes begin on page 267.

scholars seriously question the propriety of interpreting prehistoric remains by reference to the customs of modern primitive peoples. And yet, in the present instance the analogies are truly striking. It has even been remarked that in both contexts the number of neck vertebrae remaining attached to the severed skulls is generally two. But in any case, we can surely say without serious doubt that the bear is in both contexts a venerated beast, that his powers survive death and are effective in the preserved skull, that rituals serve to link those powers to the aims of the human community, and that the power of fire is in some manner associated with the rites.

The earliest known evidences of the cultivation of fire go back to a period as remote from that of Neanderthal Man as is his dim day from our own, namely, that of Pithecanthropus, some five hundred thousand years ago, in the dens of the ravenous low-browed cannibal known as Peking Man, who was particularly fond, apparently, of brains *à la nature,* gobbled raw from freshly opened skulls. His fires were not used for cooking. Neither were those of the Neanderthalers. For what, then? To furnish heat? Possibly! But possibly, also, as a fascinating fetish, kept alive in its hearth as on an altar. And this conjecture is the more likely in the light of the later appearance of domesticated fire, not only in the high Neanderthal bear sanctuaries but also in the context of the Ainu bear festivals, where it is identified explicitly with the manifestation of a goddess. Fire, then, may well have been the first enshrined divinity of prehistoric man. Fire has the property of not being diminished when halved, but increased. Fire is luminous, like the sun and lightning, the only such thing on earth. Also, it is alive: in the warmth of the human body it is life itself, which departs when the body goes cold. It is prodigious in volcanoes, and, as we know from the lore of many primitive traditions, it has been frequently identified with a demoness of volcanoes, who presides over an afterworld where the dead enjoy an everlasting dance in marvelously dancing volcanic flames.

The rugged race and life style of Neanderthal Man passed away and even out of memory with the termination of the Ice Ages, some forty thousand years ago; and there appeared then, rather abruptly, a distinctly superior race of man, Homo sapiens proper, which is directly ancestral to ourselves. It is with these men— significantly—that the beautiful cave paintings are associated of the French Pyrenees, French Dordogne, and Spanish Cantabrian hills; also, those little female figurines of stone, or of mammoth bone or ivory, that have been dubbed—amusingly—paleolithic Venuses and are, apparently, the earliest works ever produced of human art. A worshiped cave-bear skull is not an art object, nor is a burial, or a flaked tool, in the sense that I am here using the term. The figurines were fashioned without feet, because they were intended to be pressed into the earth, set up in little household shrines.

And it seems to me important to remark that, whereas when masculine figures appear in the wall paintings of the same period they are always clothed in some sort of costume, these female figurines are absolutely naked, simply standing, unadorned. This says something about the psychological and consequently mythical values of, respectively, the male and the female presences. The woman is immediately mythic in herself and is experienced as such, not only as the source and giver of life, but also in the magic of her touch and presence. The accord of her seasons with the cycles of the moon is a matter of mystery too. Whereas the male, costumed, is one who has *gained* his powers and represents some specific, limited, social role or function. In infancy—as both Freud and Jung have pointed out—the mother is experienced as a power of nature and the father as the authority of society. The mother has brought forth the child, provides it with nourishment, and in the infant's imagination may appear also (like the witch of Hansel and Gretel) as a consuming mother, threatening to swallow her product back. The father is, then, the initiator, not only inducting the boy into his social role, but also, as representing to his daughter her first and foremost experience of the character of the male, awakening her to her social role as female to male. The pa-

leolithic Venuses have been found in the precincts always of domestic hearths, while the figures of the costumed males, on the
other hand, appear in the deep, dark interiors of the painted temple-caves, among the wonderfully pictured animal herds. They re-
semble in their dress and attitudes, furthermore, the shamans of
our later primitive tribes, and were undoubtedly associated with
rituals of the hunt and of initiation.

Let me here review a legend of the North American Blackfoot
tribe that I have already recounted in *The Masks of God,* Volume I, *Primitive Mythology;* for it suggests better than any other
legend I know the manner in which the artist-hunters of the paleolithic age must have interpreted the rituals of their mysteriously
painted temple-caves. This Blackfoot legend is of a season when
the Indians found themselves, on the approach of winter, unable
to lay up a supply of buffalo meat, since the animals were refusing
to be stampeded over the buffalo fall. When driven toward the
precipice, they would swerve at the edge to right or left and gallop
away.

And so it was that, early one morning, when a young woman of
the hungering village encamped at the foot of the great cliff went
to fetch water for her family's tent and, looking up, spied a herd
grazing on the plain above, at the edge of the precipice, she cried
out that if they would only jump into the corral, she would marry
one of them. Whereupon, lo! the animals began coming over, tum-
bling and falling to their deaths. She was, of course, amazed and
thrilled, but then, when a big bull with a single bound cleared the
walls of the corral and came trotting in her direction, she was terrified. "Come along!" he said. "Oh no!" she answered, drawing
back. But insisting on her promise, he led her up the cliff, onto
the prairie, and away.

That bull had been the moving spirit of the herd, a figure rather
of mythic than of material dimension. And we find his counterparts everywhere in the legends of primitive hunters: semi-human,
semi-animal, shamanistic characters (like the serpent of Eden),

difficult to picture either as animal or as man; yet in the narratives we accept their parts with ease.

When the happy people of the village had finished slaughtering their windfall, they realized that the young woman had disappeared. Her father, discovering her tracks and noticing beside them those of the buffalo, turned back for his bow and quiver, and then followed the trail on up the cliff and out onto the plain. It was a considerable way that he had walked before he came to a buffalo wallow and, a little way off, spied a herd. Being tired, he sat down and, while considering what to do, saw a magpie flying, which descended to the wallow close by and began picking about.

"Ha!" cried the man. "You handsome bird! As you fly around, should you see my daughter, would you tell her, please, that her father is here, waiting for her at the wallow?"

The beautiful black and white bird with long graceful tail winged away directly to the herd and, seeing a young woman there, fluttered to earth nearby and resumed his picking, turning his head this way and that, until, coming very close to her, he whispered, "Your father is waiting for you at the wallow."

She was frightened and glanced about. The bull, her husband, close by, was asleep. "Sh-h-h! Go back," she whispered, "and tell my father to wait."

The bird returned with her message to the wallow, and the big bull presently woke.

"Go get me some water," the big bull said, and the young woman, rising, plucked a horn from her husband's head and proceeded to the wallow, where her father roughly seized her arm. "No, no!" she warned. "They will follow and kill us both. We must wait until he returns to sleep, when I'll come and we'll slip away."

She filled the horn and walked back with it to her husband, who drank but one swallow and sniffed. "There is a person close by," said he. He sipped and sniffed again; then stood up and bellowed. What a fearful sound!

Up stood all the bulls. They raised their short tails and shook them, tossed their great heads, and bellowed back; then pawed the dirt, rushed about in all directions, and finally, heading for the wallow, trampled to death that poor Indian who had come to seek his daughter: hooked him with their horns and again trampled him with their hoofs, until not even the smallest particle of his body remained to be seen. The daughter was screaming, "Oh, my father, my father!" And her face was streaming with tears.

"Aha!" said the bull harshly. "So you're mourning for your father! And so now, perhaps, you will understand how it is and has always been with us. We have seen our mothers, fathers, all our relatives, killed and butchered by your people. But I shall have pity on you and give you just one chance. If you can bring your father back to life, you and he can return to your people."

The unhappy girl, turning to the magpie, begged him to search the trampled mud for some little portion of her father's body; which he did, again pecking about in the wallow until his long beak came up with a joint of the man's backbone. The young woman placed this on the ground carefully and, covering it with her robe, sang a certain song. Not long, and it could be seen that there was a man beneath the robe. She lifted a corner. It was her father, not yet alive. She let the corner down, resumed her song, and when she next took the robe away he was breathing. Her father stood up, and the magpie, delighted, flew round and round with a marvelous clatter. The buffalo were astounded.

"We have seen strange things today," said the big bull to the others of his herd. "The man we trampled to death is again alive. The people's power is strong."

He turned to the young woman. "Now, before you and your father go, we shall teach you our own dance and song, which you are never to forget." For these were to be the magical means by which the buffalo killed by the people in the future would be restored to life, as the man killed by the buffalo had been restored.

All the buffalo danced; and, as befitted the dance of such great beasts, the song was slow and solemn, the step ponderous and deliberate. And when the dance was ended, the big bull said, "Now go to your home and do not forget what you have seen. Teach this dance and song to your people. The sacred object of the rite is to be a bull's head and buffalo robe: all who dance the bulls are to wear a bull's head and buffalo robe when they perform." [2]

It is amazing how many of the painted figures of the great paleolithic caves take on new life when viewed in the light of such tales of the recent hunting races. One cannot be certain, of course, that the references suggested are altogether correct. However, that the main ideas were much the same is almost certainly true. And among these we may number that of the animals killed as being willing victims, that of the ceremonies of their invocation as representing a mystic covenant between the animal world and the human, and that of song and dance as being the vehicles of the magical force of such ceremonies; further, the concept of each species of the animal world as a kind of multiplied individual, having as its seed or essential monad a semi-human, semi-animal, magically potent Master Animal; and the idea related to this, of there being no such thing as death, material bodies being merely costumes put on by otherwise invisible monadic entities, which can pass back and forth from an invisible other world into this, as though through an intangible wall; the notions, also, of marriages between human beings and beasts, of commerce and conversations between beasts and men in ancient times, and of specific covenanting episodes in those times from which the rites and customs of the peoples were derived; the notion of the magical power of such rites, and the idea that, to retain their power, they must be held true to their first and founding form—even the slightest deviation destroying their spell.

So much, then, for the mythic world of the primitive hunters. Dwelling mainly on great grazing lands, where the spectacle of nature is of a broadly spreading earth covered over by an azure dome touching down on distant horizons and the dominant image of life is of animal societies moving about in that spacious room, those nomadic tribes, living by killing, have been generally of a warlike character. Supported and protected by the hunting skills and battle courage of their males, they are dominated necessarily by a masculine psychology, male-oriented mythology, and appreciation of individual valor.

In tropical jungles, on the other hand, an altogether different order of nature prevails, and, accordingly, of psychology and mythology as well. For the dominant spectacle there is of teeming vegetable life with all else more hidden than seen. Above is a leafy upper world inhabited by winged screeching birds; below, a heavy cover of leaves, beneath which serpents, scorpions, and many other mortal dangers lurk. There is no distant clean horizon, but an ever-continuing tangle of trunks and leafage in all directions wherein solitary adventure is perilous. The village compound is relatively stable, earthbound, nourished on plant food gathered or cultivated mainly by the women; and the male psyche is consequently in bad case. For even the primary *psychological* task for the young male of achieving separation from dependency on the mother is hardly possible in a world where all the essential work is being attended to, on every hand, by completely efficient females.

It is therefore among tropical tribes that the wonderful institution originated of the men's secret society, where no women are allowed, and where curious symbolic games flattering the masculine zeal for achievement can be enjoyed in security, safe away from Mother's governing eye. In those zones, furthermore, the common sight of rotting vegetation giving rise to new green shoots seems to have inspired a mythology of death as the giver of life; whence the hideous idea followed that the way to increase life is to increase death. The result has been, for millenniums, a general rage of sacrifice through the whole tropical belt of our planet, quite in contrast to the comparatively childish ceremonies of animal-worship and -appeasement of the hunters of the great plains: brutal human as well as animal sacrifices, highly symbolic in detail; sacrifices also of fruits of the field, of the firstborn, of widows on their husbands' graves, and finally of entire courts together with their kings. The mythic theme of the Willing Victim has become associated here with the image of a primordial being that in the beginning offered itself to be slain, dismembered, and buried; and from whose buried parts then arose the food plants by which the lives of the people are sustained.

In the Polynesian Cook Islands there is an amusing local variant of this general myth in the legend of a maiden named Hina (Moon) who enjoyed bathing in a certain pool. A great big eel, one day, swam past and touched her. This occurred again, day after day, until, on one occasion, it threw off its eel costume and a beautiful youth, Te Tuna (the Eel), stood before her, whom she accepted as her lover. Thereafter he would visit her in human form, but become an eel when he swam away, until one day he announced that the time had come for him to leave forever. He would pay her one more visit, arriving in his eel form in a great flood of water, when she should cut off his head and bury it. And so indeed he came. And Hina did exactly as she was told. And every day thereafter she visited the place of the buried head, until a green sprout appeared that grew into a beautiful tree, which in the course of time produced fruits. Those were the first coconuts; and every nut, when husked, still shows the eyes and face of Hina's lover.[3]

III

The Importance of Rites

[1964]

◫ The function of ritual, as I understand it, is to give form to human life, not in the way of a mere surface arrangement, but in depth. In ancient times every social occasion was ritually structured and the sense of depth was rendered through the maintenance of a religious tone. Today, on the other hand, the religious tone is reserved for exceptional, very special, "sacred" occasions. And yet even in the patterns of our secular life, ritual survives. It can be recognized, for example, not only in the decorum of courts and regulations of military life, but also in the manners of people sitting down to table together.

All life is structure. In the biosphere, the more elaborate the structure, the higher the life form. The structure through which the energies of a starfish are inflected is considerably more complex than that of an amoeba; and as we come on up the line, say to the chimpanzee, complexity increases. So likewise in the human cultural sphere: the crude notion that energy and strength can be represented or rendered by abandoning and breaking structures is refuted by all that we know about the evolution and history of life.

Now the structuring patterns of animal conduct inhere in the in-

44

herited nervous systems of the species; and the so-called innate releasing mechanisms by which they are determined are for the most
part stereotyped. From animal to animal, the responses are consistent within a species. Moreover, the intricacy of some of the fixed
patterns of performance is amazing: the nest-building of certain
birds—the oriole, for example, fashioning its delicate hanging
nest; or among insects and arachnids, the miracle of a spider web.
Were we not so used to such things, we should be overcome with
incredulity and wonder at the sight of the mathematical regularity
and balance of a shimmering web perfectly suspended between selected twigs at the side of some forest trail, conceived and realized
(as we should say of any comparable human work) with an infallible sense for the strength of materials, tensions, balances, and so
on. All such little architectural marvels—beehives, anthills, nauti-
lus shells, and the like—are produced according to inherited skills
ingrained in the cells and nerve systems of the species.

Our human species, on the other hand, is distinguished by the
fact that the action-releasing mechanisms of its central nervous
system are for the most part not "stereotyped" but "open." They
are susceptible, consequently, to the influence of imprintings from
the society in which the individual grows up. For the human infant is born—biologically considered—some ten or twelve years
too soon. It acquires its human character, upright stature, ability
to speak, and the vocabulary of its thinking under the influence of
a specific culture, the features of which are engraved, as it were,
upon its nerves; so that the constitutional patternings which in the
animal world are biologically inherited are in the human species
matched largely by socially transmitted forms, imprinted during
what have been long known as the "impressionable years," and
rituals have been everywhere the recognized means of such imprinting. Myths are the mental supports of rites; rites, the physical
enactments of myths. By absorbing the myths of his social group
and participating in its rites, the youngster is structured to accord
with his social as well as natural environment, and turned from an
amorphous nature product, prematurely born, into a defined and

competent member of some specific, efficiently functioning social order.

This altogether extraordinary prematurity of the birth of the human infant, so that throughout the period of its infancy it is dependent on its parents, has led biologists and psychologists to compare our situation with that of marsupials: the kangaroo, for example, which gives birth to its young only three weeks after conception. The tiny unready creatures crawl instinctively up the mother's belly into her pouch, where they fix themselves—without instruction—to the nipples and remain until ready for life, nourished and protected in, so to say, a second womb. Evolution beyond that stage, in the mammals, involved the biological innovation of the placenta, which makes it possible for the young to remain within the mother until nearly ready for independence; so that mammals can generally take care of themselves almost immediately after birth, or at least within a few days or weeks. In the human species, with its great brain requiring many years to mature, on the other hand, the young are again born too soon, and instead of the pouch we have the home, which is again a sort of external second womb.

Now it is during this life stage of the home that all the basic social imprintings are established. They are there associated, however, with an attitude of dependency that has to be left behind before psychological maturity can be attained. The young human being responds to the challenges of its environment by turning to its parents for advice, support, and protection, and before it can be trusted as an adult, this patterning must be altered. Accordingly, one of the first functions of the puberty rites of primitive societies, and indeed of education everywhere, has been always that of switching the response systems of adolescents from dependency to responsibility—which is no easy transformation to achieve. And with the extension of the period of dependency in our own civilization into the middle or even late twenties, the challenge is today more threatening than ever, and our failures are increasingly apparent.

A neurotic might be defined, in this light, as one who has failed to come altogether across the critical threshold of his adult "second birth." Stimuli that should evoke in him thoughts and acts of responsibility evoke those, instead, of flight to protection, fear of punishment, need for advice, and so on. He has continually to correct the spontaneity of his response patterns and, like a child, will tend to attribute his failures and troubles either to his parents or to that handy parent substitute, the state and the social order by which he is protected and supported. If the first requirement of an adult is that he should take to himself responsibility for his failures, for his life, and for his doing, within the context of the actual conditions of the world in which he dwells, then it is simply an elementary psychological fact that no one will ever develop to this state who is continually thinking of what a great thing he would have been had only the conditions of his life been different: his parents less indifferent to his needs, society less oppressive, or the universe otherwise arranged. The first requirement of any society is that its adult membership should realize and represent the fact that it is they who constitute its life and being. And the first function of the rites of puberty, accordingly, must be to establish in the individual a system of sentiments that will be appropriate to the society in which he is to live, and on which that society itself must depend for its existence.

In the modern Western world, moreover, there is an additional complication; for we ask of the adult something still more than that he should accept without personal criticism and judgment the habits and inherited customs of his local social group. We ask and we are expecting, rather, that he should develop what Sigmund Freud has called his "reality function": that faculty of the independently observant, freely thinking individual who can evaluate without preconceptions the possibilities of his environment and of himself within it, criticizing and creating, not simply reproducing inherited patterns of thought and action, but becoming himself an innovating center, an active, creative center of the life process.

Our ideal for a society, in other words, is not that it should be a

perfectly static organization, founded in the age of the ancestors
and to remain unchanging through all time. It is rather of a process moving toward a fulfillment of as yet unrealized possibilities;
and in this living process each is to be an initiating yet cooperat-
ing center. We have, consequently, the comparatively complex
problem in educating our young of training them not simply to assume uncritically the patterns of the past, but to recognize and
cultivate their own creative possibilities; not to remain on some
proven level of earlier biology and sociology, but to represent a
movement of the species forward. And this, I would say, is in a
particular way the special charge of all who are living today as
modern Occidentals; for it is this modern Occidental civilization
which, since about the middle of the thirteenth century, has been
—quite literally—the only innovating civilization in the world.

One cannot help remarking, however, that since about the year
1914 there has been evident in our progressive world an increasing disregard and even disdain for those ritual forms that once
brought forth, and up to now have sustained, this infinitely rich
and fruitfully developing civilization. There is a ridiculous na-
ture-boy sentimentalism that with increasing force is taking over.
Its beginnings date back to the eighteenth century of Jean-Jacques
Rousseau, with its artificial back-to-nature movements and con-
ceptions of the Noble Savage. Americans abroad, from the period
of Mark Twain onward, have been notorious exemplars of the
ideal, representing as conspicuously as possible the innocent belief
that Europeans and Asians, living in older, stuffier environments,
should be refreshed and wakened to their own natural innocencies
by the unadulterated boorishness of a product of God's Country,
our sweet American soil, and our Bill of Rights. In Germany, between wars, the *Wandervögel,* with their knapsacks and guitars,
and the later Hitler Youth, were representatives of this reactionary
trend in modern life. And now, right here in God's Country itself,
idyllic scenes of barefoot white and black "Indians" camping on
our sidewalks with their tomtoms, bedrolls, and papooses are
promising to turn entire sections of our cities into fields for an-

thropological research. For, as in all societies, so among these, there are distinguishing costumes, rites of initiation, required beliefs, and the rest. They are here, however, explicitly reactionary and reductive, as though in the line of biological evolution one were to regress from the state of the chimpanzee to that of the starfish or even amoeba. The complexity of social patterning is rejected and reduced, and with that, life freedom and force have been not gained but lost.

It is in the fields of the arts that the reductive, life-diminishing effect of the loss of all sense of form is today most disquieting; for it is in their arts that the creative energies of a people are best displayed and can best be measured. One cannot help comparing the case today with that of the arts in ancient, aging Rome. Why is it that Roman works of architecture and sculpture, for all their power and facility, are less impressive, less moving, less significant formally than the Greek? Many have thought about this problem, and the other night an answer came to me in dream that I would offer now as a major illumination. It is this: that in a small community like Athens the relationship of the creative artist to the local social leaders would be forthright and direct, they would have known each other since boyhood; whereas in such a community as, say, our modern New York, London, or Paris, the artist who would be known has to go to cocktail parties to win commissions, and those who win them are the ones who are not in their studios but at parties, meeting the right people and appearing in the right places. They have not been quite enough engaged in the agony of solitary creative work to press beyond their first acquisitions of marketable styles and techniques. And the next consequence is "instant art," where some clever individual with as little formal agony as possible simply renders something unforeseen— which is then criticized and either advertised or suppressed by either friendly or unfriendly newspaper folk, who have also had a lot of socializing to attend to and, with insufficient time for extracurricular study or experience, find themselves baffled before anything really complex or significantly new.

I recall with unmitigated loathing the reviews that appeared of *Finnegans Wake* in 1939. It was not enough that that truly epochal work was dismissed as unintelligible: it was dismissed with highfaultin disdain as an arrant hoax and waste of everybody's time; whereas two years later Thornton Wilder's *The Skin of Our Teeth,* which is based entirely, from beginning to end, on the inspiration, themes, characters, plot motifs, and even incidental details drawn directly, obviously, and unashamedly from the great Irishman's *Finnegans Wake,* was awarded the journalistic Pulitzer Prize as the greatest American play of that blessed season. Practically without exception the significant modern work has, in the first place, an extremely difficult time coming to public notice at all, and, in the second place, if it ever does appear, the so-called critics will almost certainly knock it out. Is it not interesting, for example (to return to the history of James Joyce), that in the whole length of his career this greatest literary genius of our century was never awarded the Nobel Prize? Or is it any wonder that at the present moment we have no known creative work at all to match the requirements and possibilities of this fabulous period of ours—post World War II—of perhaps the greatest spiritual metamorphosis in the history of the human race? The failure is the more calamitous, since it is only from the insights of its own creative seers and artists that any people has ever derived its appropriate, life-supporting, and maturing myths and rites.

Let me recall at this point Nietzsche's statements regarding classic and romantic art. He identified two types or orders of each. There is the romanticism of true power that shatters contemporary forms to go beyond these to new forms; and there is, on the other hand, the romanticism that is unable to achieve form at all, and so smashes and disparages out of resentment. And with respect to classicism likewise, there is the classicism that finds an achievement of the recognized forms easy and can play with them at will, expressing through them its own creative aims in a rich and vital way; and there is the classicism that clings to form desperately out of weakness, dry and hard, authoritarian and cold. The point I would make—and which I believe was also Nietzsche's—is that form is the medium, the vehicle, through which life becomes manifest in its grand style, articulate and grandiose, and that the mere shattering of form is for human as well as for animal life a disaster, ritual and decorum being the structuring forms of all civilization.

In my own experience, I came to appreciate most vividly the life-amplifying service of ritual when, in Japan some years ago, I was invited to a tea ceremony of which the host was to be a distinguished master. Now if there is anything in this world more demanding of formal accuracy than the procedures of a Japanese tea ceremony, I should like to know what or where it might be. There are in Japan, I am told, people who have studied and practiced Tea all their lives without achieving perfection, so exquisite are its rules. And needless to say, in the tiny teahouse I was myself the proverbial bull in the china shop. In fact, the one outstanding general experience of the foreigner in Japan is that he will never be quite right. The forms have not been bred into his bones; even his body is the wrong shape. And the tea ceremony, which is the quintessential distillate of the whole formal wonder of that exceedingly formal civilization, comes to its own formal culmination, after a number of ritualized preliminaries, in the highly stylized act of the tea master stirring and serving his tea to a very small number of guests. I shan't go into detail, and actually couldn't, if I would. Suffice to say that every gesture and even tilt of the head is controlled; and yet, when I later talked with the other guests, they spoke with praise of the *spontaneity* of this master. The only term of comparison I could think of at the time was the poetic art of the sonnet; for there too is a very demanding form; yet the poet acquires within it a force and range of expression that he could never have gained without it, and thereby a new order of freedom. I had the privilege of observing in Japan the styles of a number of tea masters and learned to see how each was actually relaxed and free in performance. The ritual of the civilization had become organic, as it were, in the master, and he could move in it spontaneously with expressive elaboration. The effect, in its own way, was like that of a beautiful Japanese garden, where nature and art have been brought together in a common statement harmonizing and epitomizing both.

Do we have anything of the kind in our present North American civilization?

The other evening I turned on my television set and chanced upon a beautiful track meet that was then taking place in Los Angeles. It was the first such meet I had beheld since I had myself been a competitor back in the middle twenties—a lapse of about forty years, during all of which time I had paid no attention to the sport, mainly because it aroused in me more emotion than I wanted to have to control. What I had chanced upon was a mile race of six glorious runners, a really beautiful thing. But when it was over, the commentator pronounced it disappointing. I was amazed. The race had been run in four minutes, six seconds, with the next two runners within two seconds of the winner; whereas the fastest mile ever run in my own day had been just under four minutes, fifteen seconds, and I recall the excitement of that achievement. The record is now under four minutes. Reflecting, I thought: Well! where the game is played really seriously, and doesn't involve cocktail parties and the like, but confronts directly the honest challenge of the field, we still have form, and we have it in grand style! Oswald Spengler in *The Decline of the West* defines "culture" as the condition of a society "in form" in the sense in which an athlete is "in form." The way in which one holds one's arms, the angle at which the body is pitched: every detail of athletic form functions as a furthering agent for the flowering of a moment of life in fulfillment. And so it is also in the highly tuned style of a society "in form," a Japanese tea master "in form," the social decorum of a civilized people coming together "in form." The destruction of form will not produce a winner either in the field of a mile race or in the field of culture competition; and this being, finally, a serious world, it will be only where top form is maintained that civilized life will survive. Nor when a race is lost, can it be ever rerun.

And so let me now cite, in illustration of the high service of ritual to a society, the very solemn state occasion that followed, in Washington, D.C., the assassination of President Kennedy. That was a ritualized occasion of the greatest social necessity. The nation as a unit had suffered a shocking loss, a loss that had been shocking in depth—in a unanimous sense. No matter what one's opinions and feelings politically might have been, that magnificent young man representing our whole society, the living social organism of which ourselves were the members, taken away at the height of his career, at a moment of exuberant life—suddenly death, and then the appalling disorder that followed: all this required a compensatory rite to re-establish the sense of solidarity of the nation, not only as an occasion for us, here, within the nation, but also as a statement for the world, of our majesty and dignity as a modern civilized state. I count the splendid performance of the radio and television companies at that critical time an integral part of the ritual of which I speak: it was one of the spontaneous, *living* aspects of the occasion. For here was an enormous nation; yet during those four days it was made a unanimous community, all of us participating in the same way, simultaneously, in a single symbolic event. To my knowledge, this was the first and only thing of its kind in peacetime that has ever given me the sense of being a member of this whole national community, engaged as a unit in the observance of a deeply significant rite. For it has not been fashionable during the past twenty or thirty years to raise the American flag. That has been supposed to put you dangerously on the John Birch side of the aisle. But here at last was an occasion when—I should think—it would have been difficult for anyone not to have felt his own life and character magnified through participation in the life and destiny of the nation. The system of sentiments essential to our survival as an organic unit was effectively reactivated and evoked, emotionally and tellingly

represented for and to us, during that weekend of unanimous meditation.

But there ran also through my mind, as I watched those burial
rites unfold, certain extra thoughts of somewhat broader reference,
in relation particularly to the symbolism of the gun carriage bearing the flag-draped coffin, drawn by seven clattering gray steeds
with blackened hoofs, another horse prancing slowly at their side
bearing an empty saddle with stirrups reversed, also with blackened hoofs and conducted by a military groom. I saw before me, it
seemed, the seven ghostly steeds of the gray Lord Death, here
come to conduct the fallen hero youth on his last celestial journey,
passing symbolically upward through the seven celestial spheres to
the seat of eternity, whence he had once descended. The mythology of the seven spheres and of the soul's journey from its heavenly home downward to its life on earth and, when that life was
done, then upward again through all seven, is as old in this world
as our civilization itself. The steed with riderless saddle, stirrups
reversed, prancing by the dead young warrior's side, would in the
ancient days have been sacrificed, cremated along with the body of
its master in a mighty pyre symbolic of the blazing, golden sun
door through which the passing hero-soul would have gone to its
seat in the everlasting hero-hall of warrior dead. For, again symbolically, such a steed represents the body and its life, the rider,
its guiding consciousness: they are one, as are body and mind.
And as I watched that noble riderless beast of the cortege with its
blackened hoofs, I thought of the legend of the young Aryan
prince Gautama Shakyamuni's noble steed, Kantaka. When its
master, having renounced the world, rode away and into the forest
to become there the Buddha, the mount returned to the palace riderless and in sorrow expired.

Those ancient themes and legends surely were not known to
many of the modern millions who, on the occasion of their dead
young hero's burial, watched and heard the clattering hoofs of the
seven gray steeds in the silent city and saw the noble riderless
mount going by with stirrups reversed. And yet those themes and

legends were not merely background; they were the presences in those military rites, and their presence worked. That is my thesis. In addition, they brought echoes of another moment in our own American history: the gun carriages of the Civil War and the funeral of Lincoln, who also had been assassinated and was carried in exactly this manner to eternity. The force of the contemporary rite was enormously enhanced by these symbolic overtones— unheard by outward ears, perhaps, yet recognized within by all— in the slow, solemn beat of the military drums and the clattering black hoofs of those horses of King Death through the absolutely silent city.

To my mind there came, still further, as I watched those rites resounding with antique as well as with contemporary themes, considerations of the open nature of the human mind, which can find the models for its consolation in such mystery games as this of imitating the passage of the soul from earth through the ranges of the seven spheres. It had been many years before that I had encountered in the works of the great culture historian Leo Frobenius an account and discussion of what he termed the "paideumatic" or pedagogical powers by which man—the unformed, uncertain animal in whose nervous system the releasing mechanisms are not stereotyped but open to imprinting—has been governed and inspired in the shaping of his cultures throughout history. In the earliest periods, as among primitives today, man's teachers had been the animals and the plants. Later on, they became the seven heavenly spheres. For it is a curious characteristic of our unformed species that we live and model our lives through acts of make-believe. A youngster identified with a mustang goes galloping down the street with a new vitality and personality. A daughter imitates her mother; a son, his father.

In the now long-forgotten millenniums of the paleolithic Great Hunt, where man's ubiquitous nearest neighbors were the beasts in their various species, it was those animals who were his teachers, illustrating in their manners of life the powers and patternings of nature. The tribesmen assumed the names of beasts and in their

rites wore animal masks. Among those dwelling in tropical jungle
environments, on the other hand, where the spectacle of nature
was predominantly of plants, the human game of imitation was
rather of the vegetable world, and, as we have seen, the basic
myth was of a god who had yielded his body to be slain, cut up,
and buried, whence the food plants arose for the sustenance of the
people. In the rites of human sacrifice common to all planting cultures, this primal mythological scene is imitated literally—ad nau-
seam; for, as in the vegetable world life is seen to spring from
death and fresh green sprouts from decay, so too it must be in the
human. The dead are buried to be born again, and the cycles of
the plant world become models for the myths and rituals of mankind.

In the great and critical period of the rise in Mesopotamia, ca.
3500 B.C., of the earliest civilization of city-states, the center of
fascination and model for society shifted from the earth, the animal and plant kingdoms, to the heavens, when the priestly watchers of the skies discovered that the seven celestial powers—sun,
moon, and five visible planets—move at mathematically determinable rates through the fixed constellations. A new realization of
the wonder of this universe was epitomized then in the concept of
a cosmic order, which immediately became the celestial model for
the good society on earth: the king enthroned, crowned as the
moon or sun, the queen as the goddess-planet Venus, and the high
dignitaries of the court in the roles of the various celestial lights.
In the fabulous court of Christian Byzantium, as late as the fifth to
thirteenth centuries A.D., the imperial throne was surrounded by
all sorts of amazing paradisial sights: lions of gold that wagged
their tails and roared; birds of precious metals and gems, twitter-
ing in jewel trees. And when the ambassador of some barbaric
tribe who had just passed through dazzling marble corridors, long
lines of palace guards and bedizened generals and bishops, arrived
before the imposing, motionless, silent figure of the monarch, so-
lar-crowned on his radiant throne, he would cast himself in genu-
ine awe prostrate before the Presence—and while he remained

there, face down, a machine would lift the whole throne aloft, so that lo! when at last the astounded visitor rose, he would find his monarch with vestments totally changed gazing down upon him, like God, from a spangled sky. Saint Cyril of Alexandria in his letters to the Emperor addressed him as the Image of God on Earth. It was all a bit extreme, perhaps, but hardly very different from the pantomime of an imperial court today, or of a papal mass.

Monkeyshines of this kind still have an effect. They represent the projection into the daylight world—in forms of human flesh, ceremonial costume, and architectural stone—of dreamlike mythic images derived not from any actual daylight-life experience, but from depths of what we now are calling the unconscious. And, as such, they arouse and inspire in the beholder dreamlike, unreasonable responses. The characteristic effect of mythic themes and motifs translated into ritual, consequently, is that they link the individual to transindividual purposes and forces. Already in the biosphere it has been observed by students of animal behavior that where species-concerns become dominant—as in situations of courtship or of courtship combat—patterns of stereotyped, ritualized behavior move the individual creatures according to programed orders of action common to the species. Likewise, in all areas of human social intercourse, ritualized procedures depersonalize the protagonists, drop or lift them out of themselves, so that their conduct now is not their own but of the species, the society, the caste, or the profession. Hence, for example, the rituals of investiture of judges, or of officers of state: those so installed are to function in their roles, not as private individuals but as agents of collective principles and laws. And even in private business exchanges, the patternings of deeds and contracts, bargainings and threats of recourse to law constitute the ritual rules of a recognized game, relieving the confrontation—to some extent, at least —of personal accent. Without such game rules no society would exist; nor would any individual have the slightest idea how to act. And it will be only by virtue of the game rules of his local social

group that anyone's humanity will unfold from the void of undefined potentials to its one and only (temporally, spatially, and temperamentally delimited) actualization as a life.

And so let us now ask what the proper source of awe might be
for the race of mankind today. As pointed out by Frobenius, it
was first the animal world, in its various species, that impressed
mankind as a mystery, and that, in its character of admired immediate neighbor, evoked the impulse to imitative identification.
Next, it was the vegetable world and the miracle of the fruitful
earth, wherein death is changed into life. And finally, with the rise
in the ancient Near East of the earliest high civilizations, the focus
of attention shifted to the mathematics of the seven moving cosmic
lights, and it was these that gave to us those seven gray steeds of
the cavalcade of King Death and the resurrection. However, as my
historian has also remarked, our most immediate mysterious
neighbor today is not the animal or the plant; nor is it any longer
the heavenly vault with its wonderfully moving lights. Frobenius
points out that we have demythologized those through our sciences, and that the center of mystery now is man himself: man as
a Thou, one's neighbor; not as "I" might wish him to be, or may
imagine that I know and relate to him, but in himself, thus come,
as a being of mystery and wonder.

It is in the tragedies of the Greeks that one finds the earliest
recognition and celebration of this new, immediately human, center of awe. The rites of all other peoples of their time were addressed to the animal, plant, cosmic, and supernatural orders; but
in Greece, already in the period of Homer, the world had become
man's world, and in the tragedies of the great fifth-century poets
the ultimate spiritual implications of this refocusing of concern
were for all time announced and unfolded. James Joyce in *A Por-
trait of the Artist as a Young Man* has succinctly defined the essential qualities of the Greek tragedy through which the ways are
opened to an essentially mystic dimension of humanistic spirituality. Citing Aristotle's *Poetics,* he reminds us of the two classically
recognized "tragic emotions," pity and terror, noting also, how-

ever, that Aristotle had not defined them. "Aristotle has not defined pity and terror," his hero, Stephen Dedalus, declares; "I have." And he proceeds: "Pity is the feeling that arrests the mind in the presence of whatsoever is grave and constant in human sufferings and unites it with the human sufferer. Terror is the feeling that arrests the mind in the presence of whatsoever is grave and constant in human sufferings and unites it with the secret cause." The secret cause of all suffering is, of course, mortality itself, which is the prime precondition of life, and so is indeed "grave and constant." It cannot be denied if life is to be affirmed. Yet, along with the affirmation of this precondition, there is pity for the human sufferer—who is actually a counterpart, in this context, of oneself.

In those rites of burial of which I have just spoken, it was this classical and modern Occidental accent on the human object that most distinguished the occasion; and this is not what would have been experienced in any traditional Oriental event of equivalent magnitude. The reference there would have been *through* the human being to a supposed cosmological circumstance. Anyone who has ever had the experience of attending such an Oriental rite will surely have noticed that the human sufferer as an individual was in effect wiped out by the ceremonies, whereas in this instance everything was done to point up the value of the person. The old bottles carried a new wine, the wine of individual personality, and specifically, of course, that of this very special young man and what he represented, not in the timeless rounds of recurrent aeonian cycles, but in current historical time. And yet there was something of the symbolism of that older order present and effective still in those seven clattering horses of the gun carriage and the riderless steed at their side. The old imagery now carried a new song—of the unique, the unprecedented and induplicable human sufferer; yet equally a sense of the "grave and constant" in our human suffering, as well as a holy intimation of the ungainsayable "secret cause," without which the rite would have lacked its depth dimension and healing force.

And so now, in conclusion, let me conjure into final focus the prospect of unfathomed wonder to which all myths and rites—in the way of great poetry and art—introduce and unite us, by quoting the eloquent lines of a brief poem that deeply inspired me when I first read it some forty years ago, and which has steadied me in my thinking ever since. It is by the California poet Robinson Jeffers, sent to us from his watchtower on the Pacific shore, whence he had watched for years the sublime flights of pelicans winging down the coastline, heard the wet, friendly barking of the seals, and behind him the encroaching purr of increasingly numerous motors. The name of his poem is

NATURAL MUSIC

The old voice of the ocean, the bird-chatter of little rivers,
(Winter has given them gold for silver
To stain their water and bladed green for brown to line their
  banks)
From different throats intone one language.
So I believe if we were strong enough to listen without
Divisions of desire and terror
To the storm of the sick nations, the rage of the hunger-smitten
  cities,
Those voices also would be found
Clean as a child's; or like some girl's breathing who dances
  alone
By the ocean-shore, dreaming of lovers.[1]

IV

The Separation of East and West

⌘ It is not easy for Westerners to realize that
the ideas recently developed in the West of the individual, his self-
hood, his rights, and his freedom, have no meaning whatsoever in
the Orient. They had no meaning for primitive man. They would
have meant nothing to the peoples of the early Mesopotamian,
Egyptian, Chinese, or Indian civilizations. They are, in fact, re-
pugnant to the ideals, the aims and orders of life, of most of the
peoples of this earth. And yet—and here is my second point—
they are the truly great "new thing" that we do indeed represent
to the world and that constitutes our Occidental revelation of a
properly human spiritual ideal, true to the highest potentiality of
our species.

I draw the main line dividing Orient from Occident vertically
through Iran, along a longitude about 60 degrees east of Green-
wich. This can be thought of as a cultural watershed. Eastward of
that line there are two creative high-culture matrices: India and
the Far East (China and Japan); and westward, likewise, there are
two: the Levant or Near East, and Europe. In their mythologies,
religions, philosophies, and ideals, no less than in their styles of

life and dress and in their arts, these four domains have remained throughout their histories distinct. And yet they do group significantly in two orders of two: India and the Far East, on one hand; the Levant and Europe, on the other.

Now the Oriental centers, separated by great mountain wastes both from the West and from each other, have been for millenniums largely isolated, hence in a very deep way conservative. The Levant and Europe, in contrast, have been forever in fructifying conflict and commerce with each other, wide open not only to massive invasions but also to exchanges of both hard goods and ideas. The prodigious spiritual as well as physical upheavals of the present turbulent hour derive in no small measure from the fact that the isolating walls of both India and the Far East have been not merely broached but dissolved; and the world is faced in fact with the problems mythologically represented in the Bible legend of the builders of the Tower of Babel, when the Lord so confused men's tongues that they had to abandon the building of their secular city and scatter, as the book tells, "abroad, over the face of all the earth." Only there is no room today into which we might scatter away from each other; and just there, of course, is the rub and special problem of our age.

The mythical figure of Babel is in this connection doubly appropriate, since it was actually in the early city-states of Mesopotamia, ca. 3500 B.C., that the original foundations were laid of all higher (i.e., literate and monumental) civilization whatsoever; so that it was indeed from the Levant, and even specifically, those early temple cities of the towering ziggurats, that all branches of the one great tree of the four domains of civilization have stemmed. Moreover, it was there that the mythic forms of social organization came into being by which the individual in the Orient is to this day bound and restrained from the realization of a truly individual personal life. In the earlier, primitive societies of food-collecting hunters, foragers, and fishers, the precariously nurtured, nomadic social units were neither very large nor complex. The only divisions of labor were in terms of age and sex, with every man, woman, and even youngster pretty much in control of the entire cultural heritage. Every adult in such a context could—in terms at least of the local cultural model—become a total human being. Whereas with the rise and development in the ancient Near East, after ca. 7500 B.C., of comparatively well-to-do, settled communities supported by grain agriculture and stock-breeding, life became much more complex; and with the gradual increase of such communities both in number and in size, highly specialized departments of knowledge and professional skills became increasingly important. By 4500 B.C. there was a flourishing constellation of self-supporting villages throughout the Near East, and by 3500 B.C. those in the lower Tigris-Euphrates valley were becoming cities—the first cities in the history of the world. In these there were clearly distinguished governing and serving castes, wonderfully skilled specialist craftsmen, priestly orders, trading people, and so on; so that no one now could possibly hope to become a total human being. Each was but a part man. And accordingly, there appeared abruptly in the decorative arts of this period unmistakable signs of an attempt to symbolize the idea of a unification of disparate parts in relation to a whole.

Already in the pottery styles of the middle fifth millennium B.C., for example, balanced geometrical organizations of a circular field make their appearance, with a binding figure in the center symbolizing the integrating principle: a rosette, a cross, or a swastika. In later symbolic compositions this central position was occupied by the figure of a god, and in the earliest city-states the same divinity was incarnate in the king; in Egypt, in the pharaoh. Moreover, not the king alone, but all the members of his court played in their lives symbolic roles, determined not by their personal wishes but by the game rules of a ritual pantomime of identification with heavenly bodies—very much as in the earlier, primitive stages of human cultural mutation the rituals had been imitative of the animal species or of the life-and-death cycles of plants.

For, as has already been pointed out in the last chapter, it was in the early temple compounds of the Old Sumerian city-states, ca. 3500 B.C., that the priestly observers of the skies for omens first realized that the moon, the sun, and the five visible planets moved at mathematically determinable rates through the constellations. And it was then, as we have said, that the grandiose idea was conceived of a heavenly cosmic order, which should be reflected in the social order. Wearing symbolic crowns and in solemn costume, the king, his queen, and their courts duplicated in earthly mime the spectacle of celestial lights, and the force of their dedication to their roles would today be hardly credited, were it not for the astounding evidences brought to light by the late Sir Leonard Woolley from the "royal tombs" of the ancient moon-god's holy city of Ur.

Sir Leonard, as he tells, was excavating in the ancient temple cemetery of the old city from which Father Abraham is supposed to have taken his departure, when his men's spades broke into an astonishing series of multiple graves, some containing as many as sixty-five individuals laid to rest in courtly array. One of the best-preserved was of a woman named Shub-ad, buried with her court of some twenty-five attendants directly above the entombment of a male personage named A-bar-gi, with whom sixty-five or so had been laid to rest. The richly attired Shub-ad had been brought into her tomb on a sledge drawn by asses; A-bar-gi, possibly her husband, in a wagon drawn by oxen. Both the animals and the human beings had been buried in the monstrous grave alive: the court ladies lying peacefully in rows, in court regalia, wearing hair ribbons of silver and gold, red cloaks with beaded cuffs, great lunate earrings, and multiple necklaces of lapis-lazuli and gold. The girl harpists' skeleton hands were still resting on the harp strings—or where the harp strings once had been. And the instruments themselves suggested in form the body of a bull, with its beautiful golden bull's head bearing a rich lapis-lazuli beard. For this was a mythological bull: the divine lunar bull whose song of destiny had summoned these two willing companies—first of the buried king, then of his lady—to rebirth through death. And we know the name of the god of whom this bull was the animal vehicle. It was the great Near Eastern legendary god-king and universal savior Tammuz (Sumerian Dumuzi), the dates of whose annual death-and-resurrection festival are now assigned in our own mythic and ritual calendar, by the Synagogue to Passover, and by the Church to Good Friday and Easter.

We do not know what the precise occasion may have been for the burial of these two courts. Similar burials have been registered, however, for every one of the archaic civilizations. In Egypt and in China tombs have been discovered containing as many as eight hundred or more entombed, and in fact the pharaohs of the first three dynasties even had two such post-mortem estates, one at Abydos in Upper Egypt, one at Memphis in Lower: a country and a town palace, so to speak, with as many as four hundred or more skeleton attendants in each.

And now, just where, I should like to ask, is the individual in such a context? There is, in fact, in such a world, no such thing as an individual life, but only one great cosmic law by which all things are governed in their places. In Egyptian this law was known as *Maat,* in Sumerian, as *Me;* in Chinese it is *Tao;* in Sanskrit, *Dharma.* There is to be no individual choosing, willing, even thinking; no occasion to pause to ask oneself, "What is it I would now most like to do? What is it I would like to be?" One's birth determines what one is to be, as well as what one is to think and to do. And the great point that I most want to bring out is that this early Bronze Age concept of a socially manifest cosmic order, to which every individual must uncritically submit if he is to be anything at all, is fundamental in the Orient—one way or another —to this day.

The feminine present participle of the Sanskrit verb "to be" is *sati,* pronounced "suttee," and refers to the character of the virtuous Hindu wife immolating herself on her deceased husband's funeral pyre. In this selfless, thoughtless, dutiful act, fulfilling her social role, she has become something eternal, of eternal validity and life, undestroyed: that is to say, a wife. Any Indian wife refusing to fulfill her role to the end would be *a-sati,* a "non-being," a mere nothing; for one's life, one's meaning, the whole sense of one's existence on this earth is encompassed in the enactment and experience of one's social role. Only the one absolutely faultless in fulfillment can be said most truly "to be." And when we now look back to that dual multiple grave in the ancient royal cemetery of Ur—there indeed was already such a wife.

But A-bar-gi himself, it would appear, had also been ritually slain. Indubitable evidences of an ancient custom of ritual regicide have been found over a great portion of the globe. Turn, for example, to almost any page of Sir James G. Frazer's *Golden Bough.* The earliest god-kings were ritually slain every six years, eight years, or twelve, according to the various local orders; and with them the dignitaries of their courts, all casting off their bodies to be born again. It is a fantastic, noble, weirdly wonderful ideal, this of the individual who is nobody at all if not the incarnation, even unto death, of the one eternal, absolutely impersonal, cosmic law.

And it is against this that the Occidental, or, more particularly, modern European, ideal of the individual must be measured.

2

Let me now, therefore, turn directly to the question of the European individual and, for a start, cite the observations of the Swiss psychologist Carl G. Jung, throughout whose works the term "individuation" is used to designate the psychological process of achieving individual wholeness. Jung makes the point that in the living of our lives every one of us is required by his society to play some specific social role. In order to function in the world we are all continually enacting parts; and these parts Jung calls *personae,* from the Latin *persona,* meaning "mask, false face," the mask worn by an actor on the Roman stage, through which he "sounded" (*per-sonare,* "to sound through"). One has to appear in some mask or other if one is to function socially at all; and even those who choose to reject such masks can only put on others, representing rejection, "Hell no!" or something of the sort. Many of the masks are playful, opportunistic, superficial; others, however, go deep, very deep, much deeper than we know. Just as every body consists of a head, two arms, a trunk, two legs, etc., so does every living person consist, among other features, of a personality, a deeply imprinted persona through which he is made known no less to himself than to others, and without which he would not be. It is silly, therefore, to say, for example, "Let's take off our masks and be natural!" And yet—there are masks and masks. There are the masks of youth, the masks of age, the masks of the various social roles, and the masks also that we project upon others spontaneously, which obscure them, and to which we then react.

For example, let us suppose that you have been chatting comfortably with the unknown gentleman sitting beside you in an airplane seat. A stewardess stops by and respectfully addresses him as "Senator." When she leaves, you find that you are speaking to him with different feelings from those you had before, and not quite the same sense of ease. He has become for you what Jung has termed a *"mana*-personality," one charged with the magic of an imposing social mask, and you are talking now not simply to a person, but to a personage, a presence. And you have yourself become, furthermore, a subordinate personage or presence: a respectful American citizen conversing with a senator. The personae of the little scene will have changed—at least for your side of the dialogue. As far, however, as the Senator is concerned, he will still be the man he was before; and if he was putting on no airs then, he will be putting on no airs now.

To become—in Jung's terms—individuated, to live as a released individual, one has to know how and when to put on and to put off the masks of one's various life roles. "When in Rome, do as the Romans do," and when at home, do not keep on the mask of the role you play in the Senate chamber. But this, finally, is not easy, since some of the masks cut deep. They include judgment and moral values. They include one's pride, ambition, and achievement. They include one's infatuations. It is a common thing to be overly impressed by and attached to masks, either some mask of one's own or the *mana*-masks of others. The work of individuation, however, demands that one should not be compulsively affected in this way. The aim of individuation requires that one should find and then learn to live out of one's own center, in control of one's for and against. And this cannot be achieved by enacting and responding to any general masquerade of fixed roles. For, as Jung has stated: "In the last analysis, every life is the realization of a whole, that is, of a self, for which reason this realization can be called 'individuation.' All life is bound to individual carriers who realize it, and it is simply inconceivable without them. But every carrier is charged with an individual destiny and destination, and the realization of this alone makes sense of life." [1]

Which is precisely the opposite to the ideal enforced upon everyone—even the greatest saints and sages—in the great East, where the only thought is that one should become identified absolutely with the assigned mask or role of one's social place, and then, when all assigned tasks shall have been perfectly fulfilled, erase oneself absolutely, slipping (as one famous image has it) like a dewdrop into the sea. For there—in contrast to the typically West European idea of a destiny and character potential in each one of us, to be realized in our one lifetime as its "meaning" and "fulfillment"—the focus of concern is not the person but (as in the modern communist tyrant states) the established social order: not the unique, creative individual—who is regarded there as a menace—but his subjugation through identification with some local social archetype, and his inward quelling, simultaneously, of every impulse to an individual life. Education is indoctrination, or, as described today, the brainwash. The Brahmin is to be a Brahmin; the shoemaker, a shoemaker; the warrior, a warrior; the wife, a wife: nothing other, nothing less, and nothing more.

Under such a dispensation the individual never comes to the knowledge of himself as anything but the more or less competent actor of a perfectly standard part. Whatever signs of a personality may have been promising in infancy will in a few brief years have disappeared, to be replaced by the features of a social archetype, a general standard mask, a mirage personality, or—as I think we should say of such a one today—a stuffed shirt. The ideal student in such a society is the one who accepts instruction without question and, blessed with the virtue of perfect faith in his authorized instructor, is avid to assimilate not only his codified information but also his mannerisms, criteria of judgment, and general image of the persona that the student is to become—and when I say "become," that is what I mean; for there is to be nothing else remaining, no ego in our Western sense at all, with personal opinions, likes, dislikes, and unprecedented thoughts or aims.

It is interesting to remark that throughout the great *Divine Comedy* of Dante, the visionary voyager through Hell, Purgatory, and Heaven could recognize his deceased friends and talk to them of their lives. Likewise in the classical afterworlds of the *Odyssey* and *Aeneid,* Odysseus and Aeneas readily recognize and can talk with the shades of those recently dead. In the Orient, on the other hand, in the Hells and Heavens of the Hindus, Buddhists, and Jains, no such continuity of recognizable personal traits would have been found; for at death the mask of the earthly role is dropped and that of an afterlife assumed. The beings inhabiting the Hells wear demonic shapes; those in the Heavens, godly. And when the reincarnating nonentity again returns to this earth, it will assume still another mask, with no conscious recollection of any past. For whereas in the European sphere—whether in the classical epics and tragedies, Dante's *Divine Comedy,* or Jung's modern psychology of "individuation"—the focus of concern is the individual, who is born but once, lives but once, and is distinct in his willing, his thinking, and his doing from every other; in the whole great Orient of India, Tibet, China, Korea, and Japan the living entity is understood to be an immaterial transmigrant that puts on bodies and puts them off. You are not your body. You are not your ego. You are to think of these as delusory. And this funda-

mental distinction between the Oriental and our usual European
concepts of the individual touches in its implications every aspect
of social and moral as well as psychological, cosmological, and
metaphysical thought. "This objective universe," I read in a Sanskrit text, for example, "is absolutely unreal. So too is ego, the life
span of which, as seen, is but a wink. . . . Stop identifying yourself, therefore, with this lump of flesh, the gross body, and with
ego, the subtle body, which are both imagined by the mind. . . .
Destroying this egoism, your enemy, with the mighty sword of Realization, enjoy freely and directly the bliss of your own true empire, which is the majesty of the Self that is the All in all." [2]

The universe from which we are to strive thus for release is to
be known as an ever-appearing-and-disappearing dreamlike delu-
sion, rising and falling in recurrent cycles. When it is known as
such and when one has learned to play one's part in it without any
sense of ego, of desires, hopes, and fears, release from the everlasting rounds of meaningless reincarnations will have been attained. As the sun sets and rises when it should and as it should,
the moon waxes and wanes, and animals act in the manners of
their kind, so too must you and I behave in the manners proper to
our birth. It is supposed that, as a consequence of behavior in earlier lives, we have been born just where we have appeared and nowhere else. No judging deity is required to assign one to this place
or that. All is determined automatically by the spiritual weight (so
to say) of the reincarnating monad. This and this alone is what determines the level of one's social entry, the rules of life that will
be waiting for you, and all that you are to suffer and to enjoy.

In the old Sanskrit law books, *The Laws of Manu, The Insti-
tutes of Vishnu,* etc., detailed descriptions are given of the types
of study proper to each caste, the kinds of food to eat, the kind of
person to marry, when to pray, to bathe, in what direction to face
when sneezing or when yawning, how to rinse the mouth after
meals, and so on, *ad infinitum.* The assigned punishments are appalling. And in the Far East also, where, although the Way or
Order of Nature is described in terms that are not exactly the

same as those of India, they amount to pretty much the same as far as the government of one's life is concerned. For there too there is a cosmic order made known through the social order to which it is one's duty, as well as in one's nature, to conform. And there again the so-called sumptuary laws will tell in exact detail precisely how each is to live: in what size room to sleep (according to one's social status) and on a mattress of what material, how long one's sleeves are to be and of what material one's shoes, how many cups of tea one must drink in the morning, and so on. Every detail of life is prescribed to an iota, and there is so much that one *has* to do that there is no chance at all to pause and ask, "What would I *like* to do?"

In short, the principles of ego, free thought, free will, and self-responsible action are in those societies abhorred and rejected as antithetical to all that is natural, good, and true; so that the ideal of individuation, which in Jung's view is the ideal of psychological health and of an adult life fulfilled, is in the Orient simply unknown. Let me quote just one example, a passage from the Indian *Laws of Manu,* concerning the regulations for the whole life long of an orthodox Hindu wife:

Nothing is to be done, even in her own house, independently, by a girl, a young or even an aged woman. The female in childhood is to be subject to her father; in young womanhood, to her husband; and when her lord is dead, to her sons. A woman is never to be independent. She must not attempt to free herself from her father, husband, or sons. Leaving them, she would make both her own and her husband's families contemptible. She must always be cheerful, clever in the management of her household affairs, careful in cleaning her utensils, and economical in expenditure. She shall obey as long as he lives him to whom her father (or, with her father's permission, her brother) has given her; and when he is dead, she must never dishonor his memory. . . . Even a husband of no virtue, without any good qualities at all, and pursuing his pleasures elsewhere, is to be

worshiped unflaggingly as a god. . . . In reward for such conduct, the female who controls her thoughts, speech, and actions,
gains in this life highest renown and in the next a place beside
her husband.[3]

The philosophies of India have been classified by the native
teachers in four categories, according to the ends of life that they
serve, i.e., the four aims for which men strive in this world. The
first is *dharma,* "duty, virtue," of which I have just spoken, and
which, as we have seen, is defined for each by his place in the social order. The second and third are of nature and are the aims to
which all living things are naturally impelled: success or achievement, self-aggrandizement, which is called in Sanskrit *artha;* and
sensual delight or pleasure, known as *kama.* These latter two correspond to the aims of what Freud has called the id. They are expressions of the primary biological motives of the psyche, the simple "I want" of one's animal nature; whereas the principle of
dharma, impressed on each by his society, corresponds to what
Freud has called superego, the cultural "Thou shalt!" In the Indian society one's pleasures and successes are to be aimed for and
achieved under the ceiling (so to say) of one's *dharma:* "Thou
shalt!" supervising "I want!" And when mid-life has been attained, with all the duties of life fulfilled, one departs (if a male)
to the forest, to some hermitage, to wipe out through yoga every
last least trace of "I want!" and, with that, every echo also of
"Thou shalt!" Whereupon the fourth goal, the fourth and final end
of life, will have been attained, which is known as *moksha,* absolute "release" or "freedom": not "freedom," however, as we think
of it in the West, the freedom of an individual to be what he
wants to be, or to do what he wants to do. On the contrary, "freedom" in the sense of *moksha* means freedom from every impulse
to exist.

"Thou shalt!" against "I want!" and then, "Extinction!" In our
modern Occidental view, the situation represented by the first two
in tension would be thought of as proper rather to a nursery

school than to adulthood, whereas in the Orient that is the situation enforced throughout even adult life. There is no provision or allowance whatsoever for what in the West would be thought of as ego-maturation. And as a result—to put it plainly and simply—the Orient has never distinguished ego from id.

The word "I" (in Sanskrit, *aham*) suggests to the Oriental philosopher only wishing, wanting, desiring, fearing, and possessing, i.e., the impulses of what Freud has termed the id operating under pressure of the pleasure principle. Ego, on the other hand (again as Freud defines it), is that psychological faculty which relates us *objectively* to external, empirical "reality": i.e., to the fact-world, here and now, and in its present possibilities, objectively observed, recognized, judged, and evaluated; and to ourselves, so likewise known and judged, within it. A considered act initiated by a knowledgeable, responsible ego is thus something very different from the action of an avaricious, untamed id; different, too, from performances governed by unquestioning obedience to a long-inherited code—which can only be inappropriate to contemporary life or even to any unforeseen social or personal contingency.

The virtue of the Oriental is comparable, then, to that of the good soldier, obedient to orders, personally responsible not for his acts but only for their execution. And since all the laws to which he is adhering will have been handed down from an infinite past, there will be no one anywhere personally responsible for the things that he is doing. Nor, indeed, was there ever anyone personally responsible, since the laws were derived—or at least are supposed to have been derived—from the order of the universe itself. And since at the source of this universal order there is no personal god or willing being, but only an absolutely impersonal force or void, beyond thought, beyond being, antecedent to categories, there has finally never been anyone anywhere responsible for anything—the gods themselves being merely functionaries of an ever-revolving kaleidoscope of illusory appearances and disappearances, world without end.

3

Now when and how (it might be asked) did the historic turn
occur from what I have just described as the Oriental to what we
all know to be the Occidental view of the relationship of the individual to his universe? The earliest certain signs of such a turn appear in the Mesopotamian texts of about 2000 B.C., where a distinction is beginning to be made between the king as a mere
human being and the god whom he is now to serve. He is no
longer a god-king like the pharaoh of Egypt. He is called the "tenant farmer" of the god. The city of his reign is the god's earthly
estate and himself the mere chief steward or man in charge. Furthermore, it was at that time that Mesopotamian myths began to
appear of men created by gods to be their slaves. Men had become
the mere servants; the gods, absolute masters. Man was no longer
in any sense an incarnation of divine life, but of another nature
entirely, an earthly, mortal nature. And the earth itself was now
clay. Matter and spirit had begun to separate. I call this condition,
"mythic dissociation," and find it to be characteristic mainly of the
later religions of the Levant, of which the most important today
are, of course, Judaism, Christianity, and Islam.

Let me take, as an illustration of the effect on mythology of this
disenchanting turn of mind, the example of the Deluge. According
to many of the mythologies still flourishing in the Orient, a world
flood occurs inevitably at the termination of every aeon. In India
the number of years of an aeon, known as a Day of Brahma, is
reckoned as 4,320,000,000; after which there follows a Night of
Brahma, when all lies dissolved in the cosmic sea for another
4,320,000,000 years, the sum total of years of an entire cosmic
round thus being 8,640,000,000. In the Icelandic eddas it is told
that in Valhall there are 540 doors and that through each of these
there will go at the end of the world 800 battle-ready warriors to
join combat with the anti-gods.[4] But 800 times 540 is 432,000. So
it seems that there is a common mythological background theme,

here shared by pagan Europe with the ancient East. In fact, I note, with a glance at my watch, each hour with 60 minutes and each minute with 60 seconds, that in our present day of 24 hours there will be 86,400 seconds; and in the course of this day, night will automatically follow light, and, next morning, dawn follow darkness. There is no question of punishment or guilt implied in a mythology of cosmic days and nights of this kind. Everything is completely automatic and in the sweet nature of things.

But now, to press on a few steps further: according to a learned Chaldean priest, Berossos, who rendered in the early third century B.C. an account of Babylonian mythology, there elapsed 432,000 years between the crowning of the first Sumerian king and the coming of the Deluge, and there reigned during this period ten very long-lived kings. Then we observe that in the Bible it is reckoned that between the creation of Adam and coming of Noah's Flood there elapsed 1656 years, during which there lived ten very long-lived patriarchs. And if I may trust the finding of a distinguished Jewish Assyriologist of the last century, Julius Oppert (1825–1906), the number of seven-day weeks in 1656 years is 86,400.[5]

Thus the early Mesopotamian model of mathematically ordered recurrent cycles of world manifestation and disappearance, with each round terminated by a deluge, can be recognized even in the Bible. However, as we all well know, the more popular and evident explanation of Noah's Flood given in this text is that it was sent by Yahweh as a punishment for men's sins—which is a totally different concept, giving stress rather to free will than to the earlier, now hidden idea of a wholly impersonal cycle as innocent of guilt as the rounds of day and night or of the year.

The earliest extant examples of this second way of reading the Deluge legend appear in two Sumerian cuneiform texts of about 2000 to 1750 B.C. In these the name of the angry god is Enlil, and the man who builds the ark is the tenth king of the old Sumerian ziggurat-city of Kish. The period of the tablets is the same as that, already mentioned, of the designation of the ancient Mesopotamian kings as the "tenant farmers" of their deities, and the implications of the shift of view are enormous. For, in the first place, a dimension of wonder has been lost to the universe. It is no longer itself divine, radiant of a mystery beyond thought, of which all the living gods and demons, no less than the plants, animals, and cities of mankind, are functioning parts. Divinity has been removed from earth to a supernatural sphere, from which the gods, who alone are radiant, control terrestrial events.

But on the other hand, along with—and as a consequence of— this loss of essential identity with the organic divine being of a living universe, man has been given, or rather has won for himself, release to an existence of his own, endued with a certain freedom of will. And he has been set thereby in relationship to a deity, apart from himself, who also enjoys free will. The gods of the great Orient, as agents of the cycle, are hardly more than supervisors, personifying and administering the processes of a cycle that they neither put in motion nor control. But when, as now, we have a deity who, on the contrary, can decide on his own to send down a flood because the people he has made have become wicked, himself delivering laws, judging, and administering punishment, we are in a totally new situation. A radical shift of consciousness has bathed the universe and everything in it in a new, more brilliant light—like the light of a sun, blotting out the moon, the planets, and the other lights of the stars. And this new light, in the centuries then following, penetrated and transformed the whole world westward of Iran.

No longer were gods and men to be known as mere aspects of a single impersonal Being of beings beyond all names and forms. They were in nature distinct from each other, even opposed to each other, and with mankind subordinate. A personal god, furthermore, sits now behind the laws of the universe, not in front of them. Whereas in the older view, as we have seen, the god is simply a sort of cosmic bureaucrat, and the great natural laws of the universe govern all that he is and does and must do, we have now a god who himself determines what laws are to operate; who says,

"Let such-and-such come to pass!" and it comes to pass. There is, accordingly, a stress here rather on personality and on whim than on irrefragable law. The god can change his mind, as he frequently does; and this tends to bring the Levantine spirit into apparently close approach to the native individualism of Europe. However, there is even here a distinction to be made.

For in the Levant the accent is on obedience, the obedience of man to the will of God, whimsical though it might be; the leading idea being that the god has rendered a revelation, which is registered in a book that men are to read and to revere, never to presume to criticize, but to accept and to obey. Those who do not know, or who would reject, this holy book are in exile from their maker. Many nations great and small, even continents, are in actuality thus godless. Indeed, the dominant idea in all the major religions stemming from this area—Zoroastrianism, Judaism, Christianity, and Islam—is that there is but one people on earth that has received the Word, one holy people of one tradition, and that its members, then, are the members of one historic body—not such a natural, cosmic body as that of the earlier (and now Eastern) mythologies, but a supernaturally sanctified, altogether exceptional social body with its own often harshly unnatural laws. In the Levant, therefore, the essential hero is not the individual but the god-favored Chosen People or Church, of which the individual is no more than a participating member. The Christian, for example, is blessed in that he is a baptized member of the Church. The Jew is to remember ever that he is in covenant with Yahweh, by virtue of the mystery of his birth from a Jewish mother. And at the end of the world, only those faithful to the Covenant—or, in the Christian variant, those properly baptized who died in the "state of grace"—will be resurrected in the presence of God, to participate forever (as one happy version has it) in the everlasting paradisial meal of the meats of Leviathan, Behemoth, and the bird Ziz.

One striking sign of the profound difficulty experienced in Europe in assimilating this Levantine communal idea to the native

Greek and Roman, Celtic and Germanic feeling for the value of the individual may be seen in the Roman Catholic doctrine of two judgments to be endured by the soul in the afterworld: the first, the "particular judgment," immediately after death, when each will be assigned separately to his eternal reward or punishment; and the second, at the end of the world, the prodigious "general judgment," when all who will ever have lived and died on earth shall be assembled and in public judged, so that the Providence of God (which may in life have allowed the good to suffer and the wicked to seem to prosper) may in the end be shown to all men to have been eternally just.

4

Let me now, therefore, in conclusion, recount three versions of a single ancient myth, as preserved separately in India, in the Near East, and in Greece, to illustrate in an unforgettable way the contrast of the general Oriental and the two differing Occidental views of the character and highest virtue of the individual.

First the Indian myth, as preserved in a religious work, the *Brihadaranyaka Upanishad,* of about the eighth century B.C.

This tells of a time before the beginning of time, when this universe was nothing but "the Self" in the form of a man. And that Self, as we read, "looked around and saw that there was nothing but itself, whereupon its first shout was, 'It is I!'; whence the concept 'I' arose." And when that Self had thus become aware of itself as an "I," an ego, it was afraid. But it reasoned, thinking, "Since there is no one here but myself, what is there to fear?" Whereupon the fear departed.

However, that Self, as we next are told, "still lacked delight and wished there were another." It swelled and, splitting in two, became male and female. The male embraced the female, and from that the human race arose. But she thought, "How can he unite with me, who am of his own substance? Let me hide!" She became a cow, he a bull and united with her, and from that cattle arose; she a mare, he a stallion . . . and so on, down to the ants. Then he realized, "I, actually, am Creation; for I have poured forth all this." Whence arose the concept "creation" (Sanskrit *srishtih,* "what is poured forth"). "Anyone understanding this becomes, truly, himself a creator in this creation."

So the Sanskrit version of our legend. Next the Levantine, of about the same date, as preserved in the second chapter of Genesis: that melancholy tale, namely, of our simple ancestor, Adam, who had been fashioned of dust by his maker to till and to keep a garden. But the man was lonely, and his maker, hoping to please him, formed every beast of the field and every bird of the air, and brought them to the man to see what he would call them. None of them gave delight. "And so the Lord," as we read, "caused a deep sleep to fall upon the man, and while he slept took one of his ribs. . . ." And the man, when he beheld the woman, said, "This at last is bone of my bones and flesh of my flesh." We all know what next occurred—and here we all are, in this vale of tears.

But now, please notice! In this second version of the shared legend it was not the god who was split in two, but his created servant. The god did not become male and female and then pour himself forth to become all this. He remained apart and of a different substance. We have thus one tale in two totally different versions. And their implications relevant to the ideals and disciplines of the religious life are, accordingly, different too. In the Orient the guiding ideal is that each should realize that he himself and all others are of the one substance of that universal Being of beings which is, in fact, the same Self in all. Hence the typical aim of an Oriental religion is that one should experience and realize in life one's *identity* with that Being; whereas in the West, following our Bible, the ideal is, rather, to become engaged in a *relationship* with that absolutely other Person who is one's Maker, apart and "out there," in no sense one's innermost Self.

So let me now proceed to the Greek version of the legend, which is to be of still another teaching. It appears—you will re-

call—in Plato's dialogue *The Symposium,* where it is attributed
to Artistophanes; and in keeping with the lighthearted mood of
the great spirits of Plato's company, it was there offered rather
as a metaphor of the mystery of love than as an account to be
taken seriously of the actual origin of mankind.

The fantasy begins with the race of man already in existence, or rather with three distinct human races: one entirely male,
whose place of residence was the sun; one female, here on earth;
and a third, of males and females joined, whose dwelling, of
course, was the moon. And they were all as large as two human
beings of today. They had each four hands and feet, sides and
backs forming a circle, one head with two faces, and the rest to
correspond. And the gods being fearful of their strength, Zeus and
Apollo cut them in two, "like apples halved for pickling, or as
you might divide an egg with a hair." But those divided parts,
each desiring the other, came together and embraced, and would
have perished of hunger had the gods not set them far apart—the
lesson here to be learned being that "human nature was originally
one and we were a whole, and the desire and pursuit of the whole
is called love [according to its three kinds]. . . . And if we are
friends of God and reconciled to him we shall find our own true
loves, which rarely happens in this world"; whereas, "if we are
not obedient to the gods there is a danger that we shall be split up
again and go about in basso-relievo."

As in the Biblical version, so here, the being split in two is not
the ultimate divinity. We are again securely in the Occident,
where God and man are set apart, and the problem, once again, is
of relationship. However, the Greek gods were not, like Yahweh,
the *creators* of the human race. They had themselves come into
being, like men, from the bosom of the goddess Earth, and were
rather man's elder and stronger brothers than his makers. Moreover, according to this typically Greek, poetically humorous version of the archaic tales, the gods, before splitting them in two,
had been afraid of the first men, so terrible had been their might
and so great were the thoughts of their hearts. They had once even

dared to attack the gods, scaling heaven, and the pantheon had then been thrown for a time into confusion; for if with their thunderbolts the gods had annihilated man, that would have been the end of sacrifice, and they would themselves have expired from lack of worship. Hence, they settled upon the splitting idea, and might yet carry it further.

The Greeks, that is to say, are on man's side, both in sympathy and in loyalty; the Hebrews, on the contrary, on God's. Never would we have heard from a Greek such words as those of the sorely beaten "blameless and upright" Job, addressed to the god who had "destroyed him without cause" and who then came at him in the whirlwind, boasting of his power.

"Behold," pleaded Job, "I am of small account . . . I know that thou canst do all things. . . . I despise myself and repent in dust and ashes."

Repent! Repent for what?

In contrast, the great contemporary Greek playwright Aeschylus, of about the same fifth-century date as the anonymous author of the Book of Job, puts into the mouth of his Prometheus—who was also being tormented by a god that could "draw Leviathan out with a fishhook, play with him as with a bird, and fill his skin with harpoons"—the following stunning words: "He is a monster. . . . I care less than nothing for Zeus. Let him do as he likes."

And so say we all today in our hearts, though our tongues may have been taught to babble with Job.

V

The Confrontation of East and West in Religion

[1970]

One never would have thought, when I was a student back in the twenties, that in the seventies there would be intelligent people still wishing to hear and think about religion. We were all perfectly sure in those days that the world was through with religion. Science and reason were now in command. The World War had been won (the *First,* that is to say), and the earth made safe for the rational reign of democracy. Aldous Huxley in his first phase, of *Point Counter Point,* was our literary hero; Bernard Shaw, H. G. Wells, and other reasonable authors of that kind. But then, in the midst of all that optimism about reason, democracy, socialism, and the like, there appeared a work that was disturbing: Oswald Spengler's *The Decline of the West.* Other writings of uncertain import were also appearing in those happy years, from unexpected quarters: Thomas Mann's *The Magic Mountain,* James Joyce's *Ulysses,* Marcel Proust's *Remembrance of Things Past,* and T. S. Eliot's "The Waste Land." In a literary sense, those were very great years indeed. But what certain of its authors seemed to be telling us was that with all our rational triumphs and progressive political achievements, illuminating the dark quarters of the earth and so on, there was nevertheless something beginning to disintegrate at the heart of our Occidental civilization itself. And of all these warnings and pronouncements, that of Spengler was the most disquieting. For it was based on the concept of an organic pattern in the life course of a civilization, a morphology of history: the idea that every culture has its period of youth, its period of culmination, its years then of beginning to totter with age and of striving to hold itself together by means of rational planning, projects, and organization, only finally to terminate in decrepitude, petrifaction, what Spengler called "fellaheenism," and no more life. Moreover, in this view of Spengler's, we were at present on the point of passing from what he called the period of Culture to Civilization, which is to say, from our periods of youthful, spontaneous, and wonderful creativity to those of uncertainty and anxiety, contrived programs, and the beginning of the end. When he sought for analogies in the classical world, our moment today corresponded, he found, to that of the late second century B.C., the time of the Carthaginian Wars, the decline of the culture-world of Greece into Hellenism, and the rise of the military state of Rome, Caesarism, and what he termed the Second Religiousness, politics based on providing bread and circuses to the megalopolitan masses, and a general trend to violence and brutality in the arts and pastimes of the people.

Well, I can tell you, it has been for me something of a life experience to have watched the not so gradual coming into fulfillment in this world of every bit of what Spengler promised. I can remember how we used to sit around and discuss this looming prospect, trying to imagine how it might be beaten back, and trying to guess what the *positive* features might be of this period of crisis and transition. Spengler had declared that in periods like ours, of the passage from Culture to Civilization, there is a dropping off and away of the Culture forms: and indeed, in my own teaching I am today encountering more and more students who profess to find the whole history of our Western culture "irrelevant." That is the brush-off term they use. The "kids" (as they

like to call themselves) seem to lack the energy to encompass it all
and press on. One notes, or at least at times suspects, a kind of
failure of heart, a loss of nerve. But then, one can also regard
their situation from another point of view and consider the concat-
enation of new problems now to be faced, new facts and influ-
ences to be absorbed. One might then conclude that their energies
are perhaps being directed to an expanding present and problem-
atical future and, in line with Spengler's concept, recognize that
in this period Western man is not only dropping the culture forms
of the past but also shaping the civilization forms that are .to
build and support a mighty multicultural future.

I am reminded here of that very strange prophetic work of the
great Irish poet William Butler Yeats, *A Vision,* which he composed mainly during the twenty years from 1917 to 1936, and
wherein he has recognized certain affinities of his own intuitions
with those of Spengler's morphological view. Yeats there represents our present moment as the last phase of a great Christian
cycle or "gyre" of two thousand years: "And I notice," he writes,
"that when the limit is approached or past, when the moment of
surrender is reached, when the new gyre begins to stir, I am filled
with excitement." [1] On which theme he wrote and published already in 1921 a most awesome, fate-inspired poem:

THE SECOND COMING

> Turning and turning in the widening gyre
> The falcon cannot hear the falconer;
> Things fall apart; the center cannot hold;
> Mere anarchy is loosed upon the world,
> The blood-dimmed tide is loosed, and everywhere
> The ceremony of innocence is drowned;
> The best lack all conviction, while the worst
> Are full of passionate intensity.
>
> Surely some revelation is at hand;
> Surely the Second Coming is at hand.

The Second Coming! Hardly are those words out
When a vast image out of *Spiritus Mundi*
Troubles my sight: somewhere in sands of the desert
A shape with lion body and the head of a man,
A gaze blank and pitiless as the sun,
Is moving its slow thighs, while all about it
Reel shadows of the indignant desert birds.
The darkness drops again; but now I know
That twenty centuries of stony sleep
Were vexed to nightmare by a rocking cradle,
And what rough beast, its hour come round at last,
Slouches towards Bethlehem to be born? [2]

There was another German culture-historian also writing in those days, Leo Frobenius, who, like Spengler and like Yeats, conceived of culture and civilization in morphological terms as a kind of organic, unfolding process of irreversible inevitability. He was, however, an Africanist and anthropologist, and so included in his purview not only the higher civilizations but also the primitive, his leading concept being of three distinct great stages in the *total* development of the culture history of mankind. The first was of the primitive food-foragers, hunters and planting villagers, non-literate, greatly various, and of a time span extending from the first emergence of our species on this earth to (in some quarters) the very present. The second, commencing ca. 3500 B.C., was of the "monumental cultures," literate and complex—first of Mesopotamia and Egypt, then Greece and Rome, India, China and Japan, Middle and South America, the Magian-Arabic Levant, and Gothic-to-modern Europe. And now finally comes stage three, of this greatly promising, dawning global age, which Frobenius looked upon as probably the final phase of mankind's total culture history, but to last, possibly, for many tens of thousands of years. That is to say, what both Spengler and Yeats were interpreting as the end of the Western culture cycle Frobenius saw in a very much larger prospect as the opening of a new age of boundless horizons. And indeed, this present season of the coming together of all the formerly separate culture worlds may well mark not only the end of the hegemony of the West but also the beginning of an age of mankind, united and supported by the great Western gifts of science and the machine—without which no such age as our own could ever have come to pass.

However, the darker vision of Spengler foresees only desolation here too. For science and the machine are in his view expressions of the mentality of Western man, which are being taken over by non-Western peoples only as a means by which to undo and destroy the West. And when this killing of the goose that lays the golden eggs will have been accomplished, there will be no further development either of science or of industry, but a loss of competence and even of interest in both, with a resultant decline in technology and return of the various peoples to their local styles; the present great age of Europe and its promise for the world then but a broken dream. In contrast, Frobenius, like Nietzsche before him, saw the present as an epoch of irreversible advance in the one life course of the entire human race, here passing from its youthful, locally bounded stages of cultural growths to a new and general future of as yet unforeseen creative insights and realizations. But I must confess that while in my own thinking it is to the later view that I incline, I cannot quite get the other, of Spengler, out of my mind. . . .

In any case, what we all today surely recognize is that we are entering—one way or another—a new age, requiring a new wisdom: such a wisdom, furthermore, as belongs rather to experienced old age than to poetically fantasizing youth, and which every one of us, whether young or old, has now somehow to assimilate. Moreover, when we turn our thoughts to religion, the first and most obvious fact is that every one of the great traditions is today in profound disorder. What have been taught as their basic truths seem no longer to hold.

Yet there is a great religious fervor and ferment evident among not only young people but old and middle-aged as well. The fervor, however, is in a mystical direction, and the teachers who seem to be saying most to many are those who have come to us from a world that was formerly regarded as having been left altogether behind in the great press forward of modern civilization, representing only archaic, outlived manners of thinking. We have gurus galore from India; roshis from Japan; lamas from Tibet. And Chinese oracle books are outselling our own philosophers.

They are not, however, outselling our best psychologists. And this, finally, is not surprising; for the ultimate secret of the appeal of the Orient is that its disciplines are inward-pointing, mystical, and psychological.

I find an illuminating analogy to our present religious situation in that of the North American Indian tribes, when, toward the close of the nineteenth century, in the 1870s and 1880s, the buffalo were disappearing. That was the time, not yet a century past, when the railroad lines were being laid across the plains and buffalo scouts were going out to kill off the herds and make way for the new world of the Iron Horse and a population of wheat-planting settlers moved westward from the Mississippi. A second aim of the buffalo slaughter was to deprive the buffalo-hunting Indians of their food supply, so that finally they would have to submit to life on the reservations. And it was subsequently to these (for them devastating) developments that a new religion of inward visionary experiences became suddenly fashionable throughout the Indian West.

For, as with all primitive hunting peoples, so had it been with these plains tribes. The relationship of the human to the animal community that supplied its food had been the central, pivotal concern of the religiously maintained social order. Hence, with the buffalo gone, the binding symbol was gone. Within the span of a decade the religion had become archaic; and it was then that the peyote cult, the mescal cult, came pouring up from Mexico, onto and across the plains, as a psychological rescue. Many accounts have been published of the experiences of participants: how they would gather in special lodges to pray, to chant, and to eat peyote buttons, each then experiencing visions, finding within themselves what had been lost from their society, namely an imagery of holiness, giving depth, psychological security, and apparent meaning to their lives.

Now the first and most important effect of a living mythological symbol is to waken and give guidance to the energies of life. It is an energy-releasing and -directing sign, which not only "turns you on," as they say today, but turns you on in a certain direction, making you function a certain way—which will be one conducive to your participation in the life and purposes of a functioning social group. However, when the symbols provided by the social group no longer work, and the symbols that do work are no longer of the group, the individual cracks away, becomes dissociated and disoriented, and we are confronted with what can only be named a pathology of the symbol.

A distinguished professor in psychiatry at the University of California, Dr. John W. Perry, has characterized the living mythological symbol as an "affect image." It is an image that hits one where it counts. It is not addressed first to the brain, to be there interpreted and appreciated. On the contrary, if that is where it has to be read, the symbol is already dead. An "affect image" talks directly to the feeling system and immediately elicits a response, after which the brain may come along with its interesting comments. There is some kind of throb of resonance within, responding to the image shown without, like the answer of a musical string to another equally tuned. And so it is that when the vital symbols of any given social group evoke in all its members responses of this kind, a sort of magical accord unites them as one spiritual organism, functioning through members who, though separate in space, are yet one in being and belief.

Now let us ask: What about the symbolism of the Bible? Based on the Old Sumerian astronomical observations of five to six thousand years ago and an anthropology no longer credible, it is hardly fit today to turn anybody on. In fact, the famous conflict of science and religion has actually nothing to do with religion, but is

simply of two sciences: that of 4000 B.C. and that of A.D. 2000.
And is it not ironic that our great Western civilization, which has
opened to the minds of all mankind the infinite wonders of a universe of untold billions of galaxies and untold billions of years,
should have been saddled in its infancy with a religion squeezed
into the tightest little cosmological image known to any people on
earth? The ancient Mayan calendar with its recurrent aeons of
64,000,000 years would have been far more easily justified; or the
Hindu with its *kalpas* of 4,320,000,000. Moreover, in those far
more grandiose systems the ultimate divine power is neither male
nor female but transcendent of all categories; not a male personage "out there," but a power immanent in all things: that is to say,
not so alien to the imagery of modern science that it could not
have been put to acceptable use.

The Biblical image of the universe simply won't do any more;
neither will the Biblical notion of a race of God, which all others
are meant to serve (Isaiah 49:22–23; 61:5–6; etc.); nor again, the
idea of a code of laws delivered from on high and to be valid for
all time. The social problems of the world today are not those of a
corner of the old Levant, sixth century B.C. Societies are not
static, nor can the laws of one serve another. The problems of our
world are not even touched by those stone-cut Ten Command-
ments that we carry about as luggage and which, in fact, were dis-
regarded in the blessed text itself, one chapter after they were
announced (Exodus 21:12–17, following 20:13). The modern
Western concept of a legal code is not of a list of unassailable divine edicts but of a rationally contrived, evolving compilation of
statutes, shaped by fallible human beings in council, to realize rationally recognized social (and therefore temporal) aims. We understand that our laws are not divinely ordained; and we know
also that no laws of any people on earth ever were. Thus we know
—whether we dare to say so or not—that our clergies have no
more right to claim unassailable authority for their moral law than
for their science. And even, finally, in their intimate role of giving
spiritual advice, the clergy have now been overtaken by the scien-

tific psychiatrists—and indeed to such a degree that many clergy-men are themselves turning to psychologists to be taught how best to serve their pastoral function. The magic of their own traditional symbols works no longer to heal but only to confuse.

In short, then: just as the buffalo suddenly disappeared from the North American plains, leaving the Indians deprived not only of a central mythic symbol but also of the very manner of life that the symbol once had served, so likewise in our own beautiful world, not only have our public religious symbols lost their claim to au-thority and passed away, but the ways of life they once supported have also disappeared; and as the Indians then turned inward, so do many in our own baffled world—and frequently with Oriental, not Occidental, guidance in this potentially very dangerous, often ill-advised interior adventure, questing within for the affect images that our secularized social order with its incongruously archaic re-ligious institutions can no longer render.

Let me recount three personal anecdotes to illuminate the back-ground and suggest some of the problems of this confrontation of East and West in religion.

First: back in the middle fifties, when Dr. Martin Buber was in New York lecturing, I had the privilege of being among a number invited to hear him in a series of talks held in a small, very special chamber at Columbia. And there this eloquent little man—for he was, indeed, remarkably small, endowed, however, with a power-ful presence, graced with that mysterious force known nowadays as "charisma"—held forth for some five or six weekly sessions with extraordinary eloquence. In fact, in that English was not his first but his second language, his fluency and easy eloquence were astonishing. As the talks went on, however, I gradually came to realize, about the middle of talk number three, that there was one word the doctor was using that I was failing to understand. His lectures were on the history of the holy people of the Old Testa-ment, with references also to more recent times; and the word that I was failing to understand was "God." Sometimes it seemed to refer to an imagined personal creator of this magnitudinous uni-

verse which the sciences have revealed to us. Sometimes it was
clearly a reference simply to the Yahweh of the Old Testament, in
one or another of his stages of evolution. Then again, it seemed to
be somebody with whom Dr. Buber himself had been in frequent
conversation. In the midst of one lecture, for example, he broke
suddenly off and, standing for a moment bemused, shook his head
and quietly said to us, "It pains me to speak of God in the third
person." When I reported this to Dr. Gershom Scholem (now also
of Tel Aviv), he laughed and answered quizzically, "Sometimes he
does go too far!"

So with this mercurial word slipping this way and that, I cautiously raised my hand. The lecturer paused and considerately
asked, "What is it?"

"Dr. Buber," I said, "there is one word being used here this
evening that I do not understand."

"What is that word?"

"God," I answered.

His eyes widened and the bearded face came a little forward.
"You do not know what the word 'God' means!"

"I don't know what *you* mean by 'God,' " I said. "You have
been telling us this evening that God today has hidden his face
and no longer shows himself to man. Yet I have just returned
from India [and I had indeed been there, the year before], where
I found that people are experiencing God all the time."

He drew suddenly back, lifting both hands, palms upward. "Do
you mean," he said, "to compare . . ." But the M.C., Dr. Jacob
Taubes, cut quickly in: "*No,* Doctor!" (We all knew what had
been almost said, and I was just waiting to hear what the next
would be.) "Mr. Campbell," said Dr. Taubes, "only asked to
know what *you* mean by 'God.' "

The master quickly reassembled his thoughts, then said to me in
the manner of one dismissing an irrelevancy, "Everyone must
come out of his Exile in his own way."

Which was an answer perhaps good enough from Dr. Buber's
point of view, but from another standpoint altogether inappro-

priate, since the people of the Orient are not in exile from their
god. The ultimate divine mystery is there found immanent within
each. It is not "out there" somewhere. It is within you. And no
one has ever been cut off. The only difficulty is, however, that
some folk simply don't know how to look within. The fault is no
one's, if not one's own. Nor is the problem one of an original Fall
of the "first man," many thousand years ago, and of exile and
atonement. The problem is psychological. And it *can* be solved.

That, then, is the first of my three personal anecdotes.

The second is of an event that occurred some three years after
the first, when a young Hindu gentleman came to see me, and a
very pious young man he proved to be: a worshiper of Vishnu,
employed as a clerk or secretary of one of the Indian delegates at
the UN. He had been reading the works of Heinrich Zimmer on
Indian art, philosophy, and religion, works that I had edited many
years before, and which he wanted to discuss. But there was something else that he wished to talk about too.

"You know," he said after we had begun to feel at home with
each other, "when I visit a foreign country, I like to acquaint myself with its religion; so I have bought myself a Bible and for
some months now have been reading it from the beginning; but,
you know . . ." and here he paused, to regard me uncertainly,
then said, "I can't find any religion in it!"

A fitting counterpart, that—is it not?—to Dr. Buber's unspoken
word? What for one of these two gentlemen was religion, was for
the other no religion at all.

Now I had of course been brought up on the Bible, and I had
also studied Hinduism; so I thought I might be of some help.
"Well," I said, "I can see how that might be, if you had not been
given to know that a reading of the imagined history of the Jewish
race is here regarded as a religious exercise. There would then, I
can see, be very little for you of religion in the greater part of the
Bible."

I thought later that I should perhaps have referred him to the
Psalms; but when I then turned to a fresh reading of these with

Hinduism in mind, I was glad that I had not done so; for almost invariably the leading theme is either of the virtue of the singer, protected by his God, who will "smite his enemies on the cheek" and "break the teeth of the wicked"; or, on the other hand, of complaint that that God has not yet given due aid to his righteous servant: all of which is just about diametrically opposed to what an instructed Hindu would have been taught to regard as a religious sentiment.

In the Orient the ultimate divine mystery is sought beyond all human categories of thought and feeling, beyond names and forms, and absolutely beyond any such concept as of a merciful or wrathful personality, chooser of one people over another, comforter of folk who pray, and destroyer of those who do not. Such anthropomorphic attributions of human sentiments and thoughts to a mystery beyond thought is—from the point of view of Indian thought—a style of religion for children. Whereas the final sense of all adult teaching is to the point that the mystery transcendent of categories, names and forms, sentiments and thought, is to be realized as the ground of one's own very being.

That is the realization formulated in those famous words of the gentle Brahmin Aruni to his son, recorded in the *Chhandogya Upanishad* of about the eighth century B.C.: "You, my dear Shvetaketu, you are It"—*tat tvam asi.*[3]

The "you" here meant was not the you that can be named, the "you" that one's friends know and care for, that was born and one day will die. That "you" is not "It." *Neti neti,* "not that, not that." Only when that mortal "you" will have erased everything about itself that it cherishes and is holding to, will "you" have come to the brink of an experience of identity with that Being which is no being yet is the Being beyond the nonbeing of all things. Nor is It anything that you have ever known, ever named, or even thought about in this world: It is not the gods or any God, for example, that has been personified in worship. As we read in the great *Brihadaranyaka Upanishad* (of about the same age as the *Chhandogya*):

This that people say: "Worship this god! Worship that god!"
—one god after another! All this is his creation indeed! And he
himself is all the gods. . . .

He is entered in the universe even to our fingernail-tips, like
a razor in a razorcase, or fire in firewood. Him those people see
not, for as seen, he is incomplete. When breathing, he becomes
"breath" by name; when speaking, "voice"; when seeing, "the
eye"; when hearing, "the ear"; when thinking, "mind": these
are but the names of his acts. Whoever worships one or another
of these—knows not; for he is incomplete in one or another of
these.

One should worship with the thought that he is one's self, for
therein all these become one. This Self is the footprint of that
All, for by it one knows the All—just as, verily, by following a
footprint one finds cattle that have been lost. . . .[4]

I remember a vivid talk by the Japanese Zen philosopher Dr.
Daisetz T. Suzuki, which opened with an unforgettable contrast of
the Occidental and Oriental understandings of the God-man-na-
ture mystery. Commenting first on the Biblical view of the state of
man following the Fall in Eden, "Man," he observed, "is against
God, Nature is against God, and Man and Nature are against each
other. God's own likeness (Man), God's own creation (Nature)
and God himself—all three are at war." [5] Then, expounding the
Oriental view, "Nature," he said, "is the bosom whence we come
and whither we go." [6] "Nature produces Man out of itself; Man
cannot be outside of Nature." [7] "I am in Nature and Nature is in
me." [8] The Godhead as highest Being is to be comprehended, he
continued, as prior to creation, "in whom there was yet neither
Man nor Nature." "As soon as a name is given, the Godhead
ceases to be Godhead. Man and Nature spring up and we get
caught in the maze of abstract conceptual vocabulary." [9]

We in the West have named our God; or rather, we have had
the Godhead named for us in a book from a time and place that
are not our own. And we have been taught to have faith not only

in the absolute existence of this metaphysical fiction, but also in its relevance to the shaping of our lives. In the great East, on the other hand, the accent is on experience: on one's own experience, furthermore, not a faith in someone else's. And the various disciplines taught are of ways to the attainment of unmistakable experiences—ever deeper, ever greater—of one's own identity with whatever one knows as "divine": identity, and beyond that, then, transcendence.

The word Buddha means simply, "awakened, an awakened one, or the Awakened One." It is from the Sanskrit verbal root *budh,* "to fathom a depth, to penetrate to the bottom"; also, "to perceive, to know, to come to one's senses, to wake." The Buddha is one awakened to identity not with the body but with the knower of the body, nor with thought but with the knower of thoughts, that is to say, with consciousness; knowing, furthermore, that his value derives from his power to radiate consciousness—as the value of a lightbulb derives from its power to radiate light. What is important about a lightbulb is not the filament or the glass but the light which these bulbs are to render; and what is important about each of us is not the body and its nerves but the consciousness that shines through them. And when one lives for that, instead of for protection of the bulb, one is in Buddha consciousness.

Do we have any such teaching in the West? Not in our best-known teachings of religion. According to our Good Book, God made the world, God made man, and God and his creatures are *not* to be conceived of as in any sense identical. Indeed, the preaching of identity is in our best-known view the prime heresy. When Jesus said, "I and the Father are one," he was crucified for blasphemy; and when the Moslem mystic Hallaj, nine centuries later, said the same, he too was crucified. Whereas just that is the ultimate point of what is taught throughout the Orient as religion.

So, then, what is it that our religions actually teach? Not the way to an experience of *identity* with the Godhead, since that, as we have said, is the prime heresy; but the way and the means to

establish and maintain a *relationship* to a named God. And how is
such a relationship to be achieved? Only through membership in a
certain supernaturally endowed, uniquely favored social group.
The Old Testament God has a covenant with a certain historic
people, the only holy race—the only holy thing, in fact—on
earth. And how does one gain membership? The traditional answer was most recently (March 10, 1970) reaffirmed in Israel as
defining the first prerequisite to full citizenship in that mythologically inspired nation: by being born of a Jewish mother. And in
the Christian view, by what means? By virtue of the incarnation of
Christ Jesus, who is to be known as true God and true man
(which, in the Christian view, is a miracle, whereas in the Orient,
on the other hand, everyone is to be known as true God and true
man, though few may have yet awakened to the force of that wonder in themselves). Through our humanity we are related to
Christ; through his divinity he relates us to God. And how do we
confirm in life our relationship to that one and only God-Man?
Through baptism and, thereby, spiritual membership in his
Church: which is to say, once again through a social institution.

Our whole introduction to the images, the archetypes, the universally known guiding symbols of the unfolding mysteries of the
spirit has been by way of the claims of these two self-sanctified
historical social groups. And the claims of both have today been
disqualified—historically, astronomically, biologically, and every
other way—*and everybody knows it.* No wonder our clergymen
look anxious, and their congregations confused!

And so, what now of our synagogues and our churches? Many
of the latter, I note, have already been turned into theaters; others
are lecture halls, where ethics, politics, and sociology are taught
on Sundays in a stentorian tone with that special theological trem-
olo that signifies God's will. But do they have to go down this
way? Can they not serve any more their proper function?

The obvious answer, it seems to me, is that of course they can
serve—or rather, *could,* if their clerics knew wherein the magic
lay of the symbols they hold in their keep. They could serve sim-

ply by exhibiting these in a properly *affective* way. For it is the
rite, the ritual and its imagery, that counts in religion, and where
that is missing the words are mere carriers of concepts that may or
may not make contemporary sense. A ritual is an organization of
mythological symbols; and by participating in the drama of the
rite one is brought directly in touch with these, not as verbal reports of historic events, either past, present, or to be, but as revelations, here and now, of what is always and forever. Where the
synagogues and churches go wrong is by telling what their symbols
"mean." The value of an effective rite is that it leaves everyone to
his own thoughts, which dogma and definitions only confuse.
Dogma and definitions rationally insisted upon are inevitably hin-
drances, not aids, to religious meditation, since no one's sense of
the presence of God can be anything more than a function of his
own spiritual capacity. Having your image of God—the most intimate, hidden mystery of your life—defined for you in terms contrived by some council of bishops back, say, in the fifth century or
so: what good is that? But a contemplation of the crucifix works;
the odor of incense works; so do, also, hieratic attires, the tones of
well-sung Gregorian chants, intoned and mumbled Introits, Kyries,
heard and unheard consecrations. What has the "affect value" of
wonders of this kind to do with the definitions of councils, or
whether we quite catch the precise meaning of such words as *Ora-
mus te, Domine, per merita Sanctorum tuorum?* If we are curious
for meanings, they are there, translated in the other column of the
prayerbook. But if the magic of the rite is gone. . . .

Let me offer a few suggestions. Let me first present a few
thoughts from the Indian tradition; then a thought from the Japanese; and finally, a suggestion of something that we as Westerners
may require which the Orient cannot give.

The fundamental text of the Hindu tradition is, of course, the
Bhagavad Gita; and there four basic yogas are described. The
word *yoga* itself, from a Sanskrit verbal root *yuj,* meaning "to
yoke, to link one thing to another," refers to the act of linking the
mind to the source of mind, consciousness to the source of con-

sciousness; the import of which definition is perhaps best illustrated in the discipline known as knowledge yoga, the yoga, that is
to say, of discrimination between the knower and the known, between the subject and the object in every act of knowing, and the
identification of oneself, then, with the subject. "I know my body.
My body is the object. I am the witness, the knower of the object.
I, therefore, am not my body." Next: "I know my thoughts; I am
not my thoughts." And so on: "I know my feelings; I am not my
feelings." You can back yourself out of the room that way. And
the Buddha then comes along and adds: "You are not the witness
either. There is no witness." So where are you now? Where are
you between two thoughts? That is the way known as *jnana yoga*,
the way of sheer knowledge.

A second discipline is that known as *raja yoga*, the kingly,
royal, or supreme yoga, which is the one that usually comes to
mind when the word yoga is mentioned. This we might describe as
a kind of psychological gymnastic of rigorous physical as well as
mental attitudes: sitting in the "lotus posture," breathing in deeply
and out to certain counts in certain ways; in through the right nostril, hold, out through the left; in through the left nostril, hold, out
through the right, and so on: all to various meditations. The results are actual psychological transformations, culminating in a
rapturous experience of the whole sheer light of consciousness, released from all conditioning limitations and effects.

A third way, known as *bhakti*, devotional yoga, is the closest of
the disciplines to what we in the West term "worship," or "religion." It consists in giving one's life wholly in selfless devotion to
some beloved being or thing, who becomes thereby in fact one's
"chosen god." There is a charming story told of the great nineteenth-century Indian saint Ramakrishna. A lady came to him in
some distress because she had realized that she did not actually
love and truly worship God. "Is there, then, nothing you love?" he
asked her; and when she replied that she loved her baby nephew,
"There," said he, "there is your Krishna, your Beloved. In your
service to him, you are serving God." And indeed that god

Krishna himself, as we are told in one of his legends, when he was living as a child among a tribe of simple cowherds, taught and advised those folk to worship, not an abstract god above, unseen, but their own cows. "There is where your devotion is, and where God's blessing to you resides. Worship your cows." And they garlanded the cows, and paid them worship. The lesson is clear, and not a little like that of the recent teaching of the modern Christian theologian Paul Tillich, to the point that "God is your highest concern."

The fourth, finally, and principal type of yoga expounded in the *Bhagavad Gita* is that known as the yoga of action, *karma* yoga. It is prepared for already by the very setting of the famous piece: the battlefield at the opening of the legendary Great War of the Sons of India, at the close of the Vedic-Aryan chivalrous age, when the whole feudal aristocracy of the land was self-exterminated in a bloodbath of mutual slaughter. At the opening of the portentous scene, the young prince Arjuna, about to engage in the greatest action of his career, bade his charioteer, the young god Krishna, his glorious friend, to drive him out between the two assembled battle lines, where he looked to left and right and, recognizing in both armies many relatives and friends, noble comrades and heroes of virtue, he let fall his bow and, overcome with pity and great sorrow, said to the god, his driver, "My limbs fail, my mouth is parched, my hair is standing on end. Better that I myself should die here than that I should initiate this battle. I would not kill, to rule the universe: how much less for the rule of this earth?" To which the young god replied with the following piercing words: "Whence this ignoble cowardice?" And with that the great teaching began:

To that which is born, death is certain; to that which is dead, birth is certain: be not afflicted by the unavoidable. As a noble whose duty it is to protect the law, refusing to fight this righteous war you will forfeit both virtue and honor. Your proper concern is alone the *action* of duty, not the *fruits* of the action.

Cast then away all desire and fear for the fruits, and perform your duty.

After that stern talk, the god cleared Arjuna's eyes, and the youth in amazement beheld his friend transfigured—with the radiance of a thousand suns, many flashing eyes and faces, many arms uplifting weapons, many heads, many mouths with glittering tusks. And behold! those two great hosts from either side were pouring, flying into those flaming mouths, crashing on the terrible teeth, perishing; and the monster was licking all its lips. "My God! Who are you?" Arjuna cried, with every hair now standing. And there came from what had been his friend, the Lord of the World, this answer: "I am Black Time, here for the annihilation of these hosts. Even without you, those who are about to die will not live. So now, get in there! Appear to be killing those that I have already slain. Do your duty and be not distressed by any touch of fear."

"Perform your duty," in India means, "Perform without question the assigned duty of your caste." Arjuna was a noble: his duty was to fight. We in the West, however, no longer think that way; and that is why the Oriental concept of the infallible spiritual mentor, the guru, is no longer of any real use here. It does not work, and it can't work. For our notion of the mature individual is not of a person who simply accepts without question or criticism the dictates and current ideals of his social group, as a child would and should accept the orders of a parent. Our ideal is, rather, of one who through his own experience and considered judgment (and I mean *experienced* judgment, not a parroting of the lectures of some freshman sociology course under old Professor So-and-So with his program for the universe), through his own living, has arrived at some reasoned and reasonable attitudes and will function now not as the obedient servant of some unassailable authority but in terms of his own self-responsible determinations. Duty here, therefore, does not mean at all what it means throughout the Orient. It does not mean accepting like a child what has been authoritatively taught. It means thinking, evaluating, and developing an ego: a faculty, that is to say, of independent observation and rational criticism, capable of interpreting its environment as well as of estimating its own powers in relation to circumstance; and of initiating courses of action, then, that will be relevant not to ideals of the past, but to possibilities of the present. But exactly that is in the East the one forbidden thing.

Many of my professor friends are beginning to suggest that our students today are looking not for teachers but for gurus. The guru in the Orient accepts responsibility for his student's moral life, and the student's aim, reciprocally, must be to identify with the guru and become, if possible, just like him. But as far as I can see —and so I tell my academic cronies—these students of ours lack the first virtue of such a student, Oriental style, which is, namely, faith, *shraddha,* "perfect faith," in the unquestioningly revered guru. Criticism, on the other hand, and self-responsible judgment are what we have traditionally hoped to develop in students, and often enough we have succeeded. In fact, with the present crop we have to such a degree succeeded that, hardly out of diapers, they are ready now to teach teacher, which is a bit too much of a good thing. What they may be learning from the Orient, which so many are striving to emulate, I am not going to try to suggest, beyond noting that it will have to be something—the first step or two at least—of the mystic inward way into themselves; and this, if followed without losing touch with the conditions of contemporary life, might well lead in not a few cases to a new depth and wealth of creative thought and fulfillment in life and in literature and the arts.

And with that, I come to my third personal anecdote, which is again to be of the confrontation of East and West in religion; but with a suggestion now of the way in which the Orient turns the magic of religion into art. This one is of an event that occurred in the summer of 1958, when I was in Japan for the Ninth International Congress on the History of Religions. One of our leading New York social philosophers, who was a conspicuous delegate to that extraordinarily colorful assemblage—a learned, genial, and charming gentleman, who, however, had had little or no previous experience either of the Orient or of religion (in fact I wondered by what miracle he was there)—having gone along with the rest of us on our visits to a number of noble Shinto shrines and beautiful Buddhist temples, was finally ready to ask a few significant questions. There were many Japanese members of the congress, not a few of them Shinto priests, and on the occasion of a great lawn party in the precincts of a glorious Japanese garden, our friend approached one of these. "You know," he said, "I've been now to a good many ceremonies and have seen quite a number of shrines, but I don't get the ideology; I don't get your theology."

The Japanese (you may know) do not like to disappoint visitors, and this gentleman, polite, apparently respecting the foreign scholar's profound question, paused as though in deep thought, and then, biting his lips, slowly shook his head. "I think we don't have ideology," he said. "We don't have theology. We dance."

That, for me, was the lesson of the congress. What it told was that in Japan, in the native Shinto religion of the land, where the rites are extremely stately, musical, and imposing, no attempt has been made to reduce their "affect images" to words. They have been left to speak for themselves—as rites, as works of art— through the eyes to the listening heart. And that, I would say, is what we, in our own religious rites, had best be doing too. Ask an artist what his picture "means," and you will not soon ask such a question again. Significant images render insights beyond speech, beyond the kinds of meaning speech defines. And if they do not speak to you, that is because you are not ready for them, and words will only serve to make you *think* you have understood, thus cutting you off altogether. You don't ask what a dance means, you enjoy it. You don't ask what the world means, you enjoy it. You don't ask what *you* mean, you enjoy yourself; or at least, so you do when you are up to snuff.

But to enjoy the world requires something more than mere good health and good spirits; for this world, as we all now surely know, is horrendous. "All life," said the Buddha, "is sorrowful"; and so, indeed, it is. Life consuming life: that is the essence of its being, which is forever a becoming. "The world," said the Buddha, "is an ever-burning fire." And so it is. And that is what one has to affirm, with a yea! a dance! a knowing, solemn, stately dance of the mystic bliss beyond pain that is at the heart of every mythic rite.

And so, to conclude, let me recount now a really marvelous Hindu legend to this point, from the infinitely rich mythology of the god Shiva and his glorious world-goddess Parvati. The occasion was of a time when there came before this great divinity an audacious demon who had just overthrown the ruling gods of the world and now came to confront the highest of all with a non-negotiable demand, namely, that the god should hand over his goddess to the demon. Well, what Shiva did in reply was simply to open that mystic third eye in the middle of his forehead, and paff! a lightning bolt hit the earth, and there was suddenly there a second demon, even larger than the first. He was a great lean thing with a lionlike head, hair waving to the quarters of the world, and his nature was sheer hunger. He had been brought into being to eat up the first, and was clearly fit to do so. The first thought: "So what do I do now?" and with a very fortunate decision threw himself upon Shiva's mercy.

Now it is a well-known theological rule that when you throw yourself on a god's mercy the god cannot refuse to protect you; and so Shiva had now to guard and protect the first demon from the second. Which left the second, however, without meat to quell his hunger and in anguish he asked Shiva, "Whom, then, do I eat?" to which the god replied, "Well, let's see: why not eat yourself?"

And with that, no sooner said than begun. Commencing with his feet, teeth chopping away, that grim phenomenon came right on up the line, through his own belly, on up through his chest and neck, until all that remained was a face. And the god, thereupon, was enchanted. For here at last was a perfect image of the monstrous thing that is life, which lives on itself. And to that sunlike mask, which was now all that was left of that lionlike vision of hunger, Shiva said, exulting, "I shall call you 'Face of Glory,' Kirttimukha, and you shall shine above the doors to all my temples. No one who refuses to honor and worship you will come ever to knowledge of me." [10]

The obvious lesson of all of which is that the first step to the knowledge of the highest divine symbol of the wonder and mystery of life is in the recognition of the monstrous nature of life and its glory in that character: the realization that this is just how it is and that it cannot and will not be changed. Those who think —and their name is legion—that they know how the universe could have been better than it is, how it would have been had they created it, without pain, without sorrow, without time, without life, are unfit for illumination. Or those who think—as do many —"Let me first correct society, then get around to myself" are barred from even the outer gate of the mansion of God's peace. All societies are evil, sorrowful, inequitable; and so they will always be. So if you really want to help this world, what you will have to teach is how to live in it. And that no one can do who has not himself learned how to live in it in the joyful sorrow and sorrowful joy of the knowledge of life as it is. That is the meaning of the monstrous Kirttimukha, "Face of Glory," over the entrances to the sanctuaries of the god of yoga, whose bride is the goddess of life. No one can know this god and goddess who will not bow to that mask in reverence and pass humbly through.

VI

The Inspiration of Oriental Art

[1958]

In Indian textbooks of aesthetics four types of subject are recognized as appropriate for artistic treatment. They are, first, abstract qualities, such as goodness, truth, beauty, and the like; next, types of action and mood (the slaying of enemies or of monsters, the winning of a lover, moods of melancholy, bliss, and so on); third, human types (Brahmins, mendicants, holy or wicked princes, merchants, servants, lovers, outcastes, criminals, etc.); and finally, deities—all of which, we note, are abstract. For there is in the Orient no interest in the individual as such, or in unique, unprecedented facts or events. Accordingly, what the glorious spectacle of Oriental art mainly offers are repetitions, over and over, of certain tried and true themes and motifs. And when these are compared with the galaxies of Renaissance and post-Renaissance Europe, what is perhaps most striking is the absence in the Oriental traditions of anything like significant portraiture. Consider the works of Rembrandt or Titian: the attention given in these to the representation of what we call character, personality, the uniqueness, at once physical and spiritual, of an individual presence. Such a concern for what is not enduring is

utterly contrary to the informing spirit of Oriental art. Our respect
for the individual as a unique phenomenon, not to be suppressed in
his idiosyncrasies, but to be cultivated and brought to fulfillment
as a gift to the world such as never before was seen on earth, nor
will ever appear again, is contrary, *toto caelo,* to the spirit not
only of Oriental art but also of Oriental life. And in keeping with
this turn of mind, the individual is expected not to innovate or in-
vent, but to perfect himself in the knowledge and rendition of
norms.

Accordingly, the Oriental artist must not only address himself
to standard themes, but also have no interest in any such thing as
we understand by self-expression. Accounts, such as abound in the
biographies of Western masters, of an artist's solitary agony in
long quest of his own special language to bring forward his personal message, we shall search for long and in vain in the annals
of Oriental art. Such ego-oriented thinking is alien completely to
Eastern life, thought, and religiosity, which are concerned, on the
contrary, precisely with the quenching of ego and of all interest
in this evanescent thing that is merely the "I" of a passing dream.

On the negative side, this cultivation of anonymity has led to
the production of a panorama *ad infinitum* of academic ste-
reotypes—which, however, is not on the side of our subject to
which I wish to address myself. My theme is to be rather of those
orders and masterworks of consummate art that do indeed render
to mortal eyes the knowledge of an immortal presence in all
things. The song that one hears in one's ears-of-thought when
reading the *Bhagavad Gita,* of that spirit immortal that never was
born, never dies, but lives in all things that are born to die as the
actual being of their apparent being and whose radiance gives to
them their glory, is the universal song that is sung not in Indian
art alone but in Far Eastern life as well; and it is to this that I
would attune my present song.

To begin with, then (commencing in India and moving later on
to the Far East), Indian art is a yoga and its master a kind of yogi.
Having performed through years the assignments of an obedient

apprenticeship, and having gained at last recognition as a master, commissioned to erect, say, a temple or to fashion a sacred image, the artist first will meditate, to bring before his inner eye a vision of the symbolic building to be planned, or of the deity to be rendered. Indeed, there are legends even of entire cities envisioned in this way: of some saintly monarch who will have had a dream in which he will have seen, as in a revelation, the whole form of the temple or city to be built. And I wonder if that may not be the reason why, in certain Oriental cities one can feel, even today, that one is moving in a dream: the city is dreamlike because in its inception it was actually suggested by a dream, which then was rerendered in stone.

The artist craftsman about to set to work fashioning the image of a divinity—let us say, of Vishnu—will first have studied all the relevant texts, to fix in mind the canonical signs, postures, proportions, etc., of the aspect of the god to be rendered. He will then settle down, pronouncing in his heart the seed syllable of the deity's name, and if he is fortunate there will appear, in due time, a vision before his inner eye of the very form he is to render, which will be the model, then, for his work of art. Thus the greatest works of the great periods of India were actually revelations; and to appreciate them properly as the revelations not of supposed supernatural beings, but of a power of nature latent in ourselves and requiring only to be recognized to be brought to fulfillment in our lives, we need only turn to that extraordinary psychological textbook, *A Description of the Six Bodily Centers of the Unfolding Serpent Power* (*Shatchakra-nirupanam*), which has been available now for some sixty years in the superb translation of Sir John Woodroffe, published by Ganesh and Company, Madras.[1]

The basic thesis of the so-called Kundalini yoga system elucidated in this fundamental work is that there are six plus one—i.e., seven—psychological centers distributed up the body, from its base to the crown of the head, which can, through yoga, be successively activated and so caused to release ever higher realizations of spiritual consciousness and bliss. These are known as "lotuses," *padmas,* or as *chakras,* "wheels," and are to be thought of as normally hanging limp. However, when touched and activated by a rising spiritual power called the Kundalini, which can be made to ascend through a mystic channel up the middle of the spine, they awaken to life and shine. The name of this power, *kundalini,* "the coiled one," is a feminine Sanskrit noun, here referring to the idea of a coiled serpent, to be thought of as sleeping in the lowest of the seven body centers. In the mythologies of the Orient serpents generally symbolize the vital power that sloughs death, as serpents shed their skin to be (as it were) reborn. This power is thought of in India as feminine, the feminine, form-building, life-giving and -supporting force by which the universe and all its beings are rendered animate. Sleeping coiled in the lowest of the seven centers of the body, it leaves the other six unactivated. The aim, therefore, of this yoga is to wake the serpent, cause her to lift her head, and to bring her up the mystic interior channel of the spine known as Sushumna, "rich in pleasure," piercing at each stage of her thrilling ascent the lotus there located. The yogi, sitting cross-legged, erect, holding in mind certain thoughts and pronouncing mystic syllables, will be first concerned to regulate the rhythm of his breathing, inhaling deeply, holding, and exhaling to fixed counts: in through the right nostril, out through the left, etc., pervading thus the entire body with *prana,* "spiritus," "breath," the breath of life, until presently the coiled serpent stirs and the process begins.

It is said that when the coiled serpent rests in the first lotus center, asleep, the personality of the individual is characterized by spiritual torpor. His world is the world of unexhilarated waking consciousness; yet he clings with avidity to this uninspired existence, unwilling to let go, just hanging on. I always think in this connection of what we have been told of the habits of dragons: how they hoard and guard things in their caves. What they usually hoard and guard in this way are beautiful girls and treasures of gold. They can make no proper use of either, of course, yet there they remain, always there. Such people in life are called "creeps," and God knows they are numerous enough. The name of this first lotus is Muladhara, "the root base." Its element is earth, it has four crimson petals, and its situation is described as between the genitals and the anus.

Center number two, then, is at the level of the genitals, and accordingly, anyone whose energies have mounted to this stage is of a psychology perfectly Freudian. Everything means sex to him, one way or another, as it did indeed to Freud himself, who was certain that there was nothing else people lived for: and we have now even a great school of thinkers who call themselves philosophers, interpreting the whole course of human history, thought, and art in terms of sex—repressed, frustrated, sublimated, or fulfilled. The name of this station is Svadhishthana, "her favorite resort." It is a lotus of six vermilion petals, and its element is water.

Lotus three is at the level of the navel. Its name, Manipura, means "the city of the shining jewel." It is a lotus of ten petals of the color of heavy-laden storm clouds; fire is its element; and the governing interest of anyone whose unfolding serpent power has become established on this plane is in consuming, conquering, turning all into his own substance, or forcing all to conform to his way of thought. His psychology, ruled by an insatiable will to power, is of an Adlerian type. And so Freud and Adler and their followers can be said to have interpreted the phenomenology of the spirit in terms exclusively of *chakras* two and three—which is enough to explain their inability to make anything more interesting either of the mythological symbols of mankind or of the goals of human aspiration.

For it is only at the level of the fourth *chakra* that specifically human, as distinct from sublimated animal, aims and drives become envisioned and awakened; and, according to the Indian view, it is to this level and beyond (not to the concerns of *chakras* one, two, and three) that religious symbols, the imagery of art, and the questions of philosophy properly refer. The lotus of this center is at the level of the heart; its element is air; it has twelve petals of an orange-crimson hue (the color of the Bandhuka flower [*Pen-*

tapoetes Phoenicea]), and it has a very curious name. It is called Anahata, "not hit," which means, when fully interpreted, "The sound that is not made by any two things striking together." All the sounds that we hear in this world of time and space are made by two things striking together: the sound of my voice, for example, by the breath striking my vocal cords. Likewise, every other heard sound is of things, whether seen or unseen, striking together. And so, what then would be the sound *not* made that way?

The answer given is that the sound not made by any two things striking together is of that primal energy of which the universe itself is a manifestation. It is thus antecedent to things. One might think of it as comparable to the great humming sound of an electric-power station; or as the normally unheard humming of the protons and neutrons of an atom: the interior sound, that is to say, of that primal energy, vibrating, of which ourselves and all that we know and see are apparitions. And when heard, they say, the sound that it most resembles is OM.

This sacred Indian syllable of prayer and meditation is said to be composed of four symbolic elements. First, since the O, in Sanskrit, is regarded as an amalgam of the two sounds A and U, the sacred syllable can be written and heard as AUM, and when it is so displayed, three of its four elements are made visible. The fourth, then, is the Silence that surrounds the syllable so viewed, out of which it rises, back into which it falls, and which supports it as the ground of its appearance.

Now when pronounced, the A of AUM is heard proceeding from the back of the mouth. Coming forward with U, the sounding air mass fills the whole mouth cavity; and with M it is closed at the lips. When thus pronounced, they say, the syllable contains the sounds of all the vowels of speech. And since the consonants are but interruptions of these sounds, the holy syllable contains in itself—when properly pronounced—the seed sounds of all words and thus the names of all things and relationships.

There is an extremely interesting and important Upanishad, the *Manduka,* in which the four symbolic elements of the syllable—

the A, the U, the M, and the Silence—are interpreted allegorically as referring to four planes, degrees, or modes of consciousness. The A, resounding from the back of the mouth, is said to represent waking consciousness. Here the subject and the objects of its knowledge are experienced as separate from each other. Bodies are of gross matter; they are not self-luminous and they change their forms slowly. An Aristotelean logic prevails: *a* is not *not-a*. The nature of thought on this level is that of mechanistic science, positivistic reasoning, and the aims of its life are as envisioned at *chakras* 1, 2, and 3.

Next, with U, where the sound mass, moving forward, fills the whole head as it were, the Upanishad associates dream consciousness; and here the subject and object, the dreamer and his dream, though they may seem to be separate, are actually one, since the images are of the dreamer's own will. Further, they are of a subtle matter, self-luminous, and of rapidly changing form. They are of the nature of divinities: and indeed all the gods and demons, Heavens and Hells, are in fact the cosmic counterparts of dream. Moreover, since on this subtle plane the seer and the seen are one and the same, all the gods and demons, Heavens and Hells are within us; are ourselves. Turn within, therefore, if you seek your model for the image of a god. Accordingly, it is experiences of this plane of consciousness that are rendered visible in the Oriental arts.

Next, M, third element of the syllable, where the intonation of this holy sound terminates forward, at the closed lips, the Upanishad associates with deep dreamless sleep. There is here neither object seen nor seeing subject, but unconsciousness—or rather, latent, potential consciousness, undifferentiated, covered with darkness. Mythologically this state is identified with that of the universe between cycles, when all has returned to the cosmic night, the womb of the cosmic mother: "chaos," in the language of the Greeks, or in Genesis, the first "formless waste, with darkness over the seas." There is no consciousness of any objects either of waking or of dream, but only uninflected consciousness in its pristine, uncommitted state—lost, however, in darkness.

The ultimate aim of yoga, then, can be only to enter that zone awake: which is to say, to "join" or to "yoke" (Sanskrit verbal root *yuj,* whence the noun *yoga*) one's waking consciousness to its source in consciousness *per se,* not focused on any object or enclosed in any subject, whether of the waking world or of sleep, but sheer, unspecified and unbounded. And since all words refer to objects or to object-related thoughts or ideas, we have no word or words for the experience of this fourth state. Even such words as "silence" or "void" can be understood only with reference to sound or to things—as of no sound, or as of no thing. Whereas here we have come to the primal Silence antecedent to sound, containing sound as potential, and to the Void antecedent to things, containing as potential the whole of space-time and its galaxies. No word can say what the Silence tells that is all around and within us, this Silence that is no silence but to be heard resounding through all things, whether of waking, dream, or dreamless night—as surrounding, supporting, and suffusing the syllable AUM.

Listen to the sound of the city. Listen to the sound of your neighbor's voice, or of the wild geese honking skyward. Listen to any sound or silence at all without interpreting it, and the Anahata will be heard of the Void that is the ground of being, and the world that is the body of being, the Silence and the Syllable. Moreover, when once this sound has been "heard," as it were, as the sound and being of one's own heart and of all life, one is stilled and brought to peace; there is no need to quest any more, for it is here, it is there, it is everywhere. And the high function of Oriental art is to make known that this truly is so; or, as our Western poet Gerhart Hauptmann has said of the aim of all true poetry: "to let the Word be heard resounding behind words." The mystic Meister Eckhart expressed the same thought in theological terms when he told his congregation, "Any flea as it is in God is nobler than the highest of the angels in himself. Things in God are all the same: they are God Himself." ² That, in short, is the experience of Anahata, at the level of the fourth *chakra,* where things no longer hide their truth, but the marvel is experienced that Blake envisioned when he wrote, "If the doors of perception were cleansed every thing would appear to man as it is, infinite." ³

And so what, then, of *chakra* five?

Chakra five is at the level of the larynx and is called Vishuddha, "purification." It is a lotus of sixteen petals of a smoky purple hue, and its element is ether, space. The yogi at this center is leaving art, religion, philosophy, and even thought behind; for, as in the Purgatory of the Christian faith the soul is purged of residual attachments to earth in preparation for an experience of the Beatific Vision of God, so in this Indian locus of purgation the aim is to eliminate all interpositions of the world between oneself and the immediate hearing of AUM, or, expressed in visual terms, between oneself and the vision of God. The ideals and disciplines of this stage are those rather of the hermit's cell and monastery than of art and civilized life: not aesthetic, but ascetic. And when, at last, the level of the sixth center is then attained, the mystic inward eye fully opens, and the mystic inward ear. One experiences then in immediate force the whole sight and sound of the Lord whose form is the Form of forms and whose radiance resounds. The name of the lotus here is Ajna, which means "authority, command." Its petals are two, most beautifully white. Its element is mind, and its place, well known, is a little above and between the brows. One is here in Heaven, and the soul beholds its perfect object, God.

However, there is one last barrier still; for, as the great Indian saint and teacher Ramakrishna, of the last century, once told his devotees, when the accomplished yogi beholds in this way the vision of his Beloved, there is still, as it were, an invisible wall of glass between himself and that one in whom he would know eternal extinction. For his ultimate aim is not the bliss of this sixth but the absolute, nondual state beyond all categories, visions, sen-

timents, thoughts, and feelings whatsoever, which is of the seventh
and final lotus, Sahasrara, "thousand-petaled," at the crown of the
head.

Let us withdraw, therefore, the glass. The two, the soul and its
god, the inward eye and its object, are extinguished, both and
equally. There is now neither an object nor a subject, nor anything
to be known or named, but the Silence alone that is the fourth and
final grounding element of the once heard, now no longer heard,
syllable AUM.

And here, of course, one is beyond art; beyond even Indian art.
Indian art, I would say, is concerned to suggest and render experiences akin to those of the lotus centers four to six: at four, the objects and creatures of this world as they are (to use Eckhart's
phrase again) "in God"; at five, the terrifying, devastating aspects
of the cosmic powers in their ego-shattering roles, personified as
wrathful, odious, and horrific demons; and at six, their bliss-be-
stowing, fear-dispelling, wondrous, peaceful, and heroic forms.
Thus one is ever beholding in these truly sublime, visionary masterworks either creatures represented under the aspect of eternity,
or mythic personifications of the aspects of eternity known to man.

There is therefore little, very little, of empirical daylight reality
in Indian art, of the world as known to men's normal eyes. The
interest, far and away, is in gods and mythological scenes. And
when one approaches Indian temples, of whatever period or whatever style, there is something altogether remarkable about the way
they appear either to have burst out of the landscape or to have
dropped upon it from aloft—altogether in contrast, for example,
to the lovely temple gardens of the Far East. They have either
burst from beneath the earth as an eruption of subterranean landscape, or have descended merely to rest on earth as the chariot or
magical palace of some celestial divinity. Indeed, on entering any
of the numerous, altogether wonderful cave temples, chiseled, as it
were, by wizard craftsmen, deep into the sides of mountains, not
only do we leave behind the world of normal human experience to
enter one of earth-inhabiting gnomes, but we also leave behind our

normal sense of reality and find these forms to be more true, more real, more intimately our own, somehow, than the accustomed revelations of our light-world lives. Indian art, that is to say, is an art concerned with the transcendence of our normal two-eyed experiences of life, meant to open this third eye, in the middle of the forehead, of the lotus of command, and to reveal to us thus, even while we are awake, a dream-world vision of Heaven or Hell become stone.

All of which is very different from the accent of the arts of the other East, of China, Korea, and Japan. The Buddhism of those lands, of course, originated in India and came to China in the first century A.D., to Japan from Korea in the sixth. And along with Buddhism there was brought, indeed, the wonderful Indian art of depicting the powers of all the Heavens above and Hells below this plane of earth. The natural tendency of the Far Eastern mind is much more earthly, however, than the Indian, more matter-of-fact and concerned with the optical, temporal, and practical aspects of existence. As the eminent Japanese Buddhist philosopher Daisetz T. Suzuki has pointed out in his many writings on the history of the doctrine, the luxuriance of the Indian imagination, dazzling in poetic flight, indifferent to the features of time, soaring at ease through spheres and aeons measured in terms only of infinities, contrasts altogether with the manner of thought particularly of China, where the usual term for the vastness of this universe is, "the world of ten thousand things." That is number enough for the eye and for the mind concerned rather with time than with eternity: time in its practical passage, and space in terrestrial measure, not extrapolated beyond sight. Hence, even in the Buddhist arts of the Far East there is evident generally a displacement of interest from the prospect of the sixth *chakra* to the level of *chakra* four; from that moonlight lotus of two petals, where divinity is beheld unclothed of things, to the rich garden of this beautiful world itself, where things comfortable in their places may be recognized as themselves divine in their very idiosyncrasies. For, "even in a single hair," as I have heard, "there are a thousand golden lions."

Two distinct orders of art can therefore be readily recognized in
the Far East. One is the order of the Buddhist icons, continuing as
far as possible in the spirit of the Indian visionary inspiration, reduced, however, to the level of *chakra* four. The other is most no-
tably represented in the unsurpassed tradition of Chinese and Japanese landscape painting. These are works of an altogether
different spirit, representing a native Far Eastern philosophy, the
philosophy of the *Tao,* which is a Chinese word translated generally as "the Way, the Way of Nature." And this Way of Nature is
the way in which all things come into being out of darkness into
light, then pass out of light back into darkness, the two principles
—light and dark—being in perpetual interaction and, in variously
modulated combinations, constituting this whole world of "ten
thousand things."

The light and the dark of this system of thought are named respectively *yang* and *yin,* which are words referring to the sunny
and the shady sides of a stream. *Yang* is of the sunny side; *yin,*
the shady. On the sunny side there is light, there is warmth, and
the heat of the sun is dry. In the shade, there is the cool, rather, of
the earth, and the earth is moist. Dark, cold, and moist; light, hot,
and dry: earth and sun in counteraction. These are associated, further, with the female and the male as the passive and active principles. There is no *moral* verdict here intended; neither principle
is "better" than the other, neither "stronger" than the other. They
are the two equally potent grounding principles on which all the
world rests, and in their interaction they inform, constitute, and
decompose all things.

Now when our eyes survey a country scene, say, of mountains,
waterfalls, and lakes, what we see are light and dark, light and
dark: wherever they turn, it will be the inflections and various degrees of light and dark that they will see. An artist with his brush,
therefore, could place black on white, dark on light, to represent
such a view. And just that, in fact, will have been the first principle of his whole training: how, by using light and dark, he should
depict the forms that in their essence, as well as in their appear-

ance, are of the power of light and dark, the *yang* and the *yin*. The outer form, light and dark, is to be rendered as a manifestation of what is within. So the artist, with his brush, is manipulating tinctures of the very principles that underlie all nature. The art work, thus, brings forth and makes known the essence of the world itself, that essence being an interplay of these two, the *yang* and the *yin,* through no end of modulations. And the delight of contemplating this interplay is the delight of the man who does not wish to break through and beyond the walls of the world display but to remain within it, playing himself with the potentials of this infinitely and incessantly changing universal duad.

The artist's eyes in China and Japan are open to the world. Does he intend to depict bamboo? Let him assimilate the rhythm of the *yang* and *yin* in bamboo, know bamboo, live with bamboo, watch it, feel it, even eat it. In China we learn of what are known as the six canons, six principles, of the classical painter's art; and these hold true for Japan as well. The first of the six is *rhythm*. When observing bamboo, one is to get the feel of the rhythm of bamboo; when a bird, the rhythms of its bird-life, its walk, its poise, and its flight. For rendering anything, the first necessity is to have known and to have experienced its rhythm. So that rhythm, then, is the first principle of the canon, the indispensable first vehicle of art. And the second principle is *organic form*. The line, that is to say, must be a sound, continuous, living line: itself organic and not the mere imitation of something alive. But in its life it must carry, of course, the rhythm of the object represented. Canon three is *trueness to nature*. The artist eye does not turn away. It holds to nature—which does not mean, however, that the work is to be photographic. It is to the rhythm of the object's life that the artist is to remain true. If the picture is of a bird, the bird is to be birdlike; if of a bird perched on bamboo, the two natures of the bird and the bamboo are equally there. The fourth principle, then, is *color,* which includes the whole mysterious lore of light and shade, the light and the dark, rendering the essences of energy and inertia. Fifth there comes—and this, I have noticed, is

a principle strikingly honored today in Japanese photography—
the placement of the object in the field. In Japan there is, for example, a kind of painting known as "one-corner painting," where
some relatively small subject in a great emptiness (say, a fishing-
boat in a mist) is placed in just such a way, in one corner of the
work, that its influence will affect and bring to life the whole
scene. And finally there is the matter of *style,* the requirement that
the style employed—the force, roughness, or refinement of the
brushstrokes, etc.—should be appropriate to the rhythm of the
subject.

Now, of course, in order to experience what is before him, the
artist has mainly to look; and looking, finally, is an unaggressive
activity. One does not say to one's eyes, "Go out and do something to that thing out there." One looks, looks long, and the
world comes in. There is an important Chinese term, *wu-wei,* "not
doing," the meaning of which is not "doing nothing," but "not
forcing." Things will open up of themselves, according to their nature. And so, just as a god might show himself to the meditating
Indian artist, the world shows itself in its inward form to the eye
of the Far Eastern. "The *Tao* is close at hand, yet people seek it
afar," is an old saying of the Chinese philosopher Mencius. The
idea of the universe coming to form with a spontaneity of its own,
which is at one, finally, with the spontaneity of the nature of the
artist, and the spontaneity, then, of his brush as it renders in black
on white the *Tao* of things, is one that is altogether essential to
this Taoist view.

There are two contrasting Chinese words for law, defined and
elucidated in the second volume of Joseph Needham's *Science and
Civilization in China:* the word *li,* and the word *tse.* The word *li* is
believed to have referred originally to the natural markings on a
piece of jade, the veins in the jade, and, by extension, the natural
grain of life; whereas the second word, *tse,* seems originally to
have had reference, rather, to the markings made on a caldron by
a stylus, markings made by man, its reference accordingly being
to social laws, decreed and contrived, as against natural; laws

thought up by the mind, as against those experienced as of the very pattern of nature. But the function of art is to know and to make known the latter, the laws and patterns, that is to say, of nature and the way nature moves. And to know these, the artist cannot force his own intentions upon nature. Thus it is in the sensitive work of coordinating his own concept of nature, his concept of the task to be done and his disciplines of action, with the actual given patterns of nature, that the balance between doing and not doing is achieved that yields the perfect work of art.

Furthermore, this principle of doing through not forcing informs every discipline of the Far East having to do with effective action. When I was last in Japan, the Sumo wrestling championship matches were in progress in Tokyo, the bouts of those great big fat fellows—and they certainly are big: as someone has said, they illustrate the law of the survival of the fattest. During the greater part of each contest, the two are settled in a squat position, measuring each other. They assume this pose, hold it for a while, then break, walk to the side, pick up a handful of salt, toss this carelessly to the floor, and assume their positions again. They repeat this act a number of times, and the Japanese crowd, meanwhile, is in ecstasy, shouting, watching for that sudden moment—when, bang! they will have grabbed each other and one of the two will already have hit the mat. The bout is finished. And so what was it they were doing during all of those rounds of simply assuming a preparatory stance? They were both measuring each other and finding center in that point of stillness in themselves from which all action springs, each in balance in relation to the other, in a sort of *yin-yang* correlation; and the one who was caught off-center was the one who went down.

I am told that in the old days a young person desiring to learn swordsmanship in Japan would be left by the master largely unattended for a time, doing chores about the school, washing dishes, and so on; and every now and again the master himself would come popping out from somewhere and give him a smack with a stick. After a season of that sort of thing, the victim will have begun to be prepared. But that will be of no use to him, either; for when ready for the blow to come at him, say, from over there, he will get it from back here; and next, from nowhere at all. At last the baffled youth will arrive at the realization that he will do best not to ready himself in any specific direction, because if one has a notion of where the danger may be lurking, he will be attentive in the wrong direction. The only protection, then, is to be in a per-petual state of centeredness in undirected alertness, ever ready for sudden attack and immediate response.

There is an amusing anecdote of a certain master of this kind who told the young men of his school that he would himself bow before anyone who, in any way whatsoever, could catch him by surprise. Days passed, and the master was never caught. He was never off guard. But then, one day when he had returned from an afternoon in the garden, he asked for some water with which to bathe his feet, and it was brought to him by a ten-year-old. The water was a bit cold. He asked the youngster to warm it. The little fellow returned with it hot, and the master, without thinking, put his feet in, quickly pulled them out, and went down on his knees in a very deep bow before the smallest boy in his school.

The sin of inadvertence, not being alert, not quite awake, is the sin of missing the moment of life; whereas the whole of the art of the nonaction that is action (*wu-wei*) is unremitting alertness. One is then fully conscious all the time, and since life is an expression of consciousness, life is then lived, as it were, of itself. There is no need to instruct it or direct it. Of itself it moves. Of itself it lives. Of itself it speaks and acts.

And so it is that throughout the Oriental world, in India as well as in China and Japan, the ideal of art was never—as it has been largely with us of late years—of an activity set apart from life, confined to studios of sculpture, painting, dancing, music, or act-ing. Art in the ancient East was the art of life. In the words of the late Dr. A. K. Coomaraswamy, who for some thirty years was a curator of the Boston Museum of Fine Arts, "The artist, in the ancient world, was not a special kind of man, but every man a special kind of artist." In all living and working, as in all the crafts, the highest concern, the required aim, was to be in the perfection of the work—which is just the opposite (is it not?) from the contemporary union ideal of how much one is to be paid for it and how short the hours are to be. "The adult workman should be ashamed," wrote Dr. Coomaraswamy in one of his discussions of this subject, "if anything he makes falls short of the masterpiece standard." And indeed I must say, my own impression as I have studied for years the works of art of the ancients— whether of Egypt and Mesopotamia, Greece, or the great Orient —has frequently been that the craftsmen of those incredible productions must have been elves or angels; certainly, in any case, not such as we are today. And yet I think also that if even we today could acquire the knack of maintaining undistracted consciousness between coffee breaks, we too might find that we possessed angelic talents, powers, and skills.

Now as I have already said, whereas the Indian mind and Indian arts tend to soar in imagination out of this world of ten thousand things, the Chinese arts and artists of the *Tao* prefer to remain with nature, in harmony with its wonder. And as the old texts tell us of the ancient Chinese Taoist sages, they too were lovers of the hills and watercourses. They are generally pictured as having abandoned city living to retire alone into the wilderness, there to dwell in harmony with nature. However, in Japan this cannot be done. For there are there so many people everywhere that you simply cannot be alone with nature—at least, not for very long. Climb to the summit of even an inaccessible peak and you will find a jolly picnic party already up there before you. There is no escape there from mankind. There is no escape from society. Hence it is, that although the Japanese and Chinese ideograms for the concept "freedom" (Japanese *jiyu;* Chinese *tzu-yu*) are exactly the same in form, the Chinese by implication means liberation from the human nexus, but the Japanese, compliance with the same through willing devotion to secular activities: [4] on one hand, freedom *away* from society, under the great vault of the skies, on the misty mountaintop, picking mushrooms ("No one knows where I am!"); and on the other hand, freedom *within* the undeniable bonds of the given world, the social order in which, and to the ends of which, one has been raised. Remaining within that field, one yet experiences and achieves "freedom" by bringing to it the full consent and force of one's goodwill: for, after all, the life that is found on the mountaintop lives within the heart of man when in society too.

There is a curious, extremely interesting term in Japanese that refers to a very special manner of polite, aristocratic speech known as "play language," *asobase kotoba,* whereby, instead of saying to a person, for example, "I see that you have come to Tokyo," one would express the observation by saying, "I see that you are playing at being in Tokyo"—the idea being that the person addressed is in such control of his life and his powers that for him everything is a play, a game. He is able to enter into life as one would enter into a game, freely and with ease. And this idea is carried even so far that instead of saying to a person, "I hear that your father has died," you would say, rather, "I hear that your father has played at dying." [5] And now, I submit that this is truly a noble, really glorious way to approach life. What *has* to be done is attacked with such a will that in the performance one is literally "in play." That is the attitude designated by Nietzsche as *Amor fati,* love of one's fate. It is what the old Roman Seneca referred to in his often quoted saying: *Ducunt volentem fata, nolentem trahunt:* "The Fates lead him who will; him who won't, they drag."

Are you *up* to your given destiny? That is the challenge of Hamlet's troubled question. The ultimate nature of the experience of life is that toil and pleasure, sorrow and joy, are inseparably mixed in it. The very will to life that brought one to light, however, was a will to come even through pain into this world; else one never would have got here. And *that* is the notion underlying the Oriental idea of reincarnation. Since you came to birth in this world at this time, in this place, and with this particular destiny, it

was this indeed that you wanted and required for your own ultimate
illumination. That was a great big wonderful thing that you thereupon brought to pass: not the "you," of course, that you now suppose yourself to be, but the "you" that was already there before
you were born and which even now is keeping your heart beating
and your lungs breathing and doing for you all those complicated
things inside that are your life. You are not now to lose your nerve!
Go on through with it and play your own game all the way!

And of course, as everybody knows who has ever played at
games, the ones that are the most fun—to lose as well as to win
—are the ones that are the hardest, with the most complicated,
even dangerous, tasks to accomplish. And so it is that artists are
generally not content, either in the Orient or in the Occident, with
doing merely simple things—and much soon becomes simple for
an artist that for the rest of us would be difficult. The artist seeks
the challenge, the difficult thing to do; for his basic approach to
life is not of work but of play.

And so finally, now, this attitude toward art as an aspect of the
game of life, and life itself as the art of a game, is a wonderfully
joyous, invigorating approach to the mixed blessing of existence
—quite in contrast to this of our Christian West, based on a
mythology of universal guilt. There was that Fall, back there, in
the Garden, and we have all been congenital sinners ever since.
Every act of nature is an act of sin, accompanied by a knowledge
of its guilt. Whereas in the Orient there is the idea of the inherent
innocence of nature, even in what might appear to our human eyes
and sentiments to be its cruelties. The world, as they say in India,
is God's "play." It is a wondrous, thoughtless play: a rough play,
the roughest, cruelest, most dangerous, and most difficult, with no
holds barred. Often, it seems, it is the best who lose and the worst
who win. But winning, finally, is not the aim; for as we have already learned in mounting the way "rich in pleasure" of the Kundalini, winning and losing in the usual sense are experiences only
of the lower *chakras*. The aim of the ascending serpent is to clar-
ify and increase the light of consciousness within, and the first step

to the gaining of this boon—as told in the *Bhagavad Gita,* as in many another wisdom text—is to abandon absolutely all concern for the fruits of action, whether in this world or in the next. As the Lord Krishna on the battlefield said to the warrior prince Arjuna, "To the work alone are you entitled, never to its fruit. . . . He who knows that the way of renunciation and the way of action are one, he verily knows." [6]

Life as an art and art as a game—as action for its own sake, without thought of gain or of loss, praise or blame—is the key, then, to the turning of living itself into a yoga, and art into the means to such a life.

There is a little Buddhist story that will serve, I think, to drive this message home with an amusing image. It is of a young Chinese scholar, Chu, who went with a friend for a stroll in the mountains. There they chanced on the ruins of a temple, where among the broken walls an old monk had established his hermitage. Catching sight of the two arriving, the old fellow, adjusting his robe, came toddling forward to show them around. There were some statues of the immortals, as well as, here and there on the remaining walls, a number of lifelike paintings of people, animals, and flowery scenes. Both Chu and his friend were enchanted, and particularly so when, high on one of the walls, they noticed the view of a pretty little town with a lovely girl standing in the foreground, holding flowers in her hands. Her hair was down, which meant that she was unmarried, and Chu no sooner saw her than he was lost altogether in love. His imagination was holding him to the lovely smile on her lips, when, before he knew it—by the power of the foxy old monk, who thought to teach him a lesson—he was there in that little town street himself, and there too was that lovely girl.

She gladly greeted him and led him to her home. And they became engaged immediately in a passionate affair of love that went on for several days. Her friends, discovering them living that way together, laughed and teased and said to her, "Oh, oh! And your hair is still down?" They brought enameled hairpins, and when her hair had been nicely put up, poor Chu was more in love with her than ever. However, a day came when there was heard out in the street a very frightening noise of voices, rattling chains, and heavily tramping boots, which brought them to their window, and they saw a company of imperial officers coming to scout out unregistered aliens. The terrified girl told Chu to hide, which he did. He hid beneath the bed. But then, on hearing a still greater commotion outside, he leaped out from under and, rushing to the window to look, felt his sleeves suddenly fluttering and found that he had passed right out of the picture and was coming down through the air to his friend and the old monk below. The two were standing where all three had been but a few brief moments before; and when Chu, coming down, rejoined them, both he and his friend were amazed. They turned to the monk for an explanation.

"Visions are born and die in those who behold them," he said simply. "What can an old monk say?" But he raised his eyes, and they theirs, to the picture. And what do you know? The girl's hair was up.[7]

VII

Zen

[1969]

▣ In India two amusing figures are used to characterize the two principal types of religious attitude. One is "the way of the kitten"; the other, "the way of the monkey." When a kitten cries "Miaow," its mother, coming, takes it by the scruff and carries it to safety; but as anyone who has ever traveled in India will have observed, when a band of monkeys come scampering down from a tree and across the road, the babies riding on their mothers' backs are hanging on by themselves. Accordingly, with reference to the two attitudes: the first is that of the person who prays, "O Lord, O Lord, come save me!" and the second of one who, without such prayers or cries, goes to work on himself. In Japan the same two are known as *tariki,* "outside strength," or "power from without," and *jiriki,* "own strength," "effort or power from within." And in the Buddhism of that country these radically contrasting approaches to the achievement of enlightenment are represented accordingly in two apparently contrary types of religious life and thought.

The first and more popular of these two is that of the Jodo and Shinshu sects, where a transcendental, completely mythical Buddha known in Sanskrit as Amitabha, "Illimitable Radiance"—also, Amitayus, "Unending Life"—and in Japanese as Amida, is called upon to bestow release from rebirth—as is Christ, in Christian worship, to bestow redemption. *Jiriki,* on the other hand, the way of self-help, own-doing, inner energy, which neither begs nor expects aid from any deity or Buddha, but works on its own to achieve what is to be achieved, is in Japan represented pre-eminently by Zen.

There is a fable told in India of the god Vishnu, supporter of the universe, who one day abruptly summoned Garuda, his air-vehicle, the golden-feathered sun-bird; and when his wife, the goddess Lakshmi, asked why, he replied that he had just noticed that one of his worshipers was in trouble. However, hardly had he soared away when he was back, descending from the vehicle; and when the goddess again asked why, he replied that he had found his devotee taking care of himself.

Now the way of *jiriki,* as represented in the Mahayana Buddhist sect known in Japan as Zen, is a form of religion (if one may call it such) with no dependence on God or on gods, no idea of an ultimate deity, and no need even for the Buddha—in fact, no supernatural references at all. It has been described as:

> a special transmission outside the scriptures;
> not dependent on words or letters;
> a direct pointing to the heart of man;
> seeing into one's own nature; and
> the attainment thereby of Buddhahood.

The word *zen* itself is a Japanese mispronunciation of the Chinese word *ch'an,* which, in turn, is a Chinese mispronunciation of the Sanskrit *dhyana,* meaning "contemplation, meditation." Contemplation, however, of what?

Let us imagine ourselves for a moment in the lecture hall where I originally presented the material for this chapter. Above, we see the many lights. Each bulb is separate from the others, and we may think of them, accordingly, as separate from each other. Regarded that way, they are so many empirical facts; and the whole universe seen that way is called in Japanese *ji hokkai,* "the universe of things."

But now, let us consider further. Each of those separate bulbs is a vehicle of light, and the light is not many but one. The one light, that is to say, is being displayed through all those bulbs; and we may think, therefore, either of the many bulbs or of the one light. Moreover, if this or that bulb went out, it would be replaced by another and we should again have the same light. The light, which is one, appears thus through many bulbs.

Analogously, I would be looking out from the lecture platform, seeing before me all the people of my audience, and just as each bulb seen aloft is a vehicle of light, so each of us below is a vehicle of consciousness. But the important thing about a bulb is the quality of its light. Likewise, the important thing about each of us is the quality of his consciousness. And although each may tend to identify himself mainly with his separate body and its frailties, it is possible also to regard one's body as a mere vehicle of consciousness and to think then of consciousness as the one presence here made manifest through us all. These are but two ways of interpreting and experiencing the same set of present facts. One way is not truer than the other. They are just two ways of interpreting and experiencing: the first, in terms of the manifold of separate things; the second, in terms of the one thing that is made manifest through this manifold. And as, in Japanese, the first is known as *ji hokkai,* so the second is *ri hokkai,* the absolute universe.

Now the consciousness of *ji hokkai* cannot help being discriminative, and, experiencing oneself that way, one is bounded, like the light of a bulb, in this fragile present body of glass; whereas in the consciousness of *ri hokkai* there is no such delimitation. The leading aim of all Oriental mystic teaching, consequently, might be described as that of enabling us to shift our focus of self-identification from, so to say, this light bulb to its light; from this mortal person to the consciousness of which our bodies are but the vehicles. That, in fact, is the whole sense of the famous saying of the

Indian *Chhandogya Upanishad, tat tvam asi,* "Thou art That," "You yourself are that undifferentiated universal ground of all being, all consciousness, and all bliss."

Not, however, the "you" with which one normally identifies: the "you," that is to say, that has been named, numbered, and computerized for the tax collector. That is *not* the "you" that is That, but the condition that makes you a separate bulb.

It is not easy, however, to shift the accent of one's sense of being from the body to its consciousness, and from this consciousness, then, to consciousness altogether.

When I was in India I met and conversed briefly with the saintly sage Shri Atmananda Guru of Trivandrum; and the question he gave me to consider was this: *Where are you between two thoughts?* In the *Kena Upanishad* we are told: "There the eye goes not, speech goes not, nor the mind. . . . Other it is than the known. And moreover above the unknown." [1] For, on coming back from between two thoughts, one would find that all words— which, of course, can be only of thoughts and things, names and forms—only mislead. As again declared in the Upanishad: "We know not, we understand not, how It should be taught."

In fact, as I should think everyone must surely have discovered in his lifetime, it is actually impossible to communicate through speech any experience whatsoever, unless to someone who has himself enjoyed an equivalent experience of his own. Try explaining, for example, the experience of skiing down a mountain slope to a person who has never seen snow. Moreover, thoughts and definitions may annul one's own experiences even before they have been taken in: as, for instance, asking, "Can this that I feel be love?" "Is it allowed?" "Is it convenient?" Ultimately, of course, such questions may have to be asked, but the fact remains—alas! —that the moment they arise, spontaneity abates. Life defined is bound to the past, no longer pouring forward into future. And, predictably, anyone continually knitting his life into contexts of intention, import, and clarifications of meaning will in the end find that he has lost the sense of experiencing life.

The first and foremost aim of Zen, consequently, is to break the net of our concepts—which is why it has been termed by some a philosophy of "no mind." A number of schools of Occidental psychological therapy hold that what we all most need and are seeking is a meaning for our lives. For some, this may be a help; but all it helps is the intellect, and when the intellect sets to work on life with its names and categories, recognitions of relationship and definitions of meaning, what is inwardmost is readily lost. Zen, on the contrary, holds to the realization that life and the sense of life are antecedent to meaning; the idea being to let life come and not name it. It will then push you right back to where you live— where you are, and not where you are named.

There is a favorite story, frequently told by the Zen masters, of the Buddha, preaching: of how he held up a single lotus, that simple gesture being his whole sermon. Only one member of his audience, however, caught the message, a monk named Kashyapa, who is regarded now as the founder of the Zen sect. And the Buddha, noticing, gave him a knowing nod, then preached a verbal sermon for the rest: a sermon for those who required meaning, still entrapped in the net of ideas; yet pointing beyond, to escape from the net and to the way that some of them, one day or another, might find.

The Buddha himself, according to his legend, had broken the net only after years of quest and austerity, when he had arrived at last at the Bodhi-tree, the tree (so called) of enlightenment at the midpoint of the universe—that center of his own deepest silence which T. S. Eliot in his poem "Burnt Norton" has called "the still point of the turning world." In the poet's words:

I can only say, *there* we have been: but I cannot say where. And I cannot say, how long, for that is to place it in time.

There, at that tree, the god whose name is Desire and Death, by whose power the world is kept turning, approached the Blessed One to unseat him; and assuming his fair character as the inciter of desire, beautiful to look upon, he displayed before the Blessed

One his three exceedingly beautiful daughters, Yearning, Fulfillment, and Heartache; so that if the one seated there immovable
had thought, "I," he would certainly also have thought, "They,"
and been stirred. However, since he had lost all sense of the *ji
hokkai,* of things separate from each other, he remained unmoved,
and that first temptation failed.

Immediately, the Lord of Desire transformed himself into King
Death and flung at the Blessed One the whole force of his terrible
army. But again there was neither an "I" nor a "They" where the
Blessed One sat immobile, and the second temptation also failed.

Finally, assuming the form of the Lord of Dharma, Duty, the
Antagonist challenged the right of the Blessed One to be sitting
immobile on that still point of the turning world, when the duties
of his caste required him, as a prince, to be governing men from
his palace. Whereupon the prince, in response, simply changed the
position of his right hand, letting its fingers drop across the knee
to the earth in the so-called "earth-touching posture"; at which
summons the goddess Earth herself, who is Mother Nature, antecedent to society, and whose claims are antecedent too, spoke
forth and with a sound of thunder made known that the one there
sitting had, through innumerable lifetimes, so given of himself to
the world that there was no one there.

The elephant on which the Lord of Desire, Death, and Duty
was mounted bowed in reverence to the Blessed One, and the
army as well as the god himself disappeared. Whereupon the one
beneath the tree achieved that night the whole knowledge of
which I am here speaking—of himself as no "self," but identical
with the *ri hokkai,* transcendent of all names and forms, where (as
again we read in the *Kena Upanishad*) "words do not reach."

And when he had broken past the net of separate things, within
which feeling and thought are entrapped, the Buddha was so
struck by the mind-shattering sheer light that he remained seven
days seated exactly as he was, in absolute arrest; then rose and,
standing seven paces from the place where he had been sitting, remained gazing seven more days at the site of his enlightenment.

Seven days again, and he walked back and forth between the places of his standing and his sitting; after which he sat for seven days beneath a second tree, considering the irrelevance of what he had just experienced to the world-net to which he was returning. Seven days more, beneath still another tree, and he meditated on the sweetness of release; then moved to a fourth tree, where a storm of prodigious force arose that ranged over and around him, seven days. The world serpent, ascending from its station beneath the cosmic tree, gently wrapped itself around the Blessed One, spreading its great cobra-hood above his head, protecting him as a shield. The tempest abated; the cosmic serpent withdrew; and for seven days, at ease beneath a fifth tree, the Buddha, considering, thought: "This cannot be taught."

For indeed, illumination cannot be communicated.

Yet no sooner had the Buddha conceived that thought than the gods of the highest heaven—Brahma, Indra, and their angels—descended to the Blessed One to beg him, for the good of mankind, the gods, and all beings, to teach. And he consented. And for forty-nine years thereafter the Buddha taught in this world. But he did not, and he could not, teach illumination. Buddhism, therefore, is only a Way. It is called a vehicle (*yana*) to the yonder shore, transporting us from this shore of the *ji hokkai* (the experience of the separation of things, the many bulbs, the separate lights) to that, yonder, of the *ri hokkai,* beyond concepts and the net of thought, where the knowledge of a Silence beyond silences becomes actual in the blast of an experience.

And so, how then did the Buddha teach?

He went forth into the world in the character of a doctor diagnosing an illness, to prescribe for his patient a cure. First he asked, "What are the symptoms of the world disease?" And his answer was, "Sorrow!" The First Noble Truth: "All life is sorrowful."

Have we heard? Have we understood? *"All* life is sorrowful!" The important word here is "all," which cannot be translated to mean "modern" life, or (as I have recently heard) "life under cap-

italism," so that if the social order were altered, people then might
become happy. Revolution is *not* what the Buddha taught. His
First Noble Truth was that *life*—all life—is sorrowful. And his
cure, therefore, would have to be able to produce relief, no matter
what the social, economic, or geographical circumstances of the
invalid.

The Buddha's second question, accordingly, was, "Can such a
total cure be achieved?" And his answer was, "Yes!" The Second
Noble Truth: "There is release from sorrow."

Which cannot have meant release from life (life-renunciation,
suicide, or anything of that sort), since that would hardly have
been a return of the patient to health. Buddism is wrongly taught
when interpreted as a release from life. The Buddha's question
was of release not from life, but from sorrow.

So then, what would be the nature of that state of health which
he not only had envisioned but himself had already achieved?
That we learn from his Third Noble Truth: "The release from sorrow is Nirvana."

The literal meaning of this Sanskrit noun *nirvana* is "blown out";
and its reference in the Buddha's sense is to an extinction of
egoism. With that, there will have been extinguished also the desire of ego for enjoyment, its fear of death, and the sense of duties
imposed by society. For the released one is moved from within,
not by any external authority: and this motivation from within is
not out of a sense of duty, but out of compassion for all suffering
beings. Neither dead nor having quit the world, but in the full
knowledge and experience of the *ri hokkai,* the enlightened one
moves in the *ji hokkai,* where Gautama, after his enlightenment,
taught to the great old age of eighty-two.

And what was it he taught? What he taught was the *Way* to release from sorrow, the Eightfold Path, as he termed his doctrine,
of Right Views, Right Aspirations, Right Speech, Right Conduct,
Livelihood, and Effort, Right Meditation, Right Rapture.

But should you ask to know what the Buddha meant exactly by
the term "right" (Sanskrit *samyak,* "appropriate, whole, complete,

correct, proper, true"), you would learn from the various answers
of authorities that the interpretations of the Buddha's teachings
rendered by the various schools of his followers do not always
agree.

The earliest disciples of Gautama followed him literally in his
manner of life, quitting the secular world as monks, entering the
forest or going into monasteries to engage in ascetic disciplines.
Their way was the way of *jiriki,* "own effort," leaving the world
and by dint of great spiritual effort wiping out desire for its goods,
fear of death and deprivation, all sense of social obligation, and,
above all, every thought of "I" and "mine." The Buddha himself,
in his life, had seemed to represent that negative way; and the
monastic life has remained to this day a dominant force throughout the Buddhist world.

However, some five hundred years after the Buddha's life and
passing (whose dates are now given generally as ca. 563–483 B.C.)
—at just about the time, that is to say, of the opening of the
Christian era in the West—there appeared in the Buddhist centers
of North India a new trend in the interpretation of the doctrine.
The protagonists of this later view were certain late followers of
the Master who themselves had achieved illumination and could
appreciate implications of the doctrine that had been missed by
the earliest disciples. One did not have actually to leave the world
as a monk or nun, they had found, to win the gift of illumination.
One could remain in life, in the selfless performance of secular
tasks, and arrive no less securely at the goal.

With this momentous realization, there moved into the center of
Buddhist thought and imagery a new ideal and figure of fulfillment: not the monk with the shaven head in safe retreat from the
toils and tumult of society, but a kingly figure, clothed in royal
guise, wearing a jeweled crown and bearing in hand a lotus symbolic of the world itself. Addressing himself to the world of our
general life, this figure is known as a Bodhisattva. He is one, that
is to say, whose "being" (*sattva*) is "illumination" (*bodhi*), for as
the word *buddha* means "awakened," so *bodhi* is "awakening,

awakenment." And the best-known, most largely celebrated, great
wakeful being of this order is the beautiful saint of many a wondrous legend, known in Sanskrit as Avalokiteshvara. The name is
generally understood to mean "The Lord who regards the world
[in mercy]." The figure appears in Indian art always in masculine
form; in the Far East, however, as the Chinese goddess of mercy,
Kuan Yin (Japanese Kwannon); for such a being transcends the
limits of sex, and the female character, surely, is more eloquent of
mercy than the male.

The legend of this Bodhisattva tells that when he was about to
achieve complete release from this vortex of rebirths that is our
world, he heard the rocks, the trees, and all creation lamenting;
and when he asked the meaning of that sound, he was told that his
very presence here had given to all a sense of the immanence of
nirvanic rapture, which, when he left the world, would be lost. In
his selfless, boundless compassion, therefore, he renounced the release for which he had striven through innumerable lifetimes, so
that, continuing in this world, he might serve through all time as a
teacher and aid to all beings. He appears among merchants as a
merchant, among princes as a prince; even among insects as an in-
sect. And he is incarnate in us all whenever we are in converse
with each other, instructing or mercifully helping.

There is a charming Chinese legend of the infinite saving power
of this truly marvelous Bodhisattva, told of some very simple people dwelling in a village on a remote upper stream of the Yellow
River. They had never heard of religion and were interested only
in archery and swift horses. One early morning, however, an as-
tonishingly beautiful young woman appeared in their village street,
bearing a basket lined with fresh green leaves of the willow and
filled with the golden-scaled fish of the stream. Her wares, which
she cried, were immediately sold, and when they were gone, she
disappeared. Next morning she returned; and so it went for a
number of days. The young men of the village, of course, had
taken note and, having begun to watch for her, one morning
stopped her and pleaded with her to marry.

"O honorable gentlemen," she answered, "certainly I wish to marry. But I am only one woman: I cannot marry you all. So if any one of you can recite by heart the Sutra of the Compassionate Kuan Yin, he is the one I shall choose."

They had never even heard of such a thing, but that night put themselves to work; and next morning when the young woman appeared, there were thirty presenting their claim. "O honorable gentlemen, I am only one woman," she replied again. "If any one of you can explain the Sutra, he is the one I shall wed." The following morning there were ten. "If any one of you can in three days *realize* the meaning of the Sutra," she promised, "he is the one I shall marry surely." And when she arrived the third morning thereafter, there was but one there standing to greet her. His name was Mero. And when she saw him, the very beautiful young woman smiled.

"I perceive," she said, "that you have indeed realized the meaning of the blessed Sutra of the Compassionate Kuan Yin, and do gladly accept you as my husband. My house you will find this evening at the river bend, and my parents there to receive you."

Mero searched that evening as instructed, and at the river bend, among the rocks by the shore, discovered a little house. An old man and woman at the gate were beckoning, and when he approached, announcing his name, "We have been waiting for you a long time," the old man said, and the woman led him to their daughter's room.

She left him there, but the room was empty. From the open window he saw a stretch of sand as far as to the river, and in the sand, the prints of a woman's feet, which he followed, to find at the water's edge two golden sandals. He looked about in the gathering twilight and saw no house now among the rocks. There was only a cluster of reeds by the river, rustling dryly in an evening breeze. And then suddenly he knew: the fishermaid had been no other than the Bodhisattva herself. And he comprehended fully how great is the benevolence of the boundlessly compassionate Kuan Yin.[2]

That is a fable of the way of "outside help," *tariki,* the way of the kitten—which is not, however, the way of Zen.

I have already mentioned the legend of the Buddha elevating a lotus and but one member of his audience grasping the meaning. Suppose now that I were to lift a lotus and ask you for its meaning! Or suppose, rather, not a lotus—for associated with the lotus are a lot of well-known allegorical references: suppose I lifted a buttercup and asked for the meaning of a buttercup! Or a dead stick, with the question: "What is the meaning of a dead stick?" Or still again: Suppose you asked me the meaning of Buddhism or of the Buddha, and I lifted up a dead stick!

The Buddha is known as the one "Thus Come," Tathagata. He has no more "meaning" than a flower, than a tree; no more than the universe; no more than either you or I. And whenever anything is experienced that way, simply in and for and as itself, without reference to any concepts, relevancies, or practical relationships, such a moment of sheer aesthetic arrest throws the viewer back for an instant upon his own existence without meaning; for he too simply *is*—"thus come"—a vehicle of consciousness, like a spark flung out from a fire.

When Buddhism, in the first century A D , was carried from India to China, an imperial welcome was accorded the monks, monasteries were established, and the formidable labor was undertaken of translating the Indian scripture. Notwithstanding the really enormous difficulty of turning Sanskrit into Chinese, the work went forward famously and had continued for a good five hundred years when there came to China from India, about the year 520 A.D., a curiously grim old Buddhist saint and sage known as Bodhidharma, who immediately proceeded to the royal palace. According to the legend of this visit, the Emperor asked this somewhat cussed guest how much merit he had gained through his building of monasteries, support of monks and nuns, patronizing of translators, etc., and Bodhidharma answered, "None!"

"Why so?" inquired the Emperor.

"Those are inferior deeds," came the answer. "Their objects are

mere shadows. The only true work of merit is Wisdom, pure, perfect and mysterious, which is not to be won through material
acts."

"What, then," the Emperor asked, "is the Noble Truth in its
highest sense?"

"It is empty," Bodhidharma answered. "There is nothing noble
about it."

His Majesty was becoming annoyed. "And who is this monk
before me?"

To which the monk's reply was, "I do not know." And he left
the court.

Bodhidharma retreated to a monastery and settled down there,
facing a wall, where, as we are told, he remained in absolute silence for nine years—to make the point that Buddhism proper is
not a function of pious works, translating texts, or performing rituals and the like. And there came to him, as he sat there, a Confu-
cian scholar, Hui K'o by name, who respectfully addressed him,
"Master!" But the Master, gazing ever at his wall, gave no sign of
even having heard. Hui K'o remained standing—for days. Snow
fell; and Bodhidharma, in perfect silence, remained exactly as he
was. So finally, to indicate the seriousness of his purpose, the visitor drew his sword and, cutting off his own left arm, presented
this to the teacher; at which signal the monk turned.

"I seek instruction," said Hui K'o, "in the doctrine of the Buddha."

"That cannot be found through another," came the response.

"I then beg you to pacify my soul."

"Produce it, and I shall do so."

"I have sought it for years," said Hui K'o, "but when I look for
it, cannot find it."

"So there! It is at peace. Leave it alone," said the monk, returning his face to the wall. And Hui K'o, thus abruptly awakened
to his own transcendence of all daylight knowledge and concerns,
became the first Ch'an master of China.

The next crucial teacher in this Chinese Ch'an line of great

names, Hui-neng (638–713 A.D.), was an illiterate woodchopper,
we are told. His mother was a widow, whom he supported by delivering firewood. And he was standing one day at the door of a
private home, waiting for an order, when he overheard someone
inside intoning the verses of a Mahayana scripture called the
"Diamond Cutter," *Vajrachchhedika.* "Wake the mind," is what
he heard, "not fixing it anywhere." And, immediately illumined, he
was overcome.

Desiring to improve his understanding, Hui-neng then made his
way to a monastery, the Monastery of the Yellow Plum, where the
old abbot, Hung-jen, who was the leading Ch'an master of the period, sized up the illiterate youth and assigned him to the kitchen.
Eight months later, realizing that the time had arrived for him to
fix upon a successor, Hung-jen announced that that one of his
monks who could summarize best in a single stanza the essence of
Buddhist teaching would be given the abbot's robe and begging
bowl symbolic of the highest office. There were some five hundred
monks to compete, and among them one, extraordinarily gifted,
whom all expected to win: his name Shen-hsiu. And indeed, they
were *his* four lines that were selected and formally inscribed on
the wall by the door of the refectory:

> The body is the Bodhi-tree,
> The mind, a mirror bright,
> Take care to wipe them always clean,
> Lest dust on them alight.

The idea here being that the essence of the Buddhist way is dili-
gent purification.

The illiterate kitchen boy, however, having learned of the competition, asked a friend that night to read to him the poem inscribed there on the wall; and when he had heard, begged to have
the following set beside it:

> The body is no Bodhi-tree,
> The mind no mirror bright,

> Since nothing at the root exists,
> On what should what dust alight?

The abbot, next morning, hearing the excited talk of his monks, came down, stood a while before the anonymous poem, took his slipper and angrily erased it. But he had correctly guessed the author and, sending that night for the kitchen boy, presented him with the robe and bowl. "Here, my son," he said; "here are the insignia of this office. Now depart! Run away! Disappear!"

Shen-hsiu's doctrine became the founding tenet of the Northern Ch'an School of China, based on the idea of "gradual teaching" (*chien-chiao*) and the cultivation of learning. Hui-neng, on the other hand, became the founder of a Southern School of "abrupt teaching" (*tun-chiao*), based on the realization that Buddha-knowledge is achieved intuitively, by sudden insight. For this, however, the disciplines of a monastery are not only unnecessary but even possibly a hindrance, and such a doctrine, as the old abbot recognized, would discredit and finally undermine the entire monastic system. Hence his warning to disappear.

"Look within!" Hui-neng is reported to have taught. "The secret is inside you."

But how, if not through a study of the doctrine, may one come to any knowledge of that secret?

In the Zen monasteries of Japan the preferred method is meditation, guided and inspired by a curious succession of intentionally absurd meditation topics known as *koan*. These are drawn, for the most part, from the sayings of the old Chinese masters; as, for instance: "Show me the face you had before your father and mother were born!" or "What is the sound of the clapping of one hand?" Such conundrums cannot be reasoned upon. They first focus, then baffle, thought. In the monasteries the candidates for illumination are ordered by their masters to go meditate on these enigmas and return with answers. Time and time again they fail and are sent back to meditate further—until one moment, suddenly, the intellect lets go and an appropriate retort breaks spontaneously forth.

It has been said (I am told) that the ultimate koan is the universe itself, and that when this one has been answered the others come of themselves. "A koan," D. T. Suzuki has declared, "is not a logical proposition but the expression of a certain mental state." [3] It is that mental state of transrational insight that the apparently absurd, but actually carefully programed sequences of brain-busters are meant to provoke. And that they work and have worked for centuries is the answer to any question a captious critic might ask as to their sense or worth.

So let me offer now a modern Western parable of the Buddhist "wisdom of the yonder shore"—that shore beyond reason, from which "words turn back, not having attained"—of which I first learned some thirty-odd years ago, from the lips of my very great and good friend Heinrich Zimmer. As we have said, Buddhism is a vehicle or ferry to the yonder shore. So let us imagine ourselves standing on *this* shore; let us say, on Manhattan Island. We are sick of it, fed up. We are gazing westward, over the Hudson River, and there, behold! we see Jersey. We have heard a good deal about Jersey, the Garden State; and what a change that would surely be from the filthy pavements of New York! There are no bridges yet: one has to cross by ferry. And so we have begun to sit on the docks, gazing longingly over at Jersey, meditating upon it; ignorant of its true nature, yet thinking of it ever with increasing zeal. And then one day we notice a boat putting out from the Jersey shore. It comes across the waters, our way, and it docks right here at our feet. There is a ferryman aboard, and he calls, "Anyone for Jersey?" "Here!" we shout. And the boatman offers a hand.

"Are you completely sure?" he says, however, as we step down into his craft. And he warns "There is no return ticket to Manhattan. When you put out from this shore you will be leaving New York forever: all your friends, your career, your family, your name, prestige, everything and all. Are you still quite sure?"

We are perhaps a bit intimidated, but we nod and declare that we are sure, quite sure: we have had Fun City to the teeth.

My friends, that is the way of becoming a monk or nun; the way of monastic Buddhism; the way of the earliest followers of the Buddha, and, today, of the Buddhists of Ceylon, Burma, and Thailand. We are here entering what is known as the "little ferry-boat," or "lesser vehicle," *Hinayana,* so called because only those ready to renounce the world as monks or nuns can ride in this craft to the yonder shore. The members of the lay community, unwilling as yet to take the fateful step, will have to wait (that's all!) for a later incarnation, when they will have learned a little more about the vain conceits of their luxuries. This ferry is small, its benches are hard, and the name inscribed on its side is *Theravada,* "the doctrine of the ancient saints."

We embark, the ferryman hands us an oar, and the craft moves out from the dock. Ship ahoy! We are on the way, but on a rather longer voyage than we knew. In fact, it may endure for a number of lives. Nevertheless, already we are enjoying it, and already we feel superior. We are the holy ones, the voyagers, the people of the crossing, neither here nor there. We actually know, of course, no more about the Garden State than the fools (as we now call them) back on shore in the rat-maze of New York; but we are heading in the right direction, and the rules of our life are entirely different from those of the folks back home. In terms of the ladder of the Kundalini ascent (see above, pp. 107–114), we are at *chakra* five, Vishuddha, "purgation," the center of ascetic disciplines. And we are finding it, at first, very interesting and absorbing. But then gradually, in a surprising way, it begins to become frustrating—even hopeless. For the aim of it all is to get rid entirely of ego-consciousness, whereas the more we strive, the more we are building up ego, thinking of nothing, really, but ourselves: "How am *I* doing?" "Have *I* made any progress today? this hour? this week? this month? this year? this decade?" There are some who become so attached to all this self-examination that the last thing they really want to achieve is disembarkment. And yet, in some chance moment of self-forgetfulness, the miracle might indeed take place and our boat, in the spirit of the ancient saints, put to beach—in Jersey, the Garden State, Nirvana. And we step ashore. We have left the boat and all its dos and don'ts behind.

But now let us realize where we are. We have arrived at the *ri hokkai,* the shore of the knowledge of unity, nonduality, no separateness; and, turning to see what the Manhattan shore might look like from this absolute point of view . . . Astonishment! There *is* no "other" shore. There is no separating stream; no ferryboat, no ferryman; no Buddhism, no Buddha. The former, unilluminated notion that between bondage and freedom, life in sorrow and the rapture of Nirvana, a distinction is to be recognized and a voyage undertaken from one to the other, was illusory, mistaken. This world that you and I are here experiencing in pain through time, on the plane of consciousness of the *ji hokkai,* is, on the plane of *ri hokkai,* nirvanic bliss; and all that is required is that we should alter the focus of our seeing and experiencing.

But is that not exactly what the Buddha taught and promised, some twenty-five centuries ago? Extinguish egoism, with its desires and fears, and Nirvana is immediately ours! We are already there, if we but knew. This whole broad earth is the ferryboat, already floating at dock in infinite space; and everybody is on it, just as he is, already at home. That is the fact that may suddenly hit one, as "sudden illumination." Hence the name, *Mahayana*—"big ferryboat," "greater vehicle"—of the Buddhism of this nondual thinking, which is the Buddhism best known as of Tibet, medieval China, Korea, and Japan.

And so what we have now discovered is that the world of many separate things, the *ji hokkai,* is not different from the *ri hokkai.* There is between the two no division. The Mahayana Japanese term for this stage of realization is *ji-ri-mu-ge,* "things and unity: no division." Though moving in the world of the multiple, we realize also, "This is the One." We are experiencing as an actuality the unity of all—and not simply all of us human beings, but the light-bulbs up there on the ceiling as well, and the walls of the great old lecture hall, and the city outside, Manhattan, and yes! the gardens of Jersey too. We include equally the past—our numerous disparate pasts—and the future, which is already here, like an oak in the acorn. To walk about in knowledge and experience of all this is to live as in a wondrous dream.

Nor is this, finally, all; for there is still one more degree of realization possible of discovery, namely that termed in Japanese *ji-ji-mu-ge:* "thing and thing: no division": no separation between things. The analogy suggested is of a net of gems: the universe as a great spread-out net with at every joint a gem, and each gem not only reflecting all the others but itself reflected in all. An alternate image is of a wreath of flowers. In a wreath, no flower is the "cause" of any other, yet together, all are the wreath. Normally we think of causes and effects. I give this book a push and it moves. It moved because I pushed it. The cause preceded the effect. What is the cause, though, of the growth of an acorn? The oak that is to come! What is to happen in the future is then the cause of what is occurring now; and, at the same time, what occurred in the past is also the cause of what is happening now. In addition, a great number of things round about, on every side, are causing what is happening now. Everything, all the time, is causing everything else.

The Buddhist teaching in recognition of this fact is called the Doctrine of Mutual Arising. It implies that no one—nobody and no thing—is to blame for anything that ever occurs, because all is mutually arising. That fundamentally is one reason why in Japan, even shortly following World War II, I found among the people I met no resentment. Enemies mutually arise: they are two parts of the one thing. A leader and his following also are parts of the one thing. You and your enemies; you and your friends: all parts of the one thing, one wreath: "thing and thing: no division."

This, surely, is sublime. This, furthermore, is the inspiring idea that inhabits much Far Eastern Buddhist art. When you are looking, for example, at a Japanese painting of a crane, that is not simply what you or I might perceive as a crane, but the universe, a reflex of the *ri hokkai,* the one Buddha-consciousness of all things.

Moreover, anything can be looked upon and immediately experienced this way.

A monk came to Ch'i-an of Yen-kuan. "Who is Vairochana Buddha?" he asked.

Said the Master, "Will you kindly bring me that pitcher?"

The monk brought the pitcher to the Master, who then told him to put it back where he found it. The monk did so and asked the Master again to tell him of Vairochana.

Ch'i-an replied, "He is long since gone." [4]

This, finally, then, is what is meant by the Mahayana Buddhist term *zen* < *ch'an* < *dhyana* = "contemplation." It is a way of contemplation that can be just as well enjoyed while walking, working, and otherwise moving about in this world, as while sitting in a lotus posture, gazing at a wall or at nothing, in the manner of a Bodhidharma. It is a way of participation, living gladly in this secular world, both *in* the world and *of* it, our labor in the earning of a living then being our discipline; the raising of our family; our intercourse with acquaintances; our sufferings and our joys. T. S. Eliot, in his play *The Cocktail Party,* applied the idea—with a number of covert quotations from Buddhist texts—to the context of a modern social circle. And in medieval Japan this was the Buddhism of the samurai. Its influence can be felt to this day in the Japanese arts of defense: wrestling, swordsmanship, archery, and the rest. Equally in the arts of gardening, flower arrangement, cooking, even wrapping a parcel and offering a present, this Buddhism is in operation. Its way is the "way of the monkey," *jiriki,* "own power," exercised in relation not only to what might be regarded in our part of the world as concerns properly religious, but, even more deliberately and diligently, to every domain of life. Which, in fact, is what accounts in the main for the almost incredible beauty of Japanese civilization. Great poverty, suffering, cruelty, and injustices, all the usual concomitants of existence in this vale of tears, are present there in full measure—as everywhere, and as they will be, world without end. But there is also escape from suffering. The escape from suffering is Nirvana. And Nirvana is this world itself, when experienced without desire and fear, just as it is: *ji-ji-mu-ge*. It is here! It is here!

To conclude, then: There is a popular Indian fable that Ramakrishna used to like to tell, to illustrate the difficulty of holding in mind the two conscious planes simultaneously, of the multiple and transcendent. It is of a young aspirant whose guru had just brought home to him the realization of himself as identical in essence with the power that supports the universe and which in theological thinking we personify as "God." The youth, profoundly moved, exalted in the notion of himself as at one with the Lord and Being of the Universe, walked away in a state of profound absorption; and when he had passed in that state through the village and out onto the road beyond it, he beheld, coming in his direction, a great elephant bearing a howdah on its back and with the mahout, the driver, riding—as they do—high on its neck, above its head. And the young candidate for sainthood, meditating on the proposition "I am God; all things are God," on perceiving that mighty elephant coming toward him, added the obvious corollary, "The elephant also is God." The animal, with its bells jingling to the majestic rhythm of its stately approach, was steadily coming on, and the mahout above its head began shouting, "Clear the way! Clear the way, you idiot! Clear the way!" The youth, in his rapture, was thinking still, "I am God; that elephant is God." And, hearing the shouts of the mahout, he added, "Should God be afraid of God? Should God get out of the way of God?" The phenomenon came steadily on with the driver at its head still shouting at him, and the youth, in undistracted meditation, held both to his place on the road and to his transcendental insight, until the moment of truth arrived and the elephant, simply wrapping its great trunk around the lunatic, tossed him aside, off the road.

Physically shocked, spiritually stunned, the youth landed all in a heap, not greatly bruised but altogether undone; and rising, not even adjusting his clothes, he returned, disordered, to his guru, to

require an explanation. "You told me," he said, when he had explained himself, "you told me that I was God." "Yes," said the
guru, "you are God." "You told me that all things are God."
"Yes," said the guru again, "all things are God." "That elephant,
then, was God?" "So it was. That elephant was God. But why
didn't you listen to the voice of God, shouting from the elephant's
head, to get out of the way?"

VIII

The Mythology of Love

[1967]

⌘ What a wonderful theme! And what a wonderful world of myth one finds in celebration of this universal mystery! The Greeks, it will be recalled, regarded Eros, the god of love, as the eldest of the gods; but also as the youngest, born fresh and dewy-eyed in every loving heart. There were, moreover, two orders of love, according to the manners of manifestation of this divinity, in his terrestrial aspect and celestial. And Dante, following the classical lead, saw love suffusing and turning the universe, from the highest seat of the Trinity above to the lowest pits of Hell.

One of the most amazing images of love that I know is Persian —a mystical Persian representation of Satan as the most loyal lover of God. You will have heard the old legend of how, when God created the angels, he commanded them to pay worship to no one but himself; but then, creating man, he commanded them to bow in reverence to this most noble of his works, and Lucifer refused—because, we are told, of his pride. However, according to this Moslem reading of his case, it was rather because he loved and adored God so deeply and intensely that he could not bring himself to bow before anything else. And it was for that that he was flung into Hell, condemned to exist there forever, apart from his love.

Now it has been said that of all the pains of Hell, the worst is neither fire nor stench but the deprivation forever of the beatific sight of God. How infinitely painful, then, must the exile of this great lover be, who could not bring himself, even on God's own word, to bow before any other being!

The Persian poets have asked, "By what power is Satan sustained?" And the answer that they have found is this: "By his memory of the sound of God's voice when he said, 'Be gone!' " What an image of that exquisite spiritual agony which is at once the rapture and the anguish of love!

Another lesson from Persia is in the life and words of the great Sufi mystic Hallaj, who in the year 922 was tortured and crucified for having declared that he and his Beloved—namely God—were one. He had compared his love for God with that of the moth for the flame. The moth plays about the lighted lamp till dawn, and, returning with battered wings to its friends, tells of the beautiful thing it found; then, desiring to be joined to it entirely, flying into the flame the next night, becomes one with it.

Such metaphors speak of a rapture that we all, one way or another, must at one time or another, either intensely or not so intensely, have experienced or at least imagined. But there is another aspect of love, which some may also have experienced, and which is likewise illustrated in a Persian text. This one is from an ancient Zoroastrian legend of the first parents of the human race, where they are pictured as having sprung from the earth in the form of a single reed, so closely joined that they could not have been told apart. However, in time they separated; and again in time they united, and there were born to them two children, whom they loved so tenderly and irresistibly that they ate them up. The mother ate one; the father ate the other; and God, to protect the human race, then reduced the force of man's capacity for love by some ninety-nine per cent. Those first parents thereafter had seven

more pairs of children, every one of which, however—thank God!
—survived.

The old Greek idea of Love as the eldest of the gods is matched
in India by that ancient myth from the *Brihadaranyaka Upanishad*
cited above, pp. 78f., of the Primal Being as a nameless, formless
power that at first had no knowledge of itself but then thought,
"I," *aham,* and immediately felt fear that the "me" it now had in
mind might be slain. Then, reasoning, "Since I am all there is,
what should I fear?" it thought, "I wish there were another!" and,
swelling, splitting, became two, a male and a female; out of which
primal couple there came into being all the creatures of this earth.
And when all had been accomplished, the male looked about, saw
the world he had produced, and thought and said, "All this am I!"

In the meaning of this story, that Primal Being antecedent to
consciousness—which in the beginning thought, "I!" and felt fear,
then desire—is the motivating substance activating each one of us
in our unconsciously motivated lives. And the second lesson of the
myth is that through our own experiences of the union of love we
participate in the creative action of that ground of all being. For,
according to the Indian view, our separateness from each other in
space and time here on earth—our multitude—is but a secondary,
deluding aspect of the truth, which is that in essence we are of one
being, one ground; and we know and experience that truth—going
out of ourselves, outside the limits of ourselves—in the rapture of
love.

The great German philosopher Schopenhauer, in a magnificent
essay on "The Foundation of Morality," treats of this transcendental spiritual experience. How is it, he asks, that an individual can
so forget himself and his own safety that he will put himself and
his life in jeopardy to save another from death or pain—as though
that other's life were his own, that other's danger his own? Such a
one is then acting, Schopenhauer answers, out of an instinctive
recognition of the truth that he and that other in fact are one. He
has been moved not from the lesser, secondary knowledge of himself as separate from others, but from an immediate experience of

the greater, truer truth, that we are all one in the ground of our being. Schopenhauer's name for this motivation is "compassion," *Mitleid,* and he identifies it as the one and only inspiration of inherently moral action. It is founded, in his view, in a metaphysically valid insight. For a moment one is selfless, boundless, without ego. And I have lately had occasion to think frequently of this word of Schopenhauer as I have watched on television newscasts those heroic helicopter rescues, under fire in Vietnam, of young men wounded in enemy territory: their fellows, forgetful of their own safety, putting their young lives in peril as though the lives to be rescued were their own. There, I would say—if we are looking truly for an example in our day—is an *authentic* rendition of the labor of Love.

In the religious lore of India there is a formulation of five degrees of love through which a worshiper is increased in the service and knowledge of his God—which is to say, in the Indian sense, in the realization of his own identity with that Being of all beings who in the beginning said "I" and then realized, "I am all this world!" The first degree of such love is of servant to master: "O Lord, you are the Master; I am thy servant. Command, and I shall obey!" This, according to the Indian teaching, is the appropriate spiritual attitude for most worshipers of divinities, no matter where in the world. The second order of love, then, is that of friend to friend, which in the Christian tradition is typified in the relationship of Jesus and his apostles. They were friends. They could discuss and even argue questions. But such a love implies a deeper readiness of understanding, a higher spiritual development than the first. In the Hindu scriptures it is represented in the great conversation of the *Bhagavad Gita* between the Pandava prince Arjuna and his divine charioteer, the Lord Krishna. The next, or third, degree of love is that of parent for child, which in the Christian world is represented in the image of the Christmas Crib. One is here cultivating in one's heart the inward divine child of one's own awakened spiritual life—in the sense of the mystic Meister Eckhart's words when he said to his congregation: "It is

more worth to God his being brought forth spiritually in the individual virgin or good soul than that he was born of Mary bodily."
And again: "God's ultimate purpose is birth. He is not content
until he brings his Son to birth in us." In Hinduism, it is in the
popular worship of the naughty little "butter thief," Krishna the
infant among the cowherds by whom he was reared, that this
theme is most charmingly illustrated. And in the modern period
there is the instance of the troubled woman already mentioned,
supra, p. 98, who came to the Indian saint and sage Ramakrishna, saying, "O Master, I do not find that I love God." And he
asked, "Is there nothing, then, that you love?" To which she answered, "My little nephew." And he said to her, "There is your
love and service to God, in your love and service to that child."

The fourth degree of love is that of spouses for each other. The
Catholic nun wears the wedding ring of her spiritual marriage to
Christ. So too is every marriage in love spiritual. In the words attributed to Jesus, "The two shall be one flesh." For the "precious
thing" then is no longer oneself, one's individual life, but the duad
of each as both and the living of life, self-transcended in that
knowledge. In India the wife is to worship her husband as her
lord; her service to him is the measure of her religion. (However,
we do not hear there anything like as much of the duties of a husband to his wife.)

And so now, finally, what is the fifth, the highest order of love,
according to this Indian series? It is passionate, illicit love. In
marriage, it is declared, one is still possessed of reason. One still
enjoys the goods of this world and one's place in the world,
wealth, social position, and the rest. Moreover, marriage in the
Orient is a family-made arrangement, having nothing whatsoever
to do with what in the West we now think of as love. The seizure
of passionate love can be, in such a context, only illicit, breaking
in upon the order of one's dutiful life in virtue as a devastating
storm. And the aim of such a love can be only that of the moth in
the image of Hallaj: to be annihilated in love's fire. In the legend
of the Lord Krishna, the model is given of the passionate yearning

of the young incarnate god for his mortal married mistress, Radha, and of her reciprocal yearning for him. To quote once again the mystic Ramakrishna, who in his devotion to the goddess Kali was himself, all his life, such a lover: when one has loved God in this way, sacrificing all for the vision of his face, "O my Lord," one can say, "now reveal thyself!" and he will *have* to respond.

There is the figure also, in India, of the Lord Krishna playing his flute at night in the forest of Vrindavan, at the sound of whose irresistible strains young wives would slip from their husbands' beds and, stealing to the moonlit wood, dance the night through with their beautiful young god in transcendent bliss.

The underlying thought here is that in the rapture of love one is transported beyond temporal laws and relationships, these pertaining only to the secondary world of apparent separateness and multiplicity. Saint Bernard of Clairvaux, in the same spirit, sermonizing in the twelfth century on the Biblical text of the Song of Songs, represented the yearning of the soul for God as both beyond the law and beyond reason. Moreover, the excruciating separation and conflict of the two orders of moral commitment, of reason on one hand, and passionate love on the other, have been a source of Christian anxiety since the beginning. "The desires of the flesh are against the Spirit," wrote Saint Paul, for example, to the Galatians, "and the desires of the Spirit, against the flesh."

Saint Bernard's contemporary Abelard saw the highest exemplification of God's love for man in the descent of the son of God to the earth to become flesh and his submission to death on the cross. In Christian hermaneutics the crucifixion of the Savior had always presented a great problem; for Jesus, according to Christian belief, accepted death voluntarily. Why? In Abelard's view, it was not, as some in his day had proposed, as a ransom paid to Satan, to "redeem" mankind from his keep; nor was it, as others held, as a payment to the Father, in "atonement" for Adam's sin. Rather, it was an act of willing self-immolation in love, intended to invoke in response the return of mankind's love from worldly concerns to

God. And that Christ may not have actually suffered in that loving act we may take from a saying of the mystic Meister Eckhart:
"To him who suffers but not for love, to suffer is suffering and
hard to bear. But one who suffers for love suffers not, and his suffering is fruitful in God's sight."

Indeed, the very idea of a descent of God into the world in love
to invoke, in return, man's love to God, seems to me to imply exactly the contrary to the statement I have just quoted of Saint
Paul. Implied, rather, it seems to me, is the idea that as mankind
yearns for the grace of God, so God for the homage of mankind,
the two yearnings being reciprocal. And the image of the crucified
as both true God and true man would then seem to bring to focus
the matched terms of a *mutual* sacrifice—in the way not of atonement in the penal sense, but of at-one-ment in the marital. And
further: when extended to symbolize not only the one historic moment of Christ's crucifixion on Calvary, but the mystery through
all time and space of God's presence and participation in the
agony of all living things, the sign of the cross would then have to
be looked upon as the sign of an eternal affirmation of all that is,
ever was, or shall ever be. One thinks of Christ's words reported
in the Gnostic *Gospel According to Thomas:* "Cleave a piece of
wood, I am there; lift up the stone, you will find me there." Also,
those of Plato in the *Timaeus,* where he states that time is "the
moving image of Eternity." Or again, those of William Blake:
"Eternity is in love with the productions of time." And there is a
memorable passage in the writings of Thomas Mann, where he
celebrates man as "a noble meeting [*eine hohe Begegnung*] of
Spirit and Nature in their yearning way to each other."

We can safely say, therefore, that whereas some moralists may
find it possible to make a distinction between two spheres and
reigns—one of flesh, the other of the spirit, one of time, the other
of eternity—wherever love arises such definitions vanish, and a
sense of life awakens in which all such oppositions are at one.

The most widely revered Oriental personification of such a
world-affirming attitude, transcending opposites, is that figure of

boundless compassion already discussed at considerable length, the Bodhisattva Avalokiteshvara, known to China and Japan as Kuan Yin, Kwannon (*supra,* pp. 134–136). For, in contrast to the Buddha, who at the conclusion of his lifetime of teaching passed away, never to return, this infinitely compassionate one, who renounced for himself eternal release to remain forever in this vortex of rebirths, represents through all time the mystery of a knowledge of eternal release while living. The liberation thus taught is, paradoxically, not of escape from the vortex, but of full participation voluntarily in its sorrows—moved by compassion; for indeed, through selflessness one is released from self, and with release from self there is release from desire and fear. And as the Bodhisattva is thus released, so too are we, according to the measure of our experience of the perfection of compassion.

It is said that ambrosia pours from the Bodhisattva's fingertips even to the deepest pits of Hell, giving comfort there to the souls still locked in the torture chambers of their passions. We are told, furthermore, that in all our dealings with each other we are his agents, whether knowingly or not. Nor is it the aim of the Bodhisattva to change—or, as we like to say, to "improve"—this temporal world. Conflict, tension, defeats, and victories are inherent in the nature of things, and what the Bodhisattva is doing is participating in the nature of things. He is benevolence without purpose. And since *all* life is sorrowful, and necessarily so, the answer cannot lie in turning—or "progressing"—from one form of life to another, but only in dissolving the organ of suffering itself, which—as we have seen—is the idea of an ego to be preserved, committed to its own compelling concepts of what is good and what is evil, true and false, right and wrong; which dichotomies —as we have likewise seen—are dissolved in the metaphysical impulse of compassion.

Love as *passion;* love as *com*passion: these are the two extreme poles of our subject. They have been often represented as absolutely opposed—physical, respectively, and spiritual; yet in both the individual is torn out of himself and opened to an experience of rediscovered identity in a larger, more abiding format. And in both it is the work of Eros, eldest and youngest of the gods, that we must recognize: the same who in the beginning, as told in the ancient Indian myth, poured himself forth in creation.

In the Occident the most impressive representation of love as *passion* is to be found undoubtedly in the legend of the love potion of Tristan and Isolt, where it is the paradoxology of the mystery that is celebrated: the agony of love's joy, and the lover's joy in that agony, which is by noble hearts experienced as the very ambrosia of life. "I have undertaken a labor," wrote the greatest of the great Tristan poets, Gottfried von Strassburg, from whose version of the legend Wagner took the inspiration for his opera, "a labor out of love for the world and to comfort noble hearts: those that I hold dear, and the world to which my heart goes out." But then he adds: "Not the common world do I mean, of those who (as I have heard) cannot bear grief and desire but to bathe in bliss. (May God then let them dwell in bliss!) Their world and manner of life my tale does not regard: its life and mine lie apart. Another world do I hold in mind, which bears together in one heart its bitter sweetness and its dear grief, its heart's delight and its pain of longing, dear life and sorrowful death, dear death and sorrowful life. In this world let me have my world, to be damned with it, or to be saved."

Do we not recognize here an echo of that same metaphysically grounded sense of a coincidence and transcendence of opposites that we have already found symbolized in the figures of Satan in Hell, Christ on the cross, and the moth consumed in the flame?

However, in the medieval European experience and understanding of love, as interpreted not only by Gottfried and the Tristan poets, but also by the troubadours and Minnesingers of the twelfth and early thirteenth centuries, there is an altogether different tone from anything of the Orient, whether of the Far, Middle, or Near East. Essentially the Buddhist quality of "compassion," *karuna,* is equivalent to the Christian of "charity," *agape,* which is epitomized in the admonition of Christ to love your neighbor as yourself!—and even better, beyond that, in the words that I take to be the highest, the noblest and boldest, of the Christian teaching: "Love your enemies and pray for those who persecute you, so that you may be sons of your Father who is in heaven; for he makes his sun to rise on the evil and on the good, and sends rain on the just and on the unjust. . . ."

In all the great traditional representations of love as compassion, charity, or *agape,* the operation of the virtue is described as general and impersonal, transcending differences and even loyalties. And against this higher, *spiritual* order of love there is set generally in opposition the lower, of lust, or, as it is so often called, "animal passion," which is equally general and impersonal, transcending differences and even loyalties. Indeed, one could describe the latter most accurately, perhaps, simply as the zeal of the organs, male and female, for each other, and designate the writings of Sigmund Freud as the definitive modern text on the subject of such love. However, in the European twelfth and early thirteenth centuries, in the poetry first of the troubadours of Provence, and then, with a new accent, of the Minnesingers, a way of experiencing love came to expression that was altogether different from either of those two as traditionally opposed. And since I regard this typically and exclusively European chapter of our subject as one of the most important mutations not only of human feeling, but also of the spiritual consciousness of our human race, I am going to dwell on it a little, before proceeding to the final passages of this chapter.

To begin with, then: Marriage in the Middle Ages was almost exclusively a social, family concern—as it has been forever, of course, in Asia, and is to this day for many in the West. One was married according to family arrangements. Particularly in aristocratic circles, young women hardly out of girlhood were married off as political pawns. And the Church, meanwhile, was sacramentalizing such unions with its inappropriately mystical language about the two that were now to be of one flesh, united through love and by God: and let no man put asunder what God hath joined. Any actual experience of love could enter into such a system only as a harbinger of disaster. For not only could one be burned at the stake in punishment for adultery, but, according to current belief, one would also burn forever in Hell. And yet love came, even so, to such noble hearts as were celebrated by Gottfried; not only came, but was invited in. And it was the work of the troubadours to celebrate this passion, which in their view was of a divine grace altogether higher in dignity than the sacraments of the Church, higher than the sacrament of marriage, and, if excluded from Heaven, then sanctified in Hell. And that the word AMOR was the reverse in spelling of ROMA seemed marvelously to epitomize the sense of the contrast.

But wherein, then, lay the special quality of this new order of love, the love that was neither *agape* nor *eros,* but *amor?*

Debates of the troubadours on the subject were a favorite theme of their poems, and the most fitting definition achieved was that which has been preserved to us in a stanza by one of the most respected of their number, Guiraut de Borneilh, to the point that *amor* is discriminative—personal and specific—born of the *eyes* and the *heart.*

So, through the eyes love attains the heart:
For the eyes are the scouts of the heart,
And the eyes go reconnoitering
For what it would please the heart to possess.
And when they are in full accord
And firm, all three, in the one resolve,
At that time, perfect love is born
From what the eyes have made welcome to the heart.
Not otherwise can love be born or have commencement
Than by this birth and commencement moved by inclination.

To be noted well: such a noble love is *not* indiscriminate. It is not a "love thy neighbor as thyself no matter who he may be"; not *agape,* charity or compassion. Nor is it an expression of the general will to sex, which is equally indiscriminate. It is of the order, that is to say, neither of Heaven nor of Hell, but of earth; grounded in the psyche of a particular individual and, specifically, the predilection of his eyes: their perception of another specific individual and communication of her image to his heart—which is to be (as we are told in other documents of the time) a "noble" or "gentle" heart, capable of the emotion of love, *amor,* not simply lust.

And what, then, would be the nature of a love so born?

In the various contexts of Oriental erotic mysticism, whether of the Near East or of India, the woman is mystically interpreted as an occasion for the lover to experience depths beyond depths of transcendent illumination—much in the way of Dante's appreciation of Beatrice. Not so among the troubadours. The beloved to them was a woman, not the manifestation of some divine principle; and specifically, *that* woman. The love was for *her.* And the celebrated experience was an agony of earthly love: an effect of the fact that the union of love can never be absolutely realized on this earth. Love's joy is in its savor of eternity; love's pain, the passage of time; so that (as in Gottfried's words) "bitter sweetness and dear grief" are of its essence. And for those "who cannot bear grief, and desire but to bathe in bliss," the ambrosial potion of this greatest gift of life is a drink too strong. Gottfried even deified Love as a goddess, and brought his bewildered couple to her hidden wilderness-chapel, known as "The Grotto for People in Love," where stood, in the place of an altar, the noble crystalline bed of love.

Moreover—and this, to me, is the most profoundly moving passage in Gottfried's version of the legend—when, on the ship sailing from Ireland (with which scene Wagner's opera commences), the young couple unwittingly drank the potion and became gradually aware of the love that for some time had been quietly growing in their hearts, Brangaene, the faithful servant who by chance had left the fateful flask unattended, said to them in dire warning, "That flask and what it contained will be the death of you both!" To which Tristan answered, "So then, God's will be done, whether death it be or life. For that drink has poisoned me sweetly. I do not know what the death of which you tell is to be, but *this* death suits me well. And if delightful Isolt is to continue to be my death this way, I shall gladly court an eternal death."

What Brangaene had meant was only physical death. Tristan's reference to *"this* death," however, was to the rapture of his love; and his reference then to "an eternal death" was to an eternity in Hell—which for a medieval Catholic was no mere flourish of speech.

I think of that Moslem figure of Satan, the great lover of God, in God's Hell. And when I recall, furthermore, in the light of these words of Tristan, that scene of Dante's *Inferno* where the poet, describing his passage through the circle of the carnal sinners, tells of having beheld there, carried past on a burning wind, the whirling, screaming souls of all the most famous lovers of history—Semiramis, Helen, Cleopatra, Paris, and yes! Tristan, too; telling of how he had spoken there to Francesca da Rimini in the arms of her husband's brother Paolo, asking what had brought those two to that terrible eternity; and she told him of how they had been reading together of Guinevere and Lancelot and at a certain moment, looking at each other, kissed, all trembling, and read no more in the book that day. . . . When I recall, as I say, that passage in the light of Tristan's welcome of "an eternal death," I cannot help wondering whether Dante could have been quite correct in regarding the condition of his souls in Hell as of unmitigated pain. His point of view was that of an outsider; one, furthermore, whose own love was bearing him onward and upward to the summit of the highest Heaven. Whereas Paolo and Francesca had the inside point of view of a passion of a much more fiery sort, for a clue to whose terrible joy we may take the word of another visionary, William Blake, in *The Marriage of Heaven and Hell:* "As I was walking among the fires of Hell, delighted with the enjoyments of genius which to Angels look like torment and insanity. . . ." For the point about Hell—as of Heaven—is this: when there, you are in your proper place, which, finally, is exactly where you want to be.

The same point has been made in Jean-Paul Sartre's play *No Exit,* where the setting is a hotel room in Hell, sparcly furnished in Second Empire style and with an image of Eros on the mantel. Into this single chamber three permanent guests are to be introduced by the bellhop, one by one.

The first, a middle-aged pacifist journalist, has just this minute been shot as a deserter, and what his pride now most requires is to be told that his attempt to escape to Mexico and publish there a pacifist magazine was heroic; he was not a coward. The second to be ushered in, then, is a Lesbian who lost her life when a young wife whom she had seduced turned on the gas secretly in her apartment and expired with her, asphyxiated, in bed. Immediately despising the craven male who is to be her companion here forever, this coldly intellectual female gives him no comfort whatsoever in his need. Nor can the next and final entrant, a man-crazy young thing who had drowned her illegitimate child and driven her lover to suicide.

This second female, of course, becomes immediately interested in the male, who requires, however, not passion but compassion. The Lesbian blocks every attempt they make to reach some kind of accord, making moves of her own, meanwhile, toward the other female, who has neither any interest in, nor understanding of what she wants. And when these three—so exquisitely matched—have brought their unrelenting demands on each other to such a pitch of frustration that escape, one way or another, would seem to be the only thing that anyone in such a spot could desire, the locked door of their room swings open—showing outside an azure void —and nobody leaves. The door swings shut, and they are locked forever in their chosen cell.

Bernard Shaw says much the same in Act III of his *Man and Superman:* that delicious scene where a little old lady, faithful daughter of Mother Church, is informed that the landscape through which she is happily strolling is not of Heaven but Hell. She is indignant. "I tell you, I know I am not in Hell," she insists, "because I feel no pain." Well, if she likes (she is told), she can easily stroll on over the hill into Heaven. However, the strain of remaining there has been found intolerable (she is warned) for those who are happy in Hell. There are a few—and they are mostly English—who nevertheless remain, not because they are happy, but because they think they owe it to their position to be in Heaven. "An Englishman," states her informer, "thinks he is moral when he is only uncomfortable." And with that telling Shavian quip, I am carried to my final reflections on this chapter's theme.

For it was in the legend of the Holy Grail that the healing work was symbolized through which the world torn between honor and love, as represented in the Tristan legend, was to be cured of its irresolution. The intolerable spiritual disorder of the period was represented in this highly symbolic tale in the figure of a "waste land"—the same that T. S. Eliot in his poem of that name, published in 1922, adopted to characterize the condition of our own troubled time. Every natural impulse in that period of ecclesiastical despotism was branded as corrupt, with the only recognized means of "redemption" vested in sacraments administered by authorities who were themselves indeed corrupt. People were forced to profess and live by beliefs they did not always actually hold. The imposed moral order held precedence over the claims of both truth and love. The pains of Hell were illustrated on earth in the torture of adulteresses, heretics, and other villains, torn apart or set afire in public squares. And all hope of anything better was pitched high aloft to that celestial estate of which Gottfried spoke with such scorn, where those who could bear neither grief nor desire were to be bathed in a bliss everlasting.

In the legend of the Grail, as rendered in the *Parzival* of Gottfried's very great contemporary and leading literary rival, Wolfram von Eschenbach, this devastation of Christendom is symbolically attributed to the awesome wounding of the young

Grail King Anfortas, the meaning of whose name is "infirmity"; and the expected issue of the labors of the awaited Grail Knight was to be the healing of this dreadfully wounded youth. Anfortas —significantly—had only inherited, not rightly earned, the high office of guardianship of the supreme symbol of the spiritual life. He had not, that is to say, been properly proven to his role, but instead still moved in the natural way of youth. And like all noble youths of that period, he rode forth one day from the Castle of the Grail with the battle cry *"Amor!"* And he encountered immediately a pagan knight from a land not far from the walled garden of Paradise, who had come riding in quest of the Grail and with its name engraved on his spearhead. The two settled their lances, rode at each other, and the pagan knight was slain. But his lance, inscribed with the name of the Grail, had already unsexed the young king, and its head, broken off, remained in the excruciating wound.

This calamity, in Wolfram's meaning, was symbolic of the dissociation within Christendom of spirit from nature: the denial of nature as corrupt, the imposition of what was supposed to be an authority *super*naturally endowed, and the actual demolishment of both nature and truth in consequence. The healing of the maimed king, therefore, could be accomplished only by an uncorrupted youth *naturally* endowed, who would merit the supreme crown through his own authentic life work and experience, motivated by a spirit of unflinching noble love, enduring loyalty, and spontaneous compassion. Such a one was Parzival. And though we cannot in these few pages review the whole course of his symbolic career, enough can be said of four of the main episodes to suggest the burden of the poet's healing message.

The noble youth had been reared by his widowed mother in a forest aloof from the courtly world, and it was only when he chanced to see a small company of questing knights go riding past his farm that he learned of knighthood and, abandoning his mother, set forth for King Arthur's court. His training in courtesy and in the skills of knightly combat he received from Gurnemanz, an old nobleman who admired his obvious qualities and offered him his daughter in marriage. But Parzival, thinking, "I must not simply accept, I must *earn,* my wife!" courteously, gently refused the gift and, alone again, rode away.

He let the reins lie slack on his charger's neck, and was thus carried by the will of nature (his mount) to the besieged castle of an orphaned queen his own age, Condwiramurs (*conduire amour*), whom he next day heroically rescued from the undesired assaults of a king who had hoped to add her feudal estates through capture and marriage to his own. And it was she, then, that lovely young queen, who became the wife he had earned; and there was no priest to solemnize the marriage—the poet Wolfram's healing message here being that noble love alone is the sanctification of marriage, and loyalty in marriage, the confirmation of love.

Proposition two, to which the poet then addressed himself, was of human nature fulfilled—not overcome or transcended—in the achievement of that supreme spiritual goal of which the Grail was the medieval symbol. For it was only *after* Parzival had met the normal secular challenges of his day—both in knightly deeds and in marriage—that he became involved without either forewarning or intent in the unpredicted, unpredictable, context of the higher spiritual adventure symbolized in the Grail Castle and wondrous healing of its king. The mystical law governing the adventure required that the hero to achieve it should have no knowledge of its task or rules, but accomplish all spontaneously on the impulse of his nature. The castle would appear like a vision before him. Its drawbridge lowering, he would ride across it to a joyous welcome. And the task then expected of him, when the maimed king on his litter would be carried into the stately hall, would be simply to ask what ailed him. The wound would immediately heal, the waste land become green, and the saving hero himself be installed as king. However, on the occasion of his first arrival and reception, Parzival, though moved to compassion, politely held his peace; for he had been taught by Gurnemanz that a knight does not ask questions. Thus he allowed concern for his social image to inhibit the impulse of his nature—which, of course, was exactly what everyone else in the world was doing in that period and was the cause of all that was wrong.

Well, to cut a long and wonderful story very short, the result of this suppression of the dictate of his heart was that the young, misguided knight—scorned, humiliated, cursed, derided, and exiled from the precincts of the Grail—was so shamed and baffled by what had happened that he bitterly cursed God for what he took to have been a mean deception practiced upon him, and for years he rode in desperate, solitary quest, to achieve again that castle of the Grail and release its suffering king. Indeed, even after learning from a forest hermit that it was God's law of that enchantment that none seeking the castle would find it and none who had once failed should ever have a second chance, the resolute youth persisted, moved by compassion for its terribly maimed king, whom his failure had left in such pain.

But his ultimate victory followed, ironically, rather from his loyalty to Condwiramurs and fearlessness in combat than from his obdurate determination to rediscover the castle. The immediate occasion was a great and gallant wedding feast—with many a fair lady thereabout and much fashionable dalliance among colorful pavilions—from which he rode away, not in moral dudgeon but because, with the image of Condwiramurs in his heart (whom he had not seen through all these cruel years of unrelenting quest), he could not bring himself to engage in any of the pleasures of that marvelously fair occasion. He rode away alone. And he had not ridden far when there came charging at him from a nearby wood a brilliant knight of Islam.

Now Parzival had known for some time that he had an elder half-brother, a Moslem; and it happened that this was he. They clashed and gave battle fiercely. "And I mourn for this," wrote Wolfram; "for they were the two sons of one man. One could say that 'they' were fighting, if one wished to speak of two. Those two, however, were one: 'My Brother and I' is one body, like good man and good wife. Contending here from loyalty of heart, one flesh,

one blood, was doing itself much harm." [1] The battle scene is a re-
capitulation transformed of the encounter of Anfortas with the
pagan. Parzival's sword, however, here broke on the other's helmet. The Moslem flung his own blade away, scorning to murder a
defenseless knight, and the two sat down to what proved to be a
recognition scene.

Clearly implicit in this critical meeting is an allegorical reference to the two opposed religions of the time, Christianity and
Islam: "two noble sons," so to say, "of one father." And marvelously, when the two brothers have found their accord, a messenger
of the Grail appears to invite *both* to the castle—which in a
Christian work of the time of the Crusades is a detail surely remarkable! The maimed king is healed, Parzival is installed in his
stead, and the Moslem, taking the Grail Maiden to wife (in whose
virgin hands alone the symbolic vessel had been carried), departs
with her to his Orient, there to reign in truth and love—seeing to
it (as the text declares) "that his people should gain their rights."

But this wonderful *Parzival* of Wolfram von Eschenbach simply
has to be read.[2] Humorous, joyous, altogether different both in
spirit and in meaning from the ponderous opus of Richard Wagner,
it is one of the richest, greatest, most civilized works of the European Middle Ages; and as a monument, moreover, to the world-
saving power of love in all its forms, perhaps the very greatest
love story of all time.

So let me now, in conclusion, turn to the writings of an author
of our own day, Thomas Mann, who already in his earliest nov-
elette, *Tonio Kröger,* named love the controlling principle of his
art.

The young North German hero of this story, whose mother was
a woman of Latin race, found himself set apart from his blue-eyed
blond companions, not only physically, but also temperamentally.
It was with a curiously melancholy strain of intellectual contempt
that he regarded them; yet with envy also, mixed of admiration
and love. Indeed, in his secret heart, he pledged himself to them
all eternally—and particularly a certain charming blue-eyed Hans

and beautiful blonde Ingeborg, who represented to him irresistibly the appeal of fresh human beauty and youthful life.

On coming of age, Tonio left the North to seek his destiny as a writer, and, moving to a city of the South, met there a young Russian, Lisaveta by name, and her circle of heavy thinkers. He there found himself no more at home, however, among those critics and despisers of the commonalty of the human race, than he had formerly felt among the objects of their scorn. He was thus between two worlds, "a lost burgher," as he termed himself; and departing from this second scene mailed back, one day, to the critical Lisaveta an epistolary manifesto, setting forth his credo as an artist.

The right word, *le mot juste,* he had recognized, can wound; can even kill. Yet the duty of the writer must be to observe and to name exactly: wounding, even possibly killing. For what the writer must name in describing are inevitably imperfections. Perfection in life does not exist; and if it did, it would be—not lovable but admirable, possibly even a bore. Perfection lacks personality. (All the Buddhas, they say, are perfect, perfect and therefore alike. Having gained release from the imperfections of this world, they have left it, never to return. But the Bodhisattvas, remaining, regard the lives and deeds of this imperfect world with eyes and tears of compassion.) For let us note well (and here is the high point of Mann's thinking on this subject): what is lovable about any human being is precisely his imperfections. The writer is to find the right words for these and to send them like arrows to their mark—but with a balm, the balm of love, on every point. For the mark, the imperfection, is exactly what is personal, human, natural, in the object, and the umbilical point of its life.

"I admire," wrote Tonio Kröger to his intellectual friend, "those proud and cold beings who adventure on paths of great daemonic beauty and despise 'mankind'; but I do not envy them. Because [and here he lets fly his own dart] if there is anything capable of making a poet of a literary man, it is this burgherlike love that I feel for the human, the commonplace. All warmth, goodness, and humor derives from this; and it even seems to me that it must be itself that love of which it is written that one may speak with the tongues of men and of angels and yet, having it not, be as sounding brass and tinkling cymbals. . . ."

"Erotic" or "plastic irony," is the name that Thomas Mann bestowed on this principle; and through the greater part of his creative career it was the guiding principle of his art. The unflinching eye detects, the intellect names, the heart goes out in compassion; and the life-force of every life-loving heart will be finally tested, challenged, and measured by its capacity to regard with such compassion whatever has been by the eye perceived and by the intellect named. "For God," as we read in Paul to the Romans, "has consigned all men to disobedience, that he may show his mercy to all."

Moreover, life itself, we can be sure, will provide every one of us ultimately with a test of our capacity for such love—as it in time tested Thomas Mann, with its transformation of his blue-eyed Hans and blonde Ingeborg, under Hitler, into what he could only name and describe as depraved monsters. . . .

What does one do under such a test?

Saint Paul has said, "Love bears all things." We have the words, also, of Jesus: "Judge not that you may not be judged." And there is the saying, too, of Heraclitus: "To God all things are fair and good and right; but men hold some things wrong and some right. Good and evil are one."

There is a deep and terrible mystery here, which we perhaps cannot, or possibly simply will not, comprehend; yet which will have to be assimilated if we are to meet such a test. For love is exactly as strong as life. And when life produces what the intellect names evil, we may enter into righteous battle, contending "from loyalty of heart": however, if the principle of love (Christ's "Love your enemies!") is lost thereby, our humanity too will be lost.

"Man," in the words of the American novelist Hawthorne, "must not disclaim his brotherhood even with the guiltiest."

IX

Mythologies of War and Peace

[1967]

⌐ It is for an obvious reason far easier to
name examples of mythologies of war than mythologies of peace;
for not only has conflict between groups been normal to human
experience, but there is also the cruel fact to be recognized that
killing is the precondition of all living whatsoever: life lives on
life, eats life, and would otherwise not exist. To some this terrible
necessity is fundamentally unacceptable, and such people have, at
times, brought forth mythologies of a way to perpetual peace.
However, those have not been the people generally who have survived in what Darwin termed the universal struggle for existence.
Rather, it has been those who have been reconciled to the nature
of life on this earth. Plainly and simply: it has been the nations,
tribes, and peoples bred to mythologies of war that have survived
to communicate their life-supporting mythic lore to descendants.

In the long, long view of the most recent paleological researches
and discoveries, it now appears that in primeval East Africa,
where the earliest evidences of human evolution have come to
light, there were already in the beginning, some eighteen hundred
thousand years ago at least, two distinct kinds of hominid, or man-

like creature, on this earth. One, which Professor L. S. B. Leakey, his discoverer, named Zinjanthropus, appears to have been a vegetarian. His line is now extinct. The other, Homo habilis, "able or capable man," as Leakey named him, was a meat-eater, a killer, a maker of tools and weapons. And it is from his line, apparently, that we of the present human species are descended.

"Man," wrote Oswald Spengler, "is a beast of prey." That is simply a fact of nature. And another such fact is this: that throughout the animal kingdom beasts of prey, when compared with their vegetarian victims, are in general not only the more powerful but also the more intelligent. Heraclitus declared war to be the creator of all great things; and in the words again of Spengler, "The one who lacks courage to be a hammer comes off in the role of the anvil." Many a sensitive mind, reacting to this unwelcome truth, has found nature intolerable, and has cried down all those best fit to live as "wicked," "evil," or "monstrous," setting up instead, as a counter-ideal, the model of him who turns the other cheek and whose kingdom is not of this world. And so it is that finally two radically opposed basic mythologies can be identified in the broad panorama of history: one in which this monstrous precondition of all temporal life is affirmed with a will, and the other, in which it is denied.

Now when we turn to the primitive mythologies of the nonliterate peoples of this earth, what we immediately find is that, without exception, they are of the first, or affirmative kind. I know of no primitive people anywhere that either rejects and despises conflict or represents warfare as an absolute evil. The great hunting tribesmen are killing animals all the time, and since the meat supplies are limited, there are inevitably collisions between the members of contending groups coming in to slaughter the same herds. By and large, hunting people are warrior people; and not only that, but many are exhilarated by battle and turn warfare into exercises in bravura. The rites and mythologies of such tribesmen are based generally on the idea that there is actually no such thing as death. If the blood of an animal slain is returned to the soil, it will carry the life principle back to Mother Earth for rebirth, and the same beast will return next season to yield its temporal body again. The animals of the hunt are regarded in this way as willing victims who give their bodies to mankind with the understanding that adequate rites are to be performed to return the life principle to its source. Likewise, after episodes of battle special rituals are enacted to assuage and release to the land of spirits the ghosts of those that have been slain.

Such ceremonies may also include rites for toning down the war mania and battle heat of those who have done the killing. For this whole business of killing, whether killing beasts or killing men, is supposed to be fraught with danger. On one hand, there is the danger of revenge from the person or animal killed; and on the other hand, there is an equal danger of the killer himself becoming infected by a killing mania and running berserk. Along with the rites to honor and appease ghosts, accordingly, there may be also special rites enacted to reattune returning warriors to the manners of life at home.

One of the first books that I had the privilege of editing was of a Navaho war ceremonial, accompanied by its series of sand paintings (or rather, in this case, "pollen" paintings, made of the pulverized petals of flowers). The legend illustrated was of the Navaho twin war gods, whose rites were revived on the reservation during the years of the Second World War to initiate into the spirit of war the young Navahos being drafted into the United States Army. The name of the ceremony was *Where the Two Came to Their Father*. It told of the journey of the Navaho twin heroes to the home of the sun, their father, to procure from him the magic and weapons with which to eliminate the monsters that were at that time at large in the world. For it is a basic idea of practically every war mythology that the enemy is a monster and that in killing him one is protecting the only truly valuable order of human life on earth, which is that, of course, of one's own people. In the sense of this Navaho rite, the young brave being initiated is identified with the young hero gods of the mythological age, who at that time protected mankind by clearing the wilderness of poisonous serpents, giants, and other monsters. One of the great problems, I would say, of our own variously troubled society is just this, that youths brought up to function in the protected fields of peacefully domestic life, when suddenly tapped to play the warrior role, are provided with little or no psychological induction. They are therefore spiritually unprepared to play their required parts in this immemorial game of life and cannot bring their inappropriate moral feelings to support it.

But not all primitive peoples are fighters, and when we turn from the hunting and warring nomads of the ranging animal plains to the more substantially settled village peoples of the tropics—inhabiting a largely vegetable environment, where plant, not animal food has been forever the basic diet—we might expect to find a relatively peaceable world, with little or no requirement for either a psychology or a mythology of warcraft. However, as already remarked in earlier chapters, there is a very strange prevailing belief throughout those tropical zones, based on the observation that in the vegetable world new life arises from decay, life springs from death, and that from the rotting of last year's growths new plants arise. Accordingly, the dominant mythological theme of many of the peoples of those regions supports the notion that through killing one increases life, and it is, in fact, exactly in those parts of the world that the most horrible and grotesque rituals of human sacrifice obtain even to this day, their inspiration being the notion that to activate life one kills. It is in those areas that the headhunt flourishes, the basic idea there being that before a young man who is to marry can beget a life, he must take a life and bring back as trophy a head—which will be honored at the wedding, not regarded with disdain, but respectfully entertained, so to say, as the giver of the power of life to the children of this marriage, now to be conceived and born.

And with respect to this grim task of procuring sacrificial victims for the furtherance of life, we have as an extreme example the ancient Aztec civilization, where it was supposed that unless

human sacrifices were continually immolated on the numerous altars the sun itself would cease to move, time stop, and the universe fall apart. And it was simply to procure sacrifices by
hundreds and by thousands that the Aztecs waged on their neighbors continuous war. Their own warriors were honored as priests;
and a principle of combat—combats even between the elements,
wind and earth, water and fire—was the founding principle of
their universe, with the great ritual of war, known as the Flowery
War, its highest celebration.

Now in the very ancient Near East, where grain-planting and
-harvesting communities first arose and the earliest towns then
came into being, from the eighth millennium B.C. or so onward, an
altogether new order of human existence gradually took form,
based not on foraging and hunting, but on planting and harvesting
crops, with the great and good Mother Earth as the main provider
of sustenance. And it was in those times, among those people, that
the fertility rites developed that have been the basic rites of all agriculturally founded civilizations ever since: rituals having to do
with the plow and of seeding, of reaping, winnowing, and first
fruits. For the first thousand years or so of their existence, those
earliest little towns were able to survive without protective walls.
However, by the sixth millennium B.C., and more prominently
during the fifth, walls begin to be evident in the archaeology of
those centers of civilized life, and these let us know that ranging
warrior peoples were beginning to threaten and occasionally to in-
vade and plunder the now comparatively rich settlements of the
peaceable, toiling tillers of the soil.

The two most important raiding races in the western parts of
this newly developing culture field were the cattle-herding Aryans
from the grazing-plains of Eastern Europe, and the Semites from
the south, from the Syro-Arabian desert, with their flocks of goats
and sheep. Both were terribly ruthless fighters, and their raids into
the towns and cities were appalling. The Old Testament abounds
in accounts of peaceful settlements overwhelmed, ravished, and utterly destroyed. Just imagine! From the watchtowers a dust cloud

is spied on the horizon. A windstorm? No! It is a Bedouin band;
and next morning there remains not a single living soul within
those city walls.

The two greatest works of war mythology in the West are, accordingly, the *Iliad* and the Old Testament. The late Bronze and
early Iron Age Greeks were becoming masters of the ancient Ae-
gean just about when the Amorites, Moabites, and earliest Habiru
or Hebrews were overrunning Canaan. These were approximately
contemporaneous invasions; and the legends celebrating their victories were developed simultaneously too. Moreover, the basic
mythological concepts animating these two bodies of legend were
not very different, either. They both pictured a sort of two-storied
world, with the floor of earth below, and above, an upper story of
divine beings. On the earth-plane below, there were certain wars
being waged—of *our* people overcoming *those* people—the progress of these wars being directed, however, from aloft. In the case
of the *Iliad,* the various gods of a polytheistic pantheon are supporting variously both sides; for there are quarrels going on up
there too, of Poseidon against the will of Zeus, Athene against
Aphrodite, and Zeus for a time against Hera. As the arguments
fare of the gods aloft, so the fortunes below of the armies on
earth. And in fact, one of the most interesting things about the
Iliad is that, though composed to honor the Greeks, its greatest
honors and respect are for the Trojans. The noble Trojan cham-
pion Hector is the leading spiritual hero of the piece. Achilles, beside him, is a thug. And the tender episode, in Book VI, of Hector's departure into battle from Andromache his wife and their
little son Astyanax ("like a beautiful star" in his nurse's arms) is
surely the supreme moment of humanity, gentleness, and true
manliness of the entire work.

"Dear my lord," the good wife pleaded, "this thy hardihood
will undo thee; for soon will the Achaians all set upon thee and
slay thee." And her splendid husband answered: "I pray thee,
dear one, be not of oversorrowful heart. No man against my fate
shall hurl me into Hades: only destiny, which no man has ever es-

caped, whether coward or valiant, once he has been born." And when the little boy shrank in fear from his father's shining helmet with its horsehair crest, Hector laughed aloud and, removing it, laid it gleaming on the earth, then kissed his son, dandled him in his arms, and spoke a prayer for him to Zeus before departing to be slain.

Or consider that magnificent tragedy of Aeschylus, *The Persians:* what an extraordinary production to have been presented in a Greek city hardly twenty years after Aeschylus himself had fought the invading Persians at Salamis! The setting is in Persia, with the queen of Persia and her court discussing the return of their defeated king Xerxes from that battle. It is written from the Persian point of view and shows with what respect and great capacity for empathy the ancient Greeks could regard even their most threatening enemy of that time.

But when we turn from the *Iliad* and Athens to Jerusalem and the Old Testament it is to a mythology with a very different upper story and very different power up there: not a polytheistic pantheon favoring both sides simultaneously, but a single-minded single deity, with his sympathies forever on one side. And the enemy, accordingly, no matter who it may be, is handled in this literature in a manner in striking contrast to the Greek, pretty much as though he were subhuman: not a "Thou" (to use Martin Buber's term), but a thing, an "It." I have chosen a few characteristic passages that we shall all—I am sure—readily recognize, and which, rehearsed in the present context, may help us to realize that we have been bred to one of the most brutal war mythologies of all time.

First, then, as follows:

When the Lord your God brings you into the land which you are entering to take possession of it, and clears away many nations before you, the Hittites, the Girgashites, the Amorites, the Canaanites, the Perizzites, the Hivites, and the Jebusites, seven nations greater and mightier than yourselves, and when the

Lord your God gives them over to you, and you defeat them;
then you must utterly destroy them; you shall make no covenant
with them and show them no mercy. You shall not make marriages with them, giving your daughters to their sons or taking
their daughters for your sons. For they would turn away your
sons from following me, to serve other gods; then the anger of
the Lord would be kindled against you, and he would destroy
you utterly. But thus shall you deal with them: you shall break
down their altars, and dash in pieces their pillars, and hew
down their Asherim, and burn their graven images with fire.
For you are a people holy to the Lord your God; the Lord your
God has chosen you to be a people for his own possession, out
of all the peoples that are on the face of the earth [Deuteron-
omy 7:1–6].

When you draw near to a city to fight against it, offer terms
of peace to it. And if its answer to you is peace and it opens to
you, then all the people who are found in it shall do forced
labor for you and shall serve you. But if it makes no peace with
you, but makes war against you, then you shall besiege it; and
when the Lord your God gives it into your hand you shall put
all its males to the sword, but the women and the little ones, the
cattle, and everything else in the city, all its spoil, you shall
take as booty for yourselves; and you shall enjoy the spoil of
your enemies, which the Lord your God has given you. Thus
you shall do to all the cities which are very far from you, which
are not cities of the nations here. But in the cities of these people that the Lord your God gives you for an inheritance, you
shall save alive nothing that breathes, but you shall utterly destroy them, the Hittites and the Amorites, the Canaanites and
the Perizzites, the Hivites and the Jebusites, as the Lord your
God has commanded [Deuteronomy 20:10–18].

And when the Lord your God brings you into the land which
he swore to your fathers, to Abraham, to Isaac, and to Jacob,
to give you, with great and goodly cities, which you did not

build, and houses full of all good things, which you did not fill, and cisterns hewn out, which you did not hew, and vineyards and olive trees, which you did not plant, and when you eat and are full, then take heed lest you forget the Lord, who brought you out of the land of Egypt, out of the house of bondage [Deuteronomy 6:10–12].

And when, in reading, we move on from Deuteronomy to the greatest war book of all, of Joshua, there is—most famous of all —the legend of the fall of Jericho. The trumpets blew, the walls fell down. "And then," as we read, "they utterly destroyed all in the city, both men and women, young and old, oxen, sheep, and asses, with the edge of the sword. . . . And they burned the city with fire, and all within it; only the silver and gold, and the vessels of bronze and of iron, they put into the treasury of the house of the Lord" (Joshua 6:21, 24). The next city was Ai. "And Israel smote them, until there was left none that survived or escaped. . . . And all who fell that day, both men and women, were twelve thousand, all the people of Ai" (Joshua 8:22, 25). "And so Joshua defeated the whole land, the hill country and the Negeb, and the lowland and the slopes, and their kings. He left none remaining, but utterly destroyed all that breathed, as the Lord God of Israel commanded" (Joshua 10:40).

And that, the very same Lord God so frequently cited by our doves of peace today as having taught, "Thou shalt not kill!"

Moreover, we have next the Book of Judges, with that story at the end of it of how the tribe of Benjamin got their wives (Judges 21). The earliest hymn of the Bible, Deborah's song, is a war song (Judges 5). In the Book of Kings we have those utterly monstrous bloodbaths accomplished in the name, of course, of Yahweh by Elijah and Elisha. Next come the reforms of Josiah (II Kings 22–23); shortly following which, however, Jerusalem itself is besieged and taken by the King of Babylon, Nebuchadnezzar, in the year 586 B.C. (II Kings 25).

But above and beyond all this there soars that beautiful ideal of

an ultimate and universal peace, which, from the time of Isaiah
onward, has played so alluringly through all the leading war
mythologies of the West. There is, for example, that beguiling
image so frequently cited, at the close of Isaiah 65, where "the
wolf and the lamb shall feed together, the lion shall eat straw like
the ox; and dust shall be the serpent's food. They shall not hurt or
destroy in all my holy mountain, says the Lord." However, just a
little earlier in the same Isaiah we have already been given to
know what the ideal of the peace to come is actually to be: "The
foreigners," we have there to read,

> shall build up your walls and their kings shall minister to you;
> for in my wrath I smote you, but in my favor I have had mercy
> on you. Your gates shall be open continually; day and night
> they shall not be shut; that men may bring to you the wealth of
> nations, with their kings led in procession. For the nation and
> kingdom that will not serve you shall perish; those nations shall
> be utterly laid waste. The glory of Lebanon shall come to you,
> the cypress, the plane tree, and the pine, to beautify the place
> of my sanctuary; and I will make the place of my feet glorious.
> The sons of those who oppressed you shall come bending low to
> you; and all who despised you shall bow down at your feet;
> they shall call you the City of the Lord, the Zion of the Holy
> One of Israel [Isaiah 60:10–14].

Now it was strange, and not a little threatening and awesome,
to hear echoes of these same themes emanating from the jubilation
of victory in Israel, just following the six-day Blitzkrieg and Sabbath on the seventh, of recent date. This mythology, that is to say,
unlike the ancient Greek, is still very much alive. And of course,
to complete the picture, the Arabs have *their* divinely authorized
war mythology too. For they too are a people who, according to
their legend, are of the seed of Abraham: the progeny of Ishmael,
his first and elder son. Moreover, according to this history, confirmed in the Koran, it was Abraham and Ishmael, before the
birth of Isaac, who built in Mecca the sanctuary of the Ka'aba,

which is the uniting central symbol and shrine of the entire Arab world and of all Islam. The Arabs revere and derive their beliefs from the same prophets as the Hebrews. They honor Abraham, honor Moses. They greatly honor Solomon. They honor Jesus too, as a prophet. Mohammed, however, is their ultimate prophet, and from him—who was a considerable warrior himself—they have derived their fanatic mythology of unrelenting war in God's name.

The *jihad,* the duty of the Holy War, is a concept developed from certain passages of the Koran which, during the period of the Great Conquests (from the seventh to tenth centuries), were interpreted as defining the bounden duty of every Moslem male who is free, of full age, in full possession of his intellectual powers, and physically fit for service. "Fighting is prescribed for you," we read in the Koran, Sura 2, verse 216. "True, you have an antipathy to it: however, it is possible that your antipathy is to something that is nevertheless good for you. God knows, and you know not." "To fight in the cause of Truth is one of the highest forms of charity," I read in a commentary to this passage. "What can you offer that is more precious than your own life?" All lands not belonging to "the territory of Islam" (*dar al-Islam*) are to be conquered and are known, therefore, as "the territory of war" (*dar al-harb*). "I am commanded," the Prophet is reported to have said, "to fight until men bear witness, there is no god but God and his Messenger is Mohammed." According to the ideal, one campaign a year, at least, must be undertaken by every Moslem prince against unbelievers. However, where this proves to be no longer possible, it suffices if an army, efficiently maintained, is kept trained and ready for the *jihad.*

And the Jews, "the People of the Book," as they are here called, hold a special place in this thinking, since it was they who first received God's Word but then (according to Mohammed's view) repeatedly forsook it, backsliding, rejecting, and even slaying God's later prophets. In the Koran they are repeatedly addressed and threatened: of which passages I shall cite but one, from Sura 17, verses 4–8 (and wherever the word "We" appears in this text, the reference is to God; where "you," to the Jews; while the "Book" is the Bible):

> And We gave clear warning to the Children of Israel in the Book that twice would they do mischief on the earth and be elated with mighty arrogance, and twice would they be punished. When the first warnings came to pass, We sent against you Our servants given to terrible warfare [the Babylonians, 685 B.C.]: they entered the very inmost parts of your homes; and it was a warning completely fulfilled. Then did we grant you the Return as against them; We gave you increase in resources and sons, and made you the more numerous in manpower. If ye did well, ye did well for yourselves; if ye did evil, ye did it against yourselves. So when the second of the warnings came to pass, we permitted your enemies to disfigure your faces and to enter your Temple [the Romans, 70 A.D.] as it had been entered before, and to visit with destruction all that fell into their power. It may be that your Lord may yet show Mercy unto you; but if ye revert to your sins, we shall revert to Our punishments: and We have made Hell a prison for those who reject the Faith.

These, then, are the two war mythologies that are even today confronting each other in the highly contentious Near East and may yet explode our planet.

However, to return in thought to the past, of which our present is the continuation: the old Biblical ideal of offering a holocaust to Yahweh by massacring every living thing in a captured town or city was but the Hebrew version of a custom general to the early Semites: the Moabites, the Amorites, the Assyrians, and all. However, about the middle of the eighth century B.C. the Assyrian Tiglath Pilesar III (r. 745–727) seems to have noticed that when everybody in a conquered province is slain there is no one left to enslave. Yet if any remain alive, they presently pull themselves together, and one has a revolt to put down. Tiglath Pilesar invented the procedure, therefore, of transferring populations from one region to another: when a city had been taken, its entire population was to be condemned to forced labor elsewhere, and the inhabitants of that other place transferred to the vacated site. The idea was effective and caught on; so that by the time two centuries more had elapsed, the entire Near East had been unsettled. There was hardly a land-rooted people left. When Israel fell its people were not massacred, as they would have been half a century earlier. They were taken somewhere else, and another people (known later as Samaritans) was brought to inhabit their former kingdom. And so also when Jerusalem fell in the year 586, its people were not massacred but transferred to Babylon, where, as we read in the famous Psalm 137:

> By the waters of Babylon,
> there we sat down and wept,
>   when we remembered Zion.
> On the willows there we hung up our lyres.
> For there our captors required of us songs,
> and our tormentors, mirth, saying,
>   "Sing us one of the songs of Zion!"
>
> How shall we sing the Lord's song
>   in a foreign land?
> If I forget you, O Jerusalem,
>   let my right hand wither!
> Let my tongue cleave to the roof of my mouth
>   if I do not remember you,
> if I do not set Jerusalem
>   above my highest joy!
>
> Remember, O Lord, against the Edomites
>   the day of Jerusalem,
> how they said, "Raze it, raze it!
>   Down to its foundations!"

> O daughter of Babylon, you devastator!
> Happy shall he be who requites you
> with what you have done to us!
> Happy shall he be who takes your little ones
> and dashes them against the rock!

But then there came to pass, very suddenly, an altogether radical transformation of the whole mythology of the Near East, with the sudden appearance and brilliant victories of the Aryan Persians over every nation of the ancient world save Greece, from the Bosporus and Upper Nile to the Indus. Babylon fell in the year 539 B.C. to Cyrus the Great, whose idea for the government of an empire, however, was neither to massacre nor to uproot, but to return peoples to their places, restoring them to their gods and governing them through subordinate kings of their own races and traditions. Thus he became the first King of Kings. And that title of the powerful Persian monarchs became the title presently of the Lord God of Israel himself, whose people Cyrus restored to their city and encouraged to the rebuilding of their Temple. In Isaiah 45 this gentile is even celebrated as a virtual Messiah, the anointed servant of Yahweh, the work of whose hand had been the work, actually, of Yahweh's hand, for the restoration of his people to their sacred seat. And if I read that chapter rightly, what it promises through its prophet is that ultimately it would be not the Persians, but the people themselves of Yahweh who would be reigning over the world in the name of God (Isaiah 45:14–25).

The actual mythology of the Persians, on the other hand, was not of Isaiah, but of Zarathustra (Greek, Zoroaster); and since it was to exert considerable influence not only on Judaism, but also on the whole development of Christianity, we shall do well to pause with it a moment before proceeding in our survey to the mythologies of peace.

The World Creator, according to this view, was Ahura Mazda, a god of truth and light, whose original creation was perfect. However, an opposing evil power of darkness and deception,

Angra Mainyu, infused into it evils of all kinds, so that there occurred a general Fall into ignorance and there is in progress now a
continuing conflict between the powers of light and of darkness,
truth and deception. These, in the Persian view, are not particular
to any race or tribe but are cosmic, general powers, and every individual, of whatever race or tribe, must, through his own free
will, choose sides and align himself with the powers either of
goodness or of evil in this world. If with the former, he will con-
tribute through his thoughts, words, and deeds to the restoration
of the universe to perfection; if however, with the latter, to his
own great grief in a Hell appropriate to his life.

As the day of the ultimate world-victory approaches and the
powers of darkness make their final desperate stand, there will
come a season of general wars and universal catastrophe, after
which there will arrive the ultimate savior, Saoshyant. Angra
Mainyu and his demons will be utterly undone; the dead will be
resurrected in bodies of immaculate light; Hell vanishing, its souls,
purified, will be released; and there will follow an eviternity of
sheer peace, purity, joy, and perfection—forever.

According to the view of the ancient Persian kings, it was they
who, in a special way, were the representatives on earth of the
cause and will of the Lord of Light. And so we find that in the
great multiracial and multicultural empire of the Persians—which,
in fact, was the first such empire in the history of the world—
there was a religiously authorized imperialistic impulse, to the end
that, in the name of truth, goodness, and the light, the Persian
King of Kings should become the leader of mankind to the restitu-
tion of truth. The idea is one that has had a particular appeal to
kings and has been taken over, accordingly, by conquering monarchs everywhere. In India the mythic image of the Chakravartin,
for example, the universal king, the illumination of whose presence would bring peace and well-being to mankind, is a figure inspired largely by this thought. It is to be recognized in the royal
emblems of the first Buddhist monarch, Ashoka, ca. 262–248 B.C.
And in China, immediately following the turbulent period known

as Chun Kuo, "of the Warring States," the first ruler of a united empire, Shih Huang Ti (221–207 B.C.), governed, according to his claim, by the mandate of Heaven, under Heaven's law.

It is then hardly to be wondered if the enthusiastic Hebrew author of Isaiah 40–55, who was a contemporary of Cyrus the Great and living witness of the Persian restoration to Jerusalem of its people, gives evidence in his prophecies of the influence of Zoroastrian ideas; for example, in the famous passages of Chapter 45: "Thus says the Lord to his anointed, to Cyrus . . . 'I form light and create darkness, I make weal and create woe, I am the Lord, who do all these things.' " It is in these chapters of the so-called Second or Deutero Isaiah that we find the earliest celebrations of Yahweh not simply as the greatest and most powerful god among gods, but as the one God of the universe, in whom not only Jews but also the gentiles are to find salvation: "Turn to me and be saved, all the ends of the earth!" we read, for instance. "For I am God, and there is no other" (Isaiah 45:22). Moreover, whereas the earlier idea of the Messiah of the pre-exilic prophets had been simply of an ideal king on David's throne, "to uphold it," as in Isaiah 9:6–7, "with justice and with righteousness from this time forth and for evermore"; in the post-exilic period, and particularly in the very late, apocalyptic writings of the Alexandrian age—as, for instance, in the Book of Daniel 7:13–27—there is the notion of one who, at the end of historic time, should be given, over "all peoples, nations, and languages," "an everlasting dominion, which shall not pass away." And at that time, furthermore, "Many of those who sleep in the dust of the earth shall awake, some to everlasting life, and some to shame and everlasting contempt" (Daniel 12:2).

There can be no doubt of the influence of Zoroastrian eschatology on such ideas as these of the end of the world and resurrection of the dead. Moreover, in the Essene Dead Sea Scrolls of the last century B.C., the influence of Persian thought is apparent at every turn. Their period itself, in fact, was one of such terrible tumult that the end of the world and coming of the savior Saoshyant might well have been expected by anyone familiar with the old Zoroastrian theme. Even in Jerusalem there was schism, with two contending parties in rivalry for the mastery: one supported by the Hasidim, the orthodox "pious ones," who were loyal to the law; the other favoring Greek ideas. And when (as we are told in the Books of the Maccabees) those of the latter party went to the Greek Emperor Antiochus and gained from him permission to build themselves in Jerusalem a gymnasium, "according to the customs of the heathen, and made themselves uncircumcised, and forsook the holy covenant, and joined themselves to the heathen," new contentions arose within the holy city, which culminated when the Greeks, supporting the claims of an opportunistic Hellenizer to the office of the high priesthood, sacked the Temple and ordered heathen altars to be set up all over the land. For it was then, 168 B.C., in a village named Modein, that Mattathias and his five sons (the Maccabees) attacked and slew not only the first Jew who approached the heathen altar to sacrifice "according to the king's commandment," but also the Greek officer who had arrived to set it up. However, the Maccabees themselves then impudently assumed the titles of both the kingship and high priesthood, to which they were not by descent entitled, and there were perpetrated within that family a number of ugly betrayals and murders in subsequent struggles for the inheritance. The Pharisees, Hasidim, and others resenting these impieties rose presently in a revolt that was put down with the greatest cruelty by the reigning Alexander Jannaeus (r. 104–78), who crucified eight hundred of his enemies in a single night, slaughtered their wives and children before their eyes, and himself watched the executions, drinking and publicly disporting with his concubines. "Upon which so deep a terror seized on the people," wrote the Jewish historian Josephus in concluding his account of this atrocity, "that eight thousand of his opposers fled away the very next night, out of all Judea." [1]

It has been suggested that this event specifically may have been the occasion for the founding in the wilderness on the Dead Sea

shore of the apocalyptic community of Qumran and the Dead Sea
Scrolls. Its founders, in any case, foresaw the end of the world
and were in all seriousness preparing themselves to be worthy to
survive it and to continue into eternity the destiny of the remnant
of God's people. Their expectation seems to have been that they
would themselves constitute an army of such virtue that with
God's help they would conquer and purify the world. There would
be a war to be fought, of forty years, of "the Sons of Light"
against "the Sons of Darkness." (Compare the old Zoroastrian
theme!) This would commence with a battle of six years against
such immediate neighbors as the Moabites and Egyptians and,
after a year of Sabbath rest, recommence with a series of cam-
paigns against the peoples of remoter lands. On their trumpets and
their standards the Covenanters would have written inspiring, flattering slogans: "The Elect of God," "The Princes of God," "The
Chiefs of the Fathers of the Congregation," "The Hundred of
God, a Hand of War against All Erring Flesh," "The Truth of
God," "The Righteousness of God," "The Glory of God," etc. But
meanwhile, in Jerusalem, alas! two sons of Alexander Jannaeus
were contending for the kingship. One of them invited the Romans in to assist him in his cause—and that was that, 63 B.C.

Now it is of the very greatest interest to remark the sense that
seems to have prevailed throughout that period, among the Jews
of many persuasions, of the imminent end of the world. In a Zoroastrian context this would have brought the savior Saoshyant. In
the post-exilic Jewish, it would be the Anointed, the Messiah, who
appeared. The nations were to be annihilated. Even of Israel only
a remnant would survive. And it was in this atmosphere of immediate urgency that Christianity came to birth. The prophet John
the Baptist, baptizing only a few miles up the Jordan from the
Dead Sea Covenanters, was also waiting, preparing the way, and
to him it was that Jesus came; who thereafter fasted forty days in
the desert and returned to deliver his own version of the general
apocalyptic message.

And so what, then, is the outstanding difference between the message of Christ Jesus and that of the nearby Covenanters of Qumran? It would seem to me to be this: that the Covenanters were thinking of themselves as about to engage in battle as the Sons of Light with the Sons of Darkness, their posture, that is to say, being of preparation for war, whereas the gospel of Jesus was, rather, of the battle already resolved. "You have heard that it was said, 'You shall love your neighbor and hate your enemy.' But I say to you, love your enemies and pray for those that persecute you, so that you may be sons of your Father who is in heaven; for he makes his sun to rise on the evil and on the good, and sends rain on the just and on the unjust" (Matthew 5:43–45). And exactly this, I would say, is the difference between a gospel of war and one of peace.

However, we come a little later to those startling words of Matthew 10: "Do not think that I have come to bring peace on earth; I have not come to bring peace, but a sword. For I have come to set a man against his father, and a daughter against her mother, and a daughter-in-law against her mother-in-law; and a man's foes will be those of his own household. He who loves father or mother more than me is not worthy of me; and he who loves son or daughter more than me is not worthy of me." And again in Luke 14 we encounter another echo of the same: "If anyone comes to me and does not hate his own father and mother and wife and children and brothers and sisters, yes, and even his own life, he cannot be my disciple."

The key to the meaning of all this, I believe, is in the last line here cited, and in the words immediately following each of our two quotations. In Matthew: "He who does not take his cross and follow me is not worthy of me. He who finds his life will lose it, and he who loses his life for my sake will find it." And in Luke: "Whoever does not bear his own cross and come after me, cannot be my disciple." Still further, returning to Matthew (19:21): "Go sell what you possess and give to the poor . . . ; and come, follow me." And again: "Follow me, and let the dead bury their dead" (8:22).

The ideal of this teaching is of an ascetic absolute abandonment of all the concerns of normal secular life, family ties, community, and all, leaving "the dead"—i.e. those that we call the living—"to bury their dead"; and in this the earliest Christian teaching is seen to have been of the order of the early Buddhist and of the Jain. It is a "forest teaching." And what it does to the general apocalyptic theme is to transform its reference radically from a historical future to a psychological present: the end of the world and coming of the Day of God, that is to say, are not to be awaited in the field of time, but to be achieved right now in solitude, in the chamber of the heart. And in confirmation of this meaning, we find in the last lines of the Gnostic *Gospel According to Thomas* that when Christ's disciples said to him, "When will the Kingdom come?" he replied: "It will not come by expectation; they will not say: 'See here,' or 'See there.' But the Kingdom of the Father is spread upon the earth and men do not see it."

Moreover, that the allusion of Jesus's reference to the sword which he had brought cannot possibly have been to any weapon of physical warfare appears clearly in the scene of his arrest in the Garden of Gethsemane.

Judas came [we read], and with him a great crowd with swords and clubs, from the chief priests and the elders of the people. And the betrayer had given them a sign, saying, "The one I shall kiss is the man; seize him." And he came up to Jesus at once and said, "Hail Rabbi!" And he kissed him. Jesus said to him, "Friend, do that for which you have come!" Then they came up and laid hands on Jesus and seized him. And behold, one of those who were with Jesus stretched out his hand and drew his sword, and struck the slave of the high priest and cut off his ear. Then Jesus said to him, "Put up your sword; for all who take the sword will perish by the sword" [Matthew 26:47–52].

Clear enough! Is it not? And yet that stout wielder of the sword, who is identified in the John Gospel (18:10) as Peter, was not the last of Jesus's followers to betray as surely as ever Judas did their teacher and his teaching. From the period of the victories of Constantine, fourth century A.D., the Church founded on the rock of that same good Peter's name was advanced very largely by swordsmanship. And at the height of the Middle Ages, under the mighty Pope Innocent III (1198–1216), the flashing of Peter's zealous weapon attained to a blazing climax in the crackling fires of the Albigensian Crusade—where the people going up in flames were the heretic Cathari, the self-styled Pure Ones, who had explicitly rejected the sword for lives of ascetic purity in peace.

An ascetic renunciation of the world and its life—and even of the will to survive in life—may be named, then, as the best-known discipline of peace that has been proposed, as yet, to mankind. And if one may judge from the historic circumstances of its original pronouncement, it arose—or at least caught on—as a response to a desperate general sense of things falling apart. The earlier mythic notion had been of a great war, a holy terminal war, through which a universal reign of peace should be ultimately established at the end of historic time: which, however, was not properly a mythology of peace but a summons, rather, to war, perpetual war until . . . And, ironically, no sooner had the ascetic Christian message passed from the lips of Jesus to the ears of his closest follower than it became transformed into (and has remained ever since interpreted as) only another such doctrine of the Holy War, *jihad,* or crusade. So let us review and compare now, briefly, the ideals and destinies of a number of other of the best-known ascetic mythologies of peace.

Undoubtedly the most austere and ruthlessly consistent is the religion of the Jains of India, whose teacher Mahavira was a contemporary of the Buddha. Mahavira's teaching was already at that time of great age, he having been but the last of a long series of Jain teachers known as "passage-makers," Tirthankaras, dating back to prehistoric times. And according to the absolutely nonviolent teaching of this line of sages, the candidate for release from rebirth must neither kill nor hurt any being, nor eat any animal flesh. He may not even drink water at night, for fear of swallowing insects possibly floating on the surface. Vows are to be assumed, limiting the number of steps taken a day; because every time a step is taken the lives of insects, worms, and the like are endangered. Jain yogis in the forest carry little brooms with which to sweep the ground before each step; and to this day you may see in Bombay monks and nuns of the Jain sect wearing cheesecloth masks across nose and mouth (like surgeons in the operating room) to insure against their inhaling any living thing. One is not to eat fruits that have been plucked; one is to wait for the fruits to fall. Nor is one to cut living plants with a blade. Logically, the goal of the Jain monk is an early death; not, however, before his will to life has been absolutely quenched. For if he should die with the least impulse to live, to enjoy, or to protect his own life, he would surely be reborn and so be back in this dreadful world again, again hurting and murdering things.

Now Buddhism in its primitive form was closely related to the Jain sect; however, with a critical shift of accent from the literal quenching of one's life to the quenching, rather, of one's ego. What is to be got rid of is the sense of "I" and "mine," the impulse to protect oneself, one's property, and one's life. Thus the accent is rather psychological than physical, and yet here too we may find that an absolute rule of virtue maintained to the bitter end may lead ultimately to something very much like an absolute denial of life.

For example, there is the Buddhist pious tale of the case of King Vessantara, who was asked by a neighboring monarch for the loan of his imperial white elephant. White elephants attract clouds, and the clouds of course bring rain. King Vessantara, being selfless, gave the elephant away without a second thought. However, his people were indignant that he should have shown so little concern for their own welfare, and exiled him from their kingdom, together with his family. In carriages, the royal house departed; but when about to enter the forest, they were approached by a company of Brahmins, who asked for the carriages and horses; and Vessantara, selfless absolutely, with no sense whatsoever of "I" and "mine," gave up these valuables willingly and with his family entered the dangerous forest afoot. Next he was approached by an old Brahmin who asked to be given the children. The mother selfishly protested; but the king with no sense of "I" and "mine" delivered the children willingly—into slavery. Then the wife was asked for, and she too was surrendered.

One learns from this tale what Jesus meant when admonishing us to give up father and mother, son and daughter, yea, and our own lives, in following him; when asked for our coat, to give our cloak also, and when struck, to turn the other cheek. In the pious Buddhist fable everything turned out for the best, of course, since the Brahmins were actually gods testing the king; and the children, wife, and all had been taken safely to the palace of the grandparents—much as in the Bible story of Abraham, where the sacrifice of Isaac was stayed by the hand of the god, who was just testing. The question remains in both legends equally, nevertheless, as to where virtue ends and vice begins in such pious adventures. How far, for example, will the absolute pacifist go in defending absolutely no one and nothing but his own so-spiritual purity? The question is not irrelevant to our own times.

But now, moving still farther eastward, to China and Japan, we come to another cluster of mythologies of peace, particularly of Lao-tzu and Confucius. Many would term the founding thought of these mythologies romantic; for it is simply that there is through all of nature an all-suffusing spiritual harmony: an orderly interaction through all life and lives, through all history and historical institutions, of those two principles or powers, active and passive, light and dark, hot and cold, heavenly and earthly, known as *yang* and *yin.* The force of the principle of *yang* predominates in youth; that of *yin,* later, and increasingly in old age. *Yang* is dominant in summer, in the south, and at noon; *yin* in winter, in the north, and at night. The way of their alternations through all things is the Way of all things, the *Tao.* And by putting oneself in accord with the *Tao*—one's time, one's world, oneself—one accomplishes the ends of life and is at peace in the sense of being in harmony with all things.

The best known, most richly inspired statement of this Taoist philosophy is to be found in a little work of eighty-one stanzas known as the *Tao Teh Ching,* or "Book of the Virtue of the Tao," which is attributed to a legendary, long-bearded sage called Lao-tzu, "the old boy."

> When a magistrate follows the Tao [we read in the thirtieth stanza of this wisdom book] [2] he has no need to resort to force of arms to strengthen the Empire, because his business methods alone will show good returns. Briars and thorns grow rank where an army camps. Bad harvests are the sequence of a great war. The good ruler will be resolute, and then stop, he dare not take by force. One should be resolute, but not boastful; resolute, but not haughty; resolute, but not arrogant; resolute, but yielding when it cannot be avoided; resolute, but he must not resort to violence. With a resort to force, things flourish for a time, but then decay. This is not like the Tao, and that which is not Tao-like will soon cease.

And again, in stanza 31:

> Even successful arms, among all implements, are unblessed. All men come to detest them. Therefore the one who follows the Tao does not rely on them. Arms are, of all tools, unblessed. They are not the implements of a wise man. Only as a last resort does he employ them.
>
> Peace and quietude are esteemed by the wise man, and even when victorious he does not rejoice, because rejoicing over a victory is the same as rejoicing over the killing of men. If he rejoices over the killing of men, do you think he will ever really master the Empire?

However, as the world well knows, the long, long history of China has been distinguished largely by the reigns of merciless despots alternating with chaotic centuries of war; and, at least from the Period of the Warring States (453–221 B.C.) onward, the maneuvers of large professional armies have had considerably more influence on the course of Chinese politics than anything like Lao-tzu's type of "Virtue of the Tao." It is, in fact, from that greatly turbulent period that there have come down to our time two completely hardheaded, thoroughly Machiavellian works on the arts of gaining and maintaining power: the first, the so-called *Book of the Lord Shang* (translated by J. J. L. Duyvendak, London, 1928), and, second, Sun Tzu's *The Art of War* (translated by Samuel B. Griffith, Oxford University Press, 1963). Let me quote briefly, first, from Sun Tzu (I. 1–9):

War is a matter of vital importance to the State; the province of life or death; the road to survival or ruin. It is mandatory that it be thoroughly studied. Therefore, appraise it in terms of the five fundamental factors and make comparisons of the seven elements later named. So you may assess its essentials.

The first of these factors is moral influence (*tao*); the second, weather; the third, terrain; the fourth, command; and the fifth, doctrine. By moral influence (*tao*) I mean that which causes people to be in harmony with their leaders, so that they will accompany them in life and unto death without fear of mortal peril. By weather I mean the interaction of natural forces; the effects of winter's cold and summer's heat and the conduct of military operations in accordance with the seasons. By terrain I mean distances, whether the ground is traversed with ease or difficulty, whether it is open or constricted, and the chances of life or death. By command I mean the general's qualities of wisdom, sincerity, humanity, courage, and strictness. By doctrine I mean organization, control, assignment of appropriate ranks to officers, regulation of supply routes, and the provision of principal items used by the army. There is no general who has not heard of these five matters. Those who master them win; those who do not are defeated.

And from *The Book of the Lord Shang* (I.8 and 10–12):

The country depends on agriculture and war for its peace, and likewise the ruler, for his honor. . . . If, in a country, there are the following ten things: poetry and history, rites and music, virtue and the cultivation thereof, benevolence and integrity, sophistry and intelligence, then the ruler has no one whom he can employ for defence and warfare. . . . But if a country banishes these ten things, enemies will not dare to approach, and even if they should, they would be driven back. . . . A country that loves strength makes assaults with what is difficult and thus it will be successful. A country that loves sophistry makes assaults with what is easy and thus it will be in danger. . . . When a country is in peril and the ruler in anxiety, it is of no avail to the settling of this danger, for professional talkers to form battalions. The reason why a country is in danger and its ruler in anxiety lies in some strong enemy or in another big state.

Farming, trade and office are the three permanent functions in a state, and these three functions give rise to six parasitic functions, which are called: care for old age, living on others, beauty, love, ambition, and virtuous conduct. If these six parasites find an attachment, there will be dismemberment. . . .

A country where the virtuous govern the wicked will suffer from disorder, so that it will be dismembered; but a country where the wicked govern the virtuous will be orderly, so that it will become strong. . . .

If penalties are made heavy and rewards light, the ruler loves his people and they will die for him; but if rewards are made heavy and penalties light, the ruler does not love his people, nor will they die for him.

And finally:

If things are done that the enemy would be ashamed to do, there is an advantage.

In India too it has been a long history of thinking of this kind that has actually shaped and inspired the practical arts of governance and war. Students today of the *Bhagavad Gita* tend to forget that what they are reading as a religious tract is part of one of the great war epics of all time, the Indian "Book of the Great War of the Sons of Bharata," *Mahabharata,* of which the following are a few characteristic selections from another section of the work, Book XII (the *Gita* is from Book VI):

A king who knows his own strength and commanding a large army should cheerfully and courageously, without announcing his destination, give the order to march against one shorn of allies and friends, or already at war with another and hence inattentive; or against one weaker than himself: having first arranged for the protection of his own city. . . .

A king should not forever live under a more powerful king. Even though weak, he should try to unseat the stronger and, resolved upon this, continue to rule his own. He should assail the stronger with weapons, fire, and the administration of poisons. He should also create dissension among the other's ministers and servants. . . .

The king depends on his treasury and army. His army, again, depends on his treasury. His army is the source of all his religious merits. His religious merits, again, are the support of his people. The treasury can never be replenished without oppressing others. How then can the army be maintained without oppression? The king, consequently, in times of difficulty, commits no sin in oppressing his subjects for the filling of his treasury. . . . By wealth both worlds—this and the other—can be acquired, as also truth and religious merit. A person who has no wealth is more dead than alive. . . .

One should bear one's enemy on one's shoulder as long as the times are unfavorable. When the opportunity comes, however, one should smash him, like an earthen jar on a stone. . . .

A king seeking prosperity should not hesitate to kill his son, brother, father, or friend, if any one or more of these should stand in his way. . . .

Without cutting the very vitals of others, without performing many cruel deeds, without killing living creatures, as fishermen kill fish, one cannot win prosperity. . . .

There are no special orders of creatures called enemies or friends. Persons become friends or enemies according to the trend of circumstance. . . .

Every work should be done completely. . . . By killing its inhabitants, by destroying its roads, and by burning and pulling down its houses, a king should devastate his enemy's realm.

And finally:

Might is above right; right proceeds from might; right has its support in might, as living beings in the soil. As smoke the wind, so right must follow might. Right in itself has no authority; it leans on might as the creeper on the tree.

Indeed, the *Bhagavad Gita* itself, as a chapter of this warrior epic, is in aim and content a lecture of encouragement to a young prince afflicted with a qualm of conscience before giving the signal of battle, to free his mind from all sense of grief and guilt in killing. "For that which is born, death is certain," he is told; "and for that which is dead, birth is certain. You should not grieve over the unavoidable. . . . The Supreme Self, which dwells in all bodies, can never be slain." "Weapons cut it not; fire burns it not; water wets it not; the wind does not wither it. Eternal, universal, unchanging, immovable, the Self is the same forever. . . . Dwelling in all bodies, the Self can never be slain. Therefore you should not grieve for any creature." [3]

And that, in sum, is the ultimate ground, in Oriental thinking, of all peace. In the field of action—which is to say, in life—there is no peace, and there can never be. The formula, then, for the attainment of peace is to act, as one must, but without attachment. "Being established in yoga," the young warrior prince Arjuna of the *Gita* is taught, "perform your actions, casting off attachment and remaining even-minded, both in success and in failure. This evenness is what is called yoga. And far inferior is mere action to action performed with this evenness of mind. Seek refuge in this evenness. Wretched are all who work for results. Endued with evenness of mind, one casts off in this very life both good deeds and evil deeds. Strive, therefore, for yoga. Yoga is skill in action."

Abandoning both all fear of, and all desire for, the fruits of action, one is to perform without attachment the work that has to be done; and that work is the work of one's duty, whatever it may be, the duty of princes being to fight and to slay. "To a prince," we read, "nothing is better than a righteous war. Happy indeed is the prince to whom such a war comes unsought, offering itself, throwing open heaven's gate." [4]

Thus, paradoxically, in this context the mythology of peace and the mythology of war are the same. And not only in Hinduism, but also in Buddhism—the Buddhism of the Mahayana—this paradox is fundamental. For after all, since the wisdom of the yonder shore is beyond all pairs-of-opposites, it must necessarily transcend and include the opposition of war-and-peace. As stated in a Mahayana Buddhist aphorism, "This very world, with all its imperfection, is the Golden Lotus World of perfection." And if one cannot see it this way or bear to see it this way, the fault is not with the world.

Nor can the universe be justly regarded as evil. Nature is not evil but the "action body" of Buddha-consciousness. Strife, consequently, is not evil, and neither opponent in a battle is any more evil, or better, than the other.

Accordingly, the compassionate participation of the Bodhisattva in the world process is absolutely without guilt. Also, it is absolutely impersonal. And in the same sense the Mahayana Buddhist ideal for us all, of "joyous participation" in the "action body of Buddha-consciousness," is absolutely impersonal, selfless, and guiltless. I have been told that after the Battle of Port Arthur in the Russo-Japanese War of 1904, the names not only of the men but also of the horses that had given their lives in that action were inscribed on a plaque—*in memoriam*—as Bodhisattvas.

To summarize, then: There has been from earliest times the idea that war (of one kind or another) is not only inevitable and good but also the normal and most exhilarating mode of social action of civilized mankind, the waging of war being the normal delight, as well as duty, of kings. A monarch neither engaged in nor preparing to be engaged in war would be, according to this way of thinking, a fool: a "paper tiger."

But, on the other hand, in the annals of world history accounts are to be found also of a diametrically opposite point of view to this, where the aim is to become quit of war and strife altogether in a state of perpetual peace. However, the usual corollary of this aspiration is that, since strife and pain are intrinsic to temporal existence, life itself, as we know it, is to be negated. Examples of this negativism are seen most strikingly in India, in Jainism and early (Hinayana) Buddhism, but have appeared also in the West, as in certain early Christian movements, and in twelfth-century France among the Albigenses.

Reviewing the mythologies of war, we have found in both the Torah and Koran a belief that God, the creator and sole governor of the universe, was absolutely and always on the side of a certain chosen community, and that *its* wars, consequently, were Holy Wars, waged in the name and interest of God's will. A not very different notion inspired the "Flowery Wars" of the Aztecs for the capture of sacrifices to keep the sun in motion. In the *Iliad*, on the other hand, the sympathies of the Olympians are on both sides of the combat, the Trojan War itself being interpreted not in cosmic but in earthly, human terms: it was a war for the recovery of a stolen wife. And the noble ideal of the human warrior-hero was there expressed in the character and words not of a Greek, but of a Trojan hero, Hector. I see here an evident contrast to the spirit of the two Semitic war mythologies, and an affinity, on the other hand, to the Indian *Mahabharata*. The forthright resolution of Hector, going into combat in fulfillment of his clear duty to his family and city, and the "self-control" (the yoga) required of Arjuna in the *Gita,* in fulfillment of the duties of his caste, are of essentially the same order. Moreover, in the Indian as in the Greek epic, there is equal honor and respect bestowed on the combatants of both sides.

But now, and finally, we have discovered also in our survey a third point of view in relation to the ideals and aims of war and peace, neither affirming nor denying war as life, and life as war, but aspiring to a time when wars should cease. In the Persian Zoroastrian eschatological myth, which appears to have been the first in which such a prospect was seriously envisioned, the day of the great transformation was to be in the nature of a cosmic crisis, when the laws of nature would cease to operate and an eviternity of no time, no change, no life as we know life then come into being. Ironically, there would be wars enough during the centuries of struggle just antecedent to this general transfiguration. Within the Persian Empire itself, however, there was to flourish and increase, meanwhile, a prefigurative reign of relative peace— enforced by imperial spies, informants, and police; and with the expansion of this peaceful empire, the bounds of the reign of temporal peace also would expand—until . . .

But we have heard the likes of all this more recently and close at hand. The idea, as we have seen, became assimilated to the Biblical image of Israel; and in the period of the Dead Sea Scrolls passed on into apocalyptic Christianity (see Mark 13:3–37). It is the idea essentially of the *dar al-Islam* and *dar al-harb* of the Arabs. And we have it again in the peace of Moscow—spies, informers, police crackdowns, and all.

As far as I know, there is, in addition to these, only one more thought about war and peace to be found among the great traditions, and that is the one first announced by the eminent seventeenth-century Dutch legal philosopher Grotius, in 1625, in his epochal treatise on *The Rights of War and Peace.* Here, for the first time in the history of mankind, the proposal is offered of a law of nations based on ethical, not jungle principles. In India the

governing law of international relations has for centuries been
known as the *matsya nyaya,* "law of the fish," which is, to wit,
that the big ones eat the little ones and the little ones have to be
smart. War is the natural duty of princes, and periods of peace are
merely interludes, like periods of rest between boxing rounds.
Whereas war in Grotius's view is a breach of the proper civilized
norm, which is peace; and its aim should be to produce peace, a
peace not enforced by might of arms, but of rational mutual interest. This, in turn, was the ideal that Woodrow Wilson represented
when he spoke, at the end of the First World War, of "peace without victory." And we have the ideal symbolized also in the figure
of our American eagle, which is pictured with a cluster of arrows
in the talons of its left foot, an olive branch in its right, and its
head—in the spirit of Grotius—turned rightward, facing the olive
branch. Let us hope, however, in the name of peace, that he keeps
those arrowheads over there sharp until neither asceticism nor the
power of arms, but an understanding of mutual advantage, will
have become for *all* mankind the guarantee, at long last, of a
knowledge of the reign of peace.

X

Schizophrenia—the Inward Journey

[1970]

In the spring of 1968 I was invited to deliver a series of talks on schizophrenia at the Esalen Institute at Big Sur, California. I had lectured there the year before on mythology; and apparently Mr. Michael Murphy, the imaginative young director of that highly interesting enterprise, thought there should be a connection of some kind. However, since I knew next to nothing of schizophrenia, on receipt of his letter I telephoned.

"Mike, I don't know a thing about schizophrenia," I said. "How would it be if I lectured on Joyce?"

"Why, fine!" he answered. "But I'd like to hear you on schizophrenia, just the same. Let's set up a dual talk in San Francisco: you and John Perry, on mythology and schizophrenia. How's that?"

Well, I didn't then know Dr. Perry; but in my youth I had had the very great experience of kissing the Blarney Stone—which, I can tell you, is worth a dozen Ph.D. degrees; so I thought, "Okay! Why not?" And besides, I had such confidence in Mike Murphy that I was pretty sure he had something interesting in mind.

A few weeks later, and sure enough! There came in the mail an

envelope from John Weir Perry, M.D., of San Francisco, containing the reprint of a paper on schizophrenia that he had published
in 1962 in the *Annals of the New York Academy of Sciences;* [1]
and to my considerable amazement I learned, on reading it, that
the imagery of schizophrenic fantasy perfectly matches that of the
mythological hero journey, which I had outlined and elucidated,
back in 1949, in *The Hero with a Thousand Faces.*

My own had been a work based on a comparative study of the
mythologies of mankind, with only here and there passing references to the phenomenology of dream, hysteria, mystic visions,
and the like. Mainly, it was an organization of themes and motifs
common to all mythologies; and I had had no idea, in bringing
these together, of the extent to which they would correspond to
the fantasies of madness. According to my thinking, they were the
universal, archetypal, psychologically based symbolic themes and
motifs of all traditional mythologies; and now from this paper of
Dr. Perry I was learning that the same symbolic figures arise spontaneously from the broken-off, tortured state of mind of modern
individuals suffering from a complete schizophrenic breakdown:
the condition of one who has lost touch with the life and thought
of his community and is compulsively fantasizing out of his own
completely cut-off base.

Very briefly: The usual pattern is, first, of a break away or departure from the local social order and context; next, a long, deep
retreat inward and backward, backward, as it were, in time, and
inward, deep into the psyche; a chaotic series of encounters there,
darkly terrifying experiences, and presently (if the victim is fortunate) encounters of a centering kind, fulfilling, harmonizing, giving
new courage; and then finally, in such fortunate cases, a return
journey of rebirth to life. And that is the universal formula also of
the mythological hero journey, which I, in my own published
work, had described as: 1) separation, 2) initiation, and 3) return:

A hero ventures forth from the world of common day into a region of supernatural wonder: fabulous forces are there encoun-

tered and a decisive victory is won: the hero comes back from this mysterious adventure with the power to bestow boons on his fellow men.[2]

That is the pattern of the myth, and that is the pattern of these fantasies of the psyche.

Now it was Dr. Perry's thesis in his paper that in certain cases the best thing is to let the schizophrenic process run its course, not to abort the psychosis by administering shock treatments and the like, but, on the contrary, to help the process of disintegration and reintegration along. However, if a doctor is to be helpful in this way, he has to understand the image language of mythology. He has himself to understand what the fragmentary signs and signals signify that his patient, totally out of touch with rationally oriented manners of thought and communication, is trying to bring forth in order to establish some kind of contact. Interpreted from this point of view, a schizophrenic breakdown is an inward and backward journey to recover something missed or lost, and to restore, thereby, a vital balance. So let the voyager go. He has tipped over and is sinking, perhaps drowning; yet, as in the old legend of Gilgamesh and his long, deep dive to the bottom of the cosmic sea to pluck the watercress of immortality, there is the one green value of his life down there. Don't cut him off from it: help him through.

Well, I can tell you, it was a wonderful trip I had to California. The conversations with Dr. Perry and the talk we delivered together opened a whole new prospect to me. The experience started me thinking more and more about the possible import to people in trouble today of these mythic materials on which I have been working in a more or less academic, scholarly, personally enthusiastic way all these years, without any precise knowledge of the techniques by which they might be applied to the needs of others.

Dr. Perry and Mr. Murphy introduced me to a paper on "Shamans and Acute Schizophrenia," by Dr. Julian Silverman of the National Institute of Mental Health, which had appeared in 1967

in the *American Anthropologist*,[3] and there again I found something of the greatest interest and of immediate relevance to my
studies and thinking. In my own writings I had already pointed
out [4] that among primitive hunting peoples it is largely from the
psychological experiences of shamans that the mythic imagery and
rituals of their ceremonial life derive. The shaman is a person (either male or female) who in early adolescence underwent a severe
psychological crisis, such as today would be called a psychosis.
Normally the child's apprehensive family sends for an elder shaman to bring the youngster out of it, and by appropriate measures,
songs, and exercises, this experienced practitioner succeeds. As
Dr. Silverman remarks and demonstrates in his paper, "In primitive cultures in which such a unique life crisis resolution is toler-
ated, the abnormal experience (shamanism) is typically beneficial
to the individual, cognitively and affectively; he is regarded as one
with expanded consciousness." Whereas, on the contrary, in such
a rationally ordered culture as our own—or, to phrase the proposition again in Dr. Silverman's words, "in a culture that does not
provide referential guides for comprehending this kind of crisis
experience, the individual (schizophrenic) typically undergoes an
intensification of his suffering over and above his original anxie-
ties."

Now let me describe to you the case of an Eskimo shaman who
was interviewed in the early 1920s by the great Danish scholar
and explorer Knud Rasmussen. Rasmussen was a man of the
broadest human sympathy and understanding, who was able to
talk in a marvelous way, man to man, with the characters he encountered all the way across the Arctic lands of North America in
the course of the Fifth Danish Thule Expedition, which from
1921 to 1924 trekked the whole long stretch from Greenland to
Alaska.

Igjugarjuk was a Caribou Eskimo shaman of a tribe inhabiting
the North Canadian tundras. When young, he had been visited
constantly by dreams that he could not interpret. Strange unknown
beings came and spoke to him; and when he woke he remembered

all so vividly that he could describe to his friends and family exactly what he had seen. The family, disturbed, but knowing what
was happening, sent for an old shaman named Peqanaoq, who, on
diagnosing the case, placed the youngster on a sledge just large
enough for him to sit on, and in the depth of winter—the absolutely dark and freezing Arctic winter night—dragged him far out
onto a lonely Arctic waste and built for him there a tiny snow hut
with barely room for him to sit cross-legged. He was not allowed
to set foot on the snow, but was lifted from the sledge into the hut
and there set down on a piece of skin just large enough to contain
him. No food or drink was left with him. He was instructed to
think only of the Great Spirit, who would presently appear, and
was left there alone for thirty days. After five days the elder returned with a drink of lukewarm water, and after another fifteen,
with a second drink and with a bit of meat. But that was all. The
cold and the fasting were so severe that, as Igjugarjuk told Rasmussen, "sometimes I died a little." And during all that time he
was thinking, thinking, thinking of the Great Spirit, until, toward
the end of the ordeal, a helping spirit did in fact arrive in the
form of a woman who seemed to hover in the air above him. He
never saw her again, but she became his helping spirit. The elder
shaman then brought him home, where he was required to diet
and fast for another five months; and, as he told his Danish guest,
such fasts, often repeated, are the best means of attaining to a
knowledge of hidden things. "The only true wisdom," Igjugarjuk
said, "lives far from mankind, out in the great loneliness, and can
be reached only through suffering. Privation and suffering alone
open the mind of a man to all that is hidden to others."

Another powerful shaman, whom Dr. Rasmussen met in Nome,
Alaska, told him of a similar venture into the silence. But this old
fellow, Najagneq by name, had fallen upon bad times in relation
to the people of his village. For shamans, you must know, live in a
rather perilous position. When things anywhere go wrong, people
tend to blame the local shaman. They imagine he is working
magic. And this old man, to protect himself, had invented a num-

ber of trick devices and mythological spooks to frighten his neighbors off and keep them safely at bay.

Dr. Rasmussen, recognizing that most of Najagneq's spirits
were outright frauds of this kind, one day asked him if there were
any in whom he himself believed; to which he replied, "Yes, a
power that we call Sila, one that cannot be explained in so many
words: a very strong spirit, the upholder of the universe, of the
weather, in fact of all life on earth—so mighty that his speech to
man comes not through ordinary words, but through storms, snow-
fall, rain showers, the tempests of the sea, all the forces that man
fears, or through sunshine, calm seas, or small, innocent, playing
children who understand nothing. When times are good, Sila has
nothing to say to mankind. He has disappeared into his infinite
nothingness and remains away as long as people do not abuse life
but have respect for their daily food. No one has ever seen Sila.
His place of sojourn is so mysterious that he is with us and infinitely far away at the same time."

And what does Sila say?

"The inhabitant or soul of the universe," Najagneq said, "is
never seen; its voice alone is heard. All we know is that it has a
gentle voice, like a woman, a voice so fine and gentle that even
children cannot become afraid. And what it says is: *Sila ersinarsi-
nivdluge,* 'Be not afraid of the universe.' " [5]

Now these were very simple men—at least in our terms of culture, learning, and civilization. Yet their wisdom, drawn from
their own most inward depths, corresponds in essence to what we
have heard and learned from the most respected mystics. There is
a deep and general human wisdom here, of which we do not often
come to know in our usual ways of active rational thinking.

In his article on shamanism Dr. Silverman had distinguished
two very different types of schizophrenia. One he calls "essential
schizophrenia"; the other, "paranoid schizophrenia"; and it is in
essential schizophrenia alone that analogies appear with what I
have termed "the shaman crisis." In essential schizophrenia the
characteristic pattern is of withdrawal from the impacts of experi-

ence in the outside world. There is a narrowing of concern and focus. The object world falls back and away, and invasions from the unconscious overtake and overwhelm one. In "paranoid schizophrenia," on the other hand, the person remains alert and extremely sensitive to the world and its events, interpreting all, however, in terms of his own projected fantasies, fears, and terrors, and with a sense of being in danger from assaults. The assaults, actually, are from within, but he projects them outward, imagining that the world is everywhere on watch against him. This, states Dr. Silverman, is not the type of schizophrenia that leads to the sorts of inward experience that are analogous to those of shamanism. "It is as if the paranoid schizophrenic," he explains, "unable to comprehend or tolerate the stark terrors of his inner world, prematurely directs his attention to the outside world. In this type of abortive crisis solution, the inner chaos is not, so to speak, worked through, *or* is not capable of being worked through." The lunatic victim is at large, so to say, in the field of his own projected unconscious.

The opposite type of psychotic patient, on the other hand, a pitiful thing to behold, has dropped into a snake-pit deep within. His whole attention, his whole being, is down there, engaged in a life-and-death battle with the terrible apparitions of unmastered psychological energies—which, it would appear, is exactly what the potential shaman also is doing in the period of his visionary journey. And so, we have next to ask what the difference is between the predicament of the "essential schizophrenic" and that of the trance-prone shaman: to which the answer is simply that the primitive shaman does not reject the local social order and its forms; that, in fact, it is actually by virtue of those forms that he is brought back to rational consciousness. And when he has returned, furthermore, it is generally found that his inward personal experiences reconfirm, refresh, and reinforce the inherited local forms; for his personal dream-symbology is at one with the symbology of his culture. Whereas, in contrast, in the case of a modern psychotic patient, there is a radical break-off and no effective association at all with the symbol system of his culture. The established symbol system here provides no help at all to the poor lost schizophrenic, terrified by the figments of his own imagination, to which he is a total stranger; whereas, in the case of the primitive shaman, there is between his outward life and his inward a fundamental accord.

Well, as I have said and you may imagine, that was an extremely interesting trip for me to California; and when I returned to New York (it was all happening as though some guiding spirit were setting everything up for me), a leading psychiatrist in our own tortured city, Dr. Mortimer Ostow, invited me to be discussant to a paper that he was about to read before a meeting of The Society for Adolescent Psychiatry. This turned out to be a study of certain common characteristics that Dr. Ostow had remarked, which seemed to relate, as of one order, the "mechanisms" (as Dr. Ostow termed them) of schizophrenia, mysticism, the LSD experience, and the "antinomianism" of contemporary youth: those aggressively antisocial attitudes that have become so prominent in the behavior and accomplishments of a significant number of campus adolescents and their faculty advisers of the present hour. And this invitation, too, was a major experience for me, opening my own thinking to another critical field into which my mythic studies might play—one, moreover, with which I was already in personal touch in my role as a college professor.

What I learned now was that the LSD retreat and inward plunge can be compared to an essential schizophrenia, and the antinomianism of contemporary youth to a paranoid schizophrenia. The sense of threat from every quarter of what is known as the Establishment—which is to say, of modern civilization—is not altogether a put-on or an act for many of these young folk, but an actual condition of soul. The break-off is real, and what is being bombed and blown up outside are actual symbols of interior fears. Moreover, many are unable even to communicate, every thought being so charged for them with feeling that in rational speech there is no name for it. An astonishing number cannot bring forth

even a simple declarative sentence, but, interrupting every at-
tempted phrase with the irrelevant syllable "like," they are reduced to mute signs and feeling-loaded silences, pleading for appreciation. One feels, sometimes, in dealing with them, that one is
indeed in a lunatic asylum without walls. And the indicated cure
for the ills that they are shouting about is not sociological at all
(as our news media and many of our politicians claim) but psychiatric.

The LSD phenomenon, on the other hand, is—to me at least
—more interesting. It is an intentionally achieved schizophrenia,
with the expectation of a spontaneous remission—which, however, does not always follow. Yoga, too, is an intentional schizophrenia: one breaks away from the world, plunging inward, and
the ranges of vision experienced are in fact the same as those of a
psychosis. But what, then, is the difference? What is the difference
between a psychotic or LSD experience and a yogic, or a mystical? The plunges are all into the same deep inward sea; of that
there can be no doubt. The symbolic figures encountered are in
many instances identical (and I shall have something more to say
about those in a moment). But there *is* an important difference.
The difference—to put it sharply—is equivalent simply to that
between a diver who can swim and one who cannot. The mystic,
endowed with native talents for this sort of thing and following,
stage by stage, the instruction of a master, enters the waters and
finds he can swim; whereas the schizophrenic, unprepared, un-
guided, and ungifted, has fallen or has intentionally plunged, and
is drowning. Can he be saved? If a line is thrown to him, will he
grab it?

Let us first ask about the waters into which he has descended.
They are the same, we have said, as those of the mystical experi-
ence. What, then, is their character? What are their properties?
And what does it take to swim?

They are the waters of the universal archetypes of mythology.
All my life, as a student of mythologies, I have been working with
these archetypes, and I can tell you, they *do* exist and are the

same all over the world. In the various traditions they are variously represented; as, for instance, in a Buddhist temple, medieval cathedral, Sumerian ziggurat, or Mayan pyramid. The images of divinities will vary in various parts of the world according to the local flora, fauna, geography, racial features, etc. The myths and rites will be given different interpretations, different rational applications, different social customs to validate and enforce. And yet the archetypal, essential forms and ideas are the same—often stunningly so. And so what, then, *are* they? What do they represent?

The psychologist who has best dealt with these, best described and best interpreted them, is Carl G. Jung, who terms them "archetypes of the collective unconscious," as pertaining to those structures of the psyche that are not the products of merely individual experience but are common to all mankind. In his view, the basal depth or layer of the psyche is an expression of the instinct system of our species, grounded in the human body, its nervous system and wonderful brain. All animals act instinctively. They act also, of course, in ways that have to be learned, and in relation to circumstance; yet every species differently, according to its "nature." Watch a cat enter a living room, and then, for example, a dog. Each is moved by impulses peculiar to its species, and these, finally, are the ultimate shapers of its life. And so man too is governed and determined. He has both an inherited biology and a personal biography, the "archetypes of the unconscious" being expressions of the first. The repressed personal memories, on the other hand, of the shocks, frustrations, fears, etc., of infancy, to which the Freudian school gives such attention, Jung distinguishes from that other and calls the "personal unconscious." As the first is biological and common to the species, so this second is biographical, socially determined, and specific to each separate life. Most of our dreams and daily difficulties will derive, of course, from the latter; but in a schizophrenic plunge one descends to the "collective," and the imagery there experienced is largely of the order of the archetypes of myth.

Now with respect to the power of instinct: I recall once having seen one of those beautiful Disney nature-films, of a sea turtle lay- ing her eggs in the sand, some thirty feet or so from the water. A number of days later, out of the sand there came a little multitude of tiny just-born turtles, each about as big as a nickel; and without an instant's hesitation they all started for the sea. No hunting around. No trial-and-error. No asking, "Now what would be a reasonable place for me to head for first?" Not a single one of those little things went the wrong way, fumbling first into the bushes, and there saying, "Oh!" and turning around, thinking, "I'm made for something better than this!" No, indeed! They went directly as their mother must have known they all would go: mother turtle, or Mother Nature. A flock of seagulls, meanwhile, having screamed the news to each other, came zooming like dive bombers down on those little nickels that were making for the water. The turtles knew perfectly well that that was where they had to get, and they were going as fast as their very little legs could push them: the legs, by the way, already knowing just how to push. No training or experimenting had been necessary. The legs knew what to do, and the little eyes knew that what they were seeing out in front of them was where they were going. The whole system was in perfect operation, with the whole fleet of tiny tanks heading clumsily, yet as fast as they could, for the sea: and then . . . Well now, one surely would have thought that for such little things those great big waves might have seemed threatening. But no! They went right on into the water and already knew how to swim. And as soon as they were there, of course, the fish began coming at them. Life is tough!

When people talk of going back to nature, do they really know what they are asking for?

There is another impressive example of the infallible rule of in- stinct; again of some tiny things just born: a brood of chicks just hatched, some even with fragments of their eggshells still adhering to their tails. If a hawk flies over their coop, they scurry to shel- ter; if a pigeon, they do not. Where did they learn the difference?

Who or what, shall we say, is deciding when such determinations are made? Experimenters have fashioned imitation hawks of wood and have drawn these across such coops on a wire. The chicks all scurry to shelter; but if the same models are drawn backward, they do not.

Both the readiness to respond to specific triggering stimuli and the ensuing patterns of appropriate action are in all such cases inherited with the physiology of the species. Known as "innate releasing mechanisms" (IRMs), they are constitutional to the central nervous system. And there are such in the physical make-up of the species Homo sapiens as well.

This, then, is what is meant by instinct. And if you should still have to be shown, if you are from Missouri and still doubtful of the governing force and wisdom of sheer instinct, just read in any biology book about the life cycles of parasites. Read, for example, about the hydrophobia parasite, and you will ask yourself whether a human being is worthy to play host to such a prodigy. It knows exactly what to do, where to go, and what to attack in the human nervous system, how to get there and just when to get there, to convert what we have been taught to believe is the highest creation of God's hand into its abject slave, rabid to bite and so to communicate the virus to the bloodstream of the next victim, whence it will proceed again to the salivary glands for the next event.

Now in every human being there is a built-in human instinct system, without which we should not even come to birth. But each of us has also been educated to a specific local culture system. The peculiar thing about man, which distinguishes us from all other beasts of the kingdom, is that we are born, as already remarked (*supra*, p. 45), twelve years too soon. No mother would wish it to be otherwise; but so it is, and that is our problem. The newly born has the wit neither of a newly hatched turtle, size of a nickel, nor of a chick with a piece of eggshell still adhering to its tail. Absolutely unable to fend for itself, the infant Homo sapiens is committed for twelve years to a season of dependency on parents or parent substitutes; and it is during these twelve dependent years that we are turned into human beings. We learn to walk as people walk, as well as to speak, think, and cogitate in terms of the local vocabulary. We are taught to respond to certain signals positively, to others negatively or with fear; and most of these signals taught are not of the natural, but of some local social order. They are socially specific. Yet the impulses that they activate and control are of nature, biology, and instinct. Every mythology is an organization, consequently, of culturally conditioned releasing signs, the natural and the cultural strains in them being so intimately fused that to distinguish one from the other is in many cases all but impossible. And such culturally determined signals motivate the culturally imprinted IRMs of the human nervous system, as the sign stimuli of nature do the natural reflexes of a beast.

A functioning mythological symbol I have defined as "an energy-evoking and -directing sign." Dr. Perry has termed such signals "affect images." Their messages are addressed not to the brain, to be interpreted there and passed on; but directly to the nerves, the glands, the blood, and the sympathetic nervous system. Yet they pass *through* the brain, and the educated brain may interfere, misinterpret, and so short-circuit the messages. When that occurs the signs no longer function as they should. The inherited mythology is garbled, and its guiding value lost or misconstrued. Or, what is worse, one may have been brought up to respond to a set of signals not present in the general environment; as is frequently the case, for example, with children raised in the circles of certain special sects, not participating in—and even despising or resenting—the culture forms of the rest of the civilization. Such a person will never quite feel at home in the larger social field, but always uneasy and even slightly paranoid. Nothing touches him as it should, means to him what it should, or moves him as it moves others. He is compelled to retreat for his satisfactions back to the restricted and accordingly restricting context of the sect, family, commune, or reservation to which he was attuned. He is disoriented, and even dangerous, in the larger field.

And so, it seems to me, there is a critical problem indicated here, which parents and families have to face squarely: that, namely, of insuring that the signals which they are imprinting on their young are such as will attune them to, and not alienate them from, the world in which they are going to have to live; unless, of course, one is dead set on bequeathing to one's heirs one's own paranoia. More normally, rational parents will wish to have produced socially as well as physically healthy offspring, well enough attuned to the system of sentiments of the culture into which they are growing to be able to appraise its values rationally and align themselves constructively with its progressive, decent, life-fostering, and fructifying elements.

And so we have this critical problem, as I say, this critical problem as human beings, of seeing to it that the mythology—the constellation of sign signals, affect images, energy-releasing and -directing signs—that we are communicating to our young will deliver directive messages qualified to relate them richly and vitally to the environment that is to be theirs for life, and not to some period of man already past, some piously desiderated future, or—what is worst of all—some querulous, freakish sect or momentary fad. And I call this problem critical because, when it is badly resolved, the result for the miseducated individual is what is known, in mythological terms, as a Waste Land situation. The world does not talk to him; he does not talk to the world. When that is the case, there is a cut-off, the individual is thrown back on himself, and he is in prime shape for that psychotic break-away that will turn him into either an essential schizophrenic in a padded cell, or a paranoid screaming slogans at large, in a bughouse without walls.

Let me now, therefore, before proceeding to an account of the general course or history of such a break-off—the inward journey (let us call it) of descent and return—just say one more word about the functions normally served by a properly operating mythology. They are, in my judgment, four.

The first is what I have called the mystical function: to waken

and maintain in the individual a sense of awe and gratitude in relation to the mystery dimension of the universe, not so that he
lives in fear of it, but so that he recognizes that he participates in
it, since the mystery of being is the mystery of his own deep being
as well. That is what the old Alaskan medicine man heard when
Sila, the soul of the universe, said to him, "Be not afraid." For, as
beheld by our temporal eyes, nature, as we have seen, is tough. It
is terrible, terrific, monstrous. It is the kind of thing that makes
reasonable, existentialist Frenchmen call it "absurd!" (The wonderful thing about the French is that they have been so imprinted
by Descartes that anything that cannot be parsed to Cartesian co-
ordinates must be absurd. Who or what, however, is absurd, we
may ask, when judgments of that kind are set forth as philosophy?)

The second function of a living mythology is to offer an image
of the universe that will be in accord with the knowledge of the
time, the sciences and the fields of action of the folk to whom the
mythology is addressed. In our own day, of course, the world pictures of *all* the major religions are at least two thousand years out
of date, and in that fact alone there is ground enough for a very
serious break-off. If, in a period like our own, of the greatest religious fervor and quest, you would wonder why the churches are
losing their congregations, one large part of the answer surely is
right here. They are inviting their flocks to enter and to find peace
in a browsing-ground that never was, never will be, and in any
case is surely not that of any corner of the world today. Such a
mythological offering is a sure pill for at least a mild schizophrenia.

The third function of a living mythology is to validate, support,
and imprint the norms of a given, specific moral order, that,
namely, of the society in which the individual is to live. And the
fourth is to guide him, stage by stage, in health, strength, and harmony of spirit, through the whole foreseeable course of a useful
life.

Let us review, briefly, the sequence of these stages.

The first is, of course, that of the child, dependent for those twelve years, both physically and psychologically, on the guidance and protection of its family. As I have already remarked in Chapter III, the most obvious biological analogy is to be found among the marsupials: kangaroos, opossums, wallabies, etc. Since these are not placental animals, the fetus cannot remain in the womb after the food provision (the yolk) of the egg has been absorbed, and the little things have to be born, therefore, long before they are ready for life. The infant kangaroo is born after only three weeks of gestation, but already has strong front legs, and these know exactly what to do. The tiny creature—by instinct, again please observe!—crawls up its mother's belly to her pouch, climbs in there, attaches itself to a nipple that swells (instinctively) in its mouth, so that it cannot get loose, and there, until ready to hop forth, remains in a second womb: a "womb with a view."

An exactly comparable biological function is served in our own species by a mythology, which is a no less indispensable biological organ, no less a nature product, though apparently something else. Like the nest of a bird, a mythology is fashioned of materials drawn from the local environment, apparently altogether consciously, but according to an architecture unconsciously dictated from within. And it simply does not matter whether its comforting, fostering, guiding images would be appropriate for an adult. It is not intended for adults. Its first function is to foster an unready psyche to maturity, preparing it to face its world. The proper question to ask, therefore, is whether it is training up a character fit to live in this world as it is, or only in some Heaven or imagined social field. The next function, accordingly, must be to help the ready youth step out and away, to leave the myth, this second womb, and to become, as they say in the Orient, "twice born," a competent adult functioning rationally in his present world, who has left his childhood season behind.

And now, to say just one more nasty thing about our religious institutions: what they require and expect is that one should *not* leave the womb that they provide. It is as though young kangaroos should be required to remain in their mother's pouch. And we all know what happened in the sixteenth century as a result: the whole pouch of Mother Church went to pieces, and not all the king's horses or all the king's men have been able to put it together again. So it is now destroyed, and we have no adequate pouch any more for even our littlest kangaroos. We do, however, have "reading, 'riting, and 'rithmetic" as a sort of plastic substitute. And if you are going on for your Ph.D., you may be in that inorganic incubator until you are forty-five. I have noticed (haven't you?) on television that when professors are asked questions they usually hum and haw and mmmm and uh, until you have to ask yourself whether it is some kind of interior crisis they are experiencing, or just a loss of words for exquisite thoughts; whereas when a professional baseball or football player is asked even a pretty complicated question, he can usually answer with ease and grace. He graduated from the womb when he was nineteen or so and the best player in the sandlot. But this other poor chap was held sitting under a canopy of professors until well into middle age, and even though he must now have acquired that degree, it came too late for him ever to begin developing what used to be called self-confidence. He has the imprint of that professorial canopy in his IRMs forever and is still hoping that no one is going to be giving him bad marks for his answer.

Then next, no sooner have you learned your adult job and gained a place for yourself in this society of ours, than you begin to feel the creak of age, retirement is in prospect, and remarkably soon it arrives with its Medicare, old-age pensions, and all. You have now a disengaged psyche on your hands, your own; a load of what Jung termed "disposable libido." What to do with it? The classical period has arrived of the late-middle-age nervous breakdown, divorce, alcoholic debacle, and so forth: when the light of your life has descended, unprepared, into an unprepared unconscious, and you there drown. It would have been a very much better situation if, during your childhood years, you had been given a sound imprinting of childhood myths, so that when the time came for this backward, downward plunge the scenery down there would have been a bit more familiar. At least for some of the monsters encountered you would have been given names and perhaps even weapons: for it is simply a fact, and a very important one, that the images of mythology that in childhood are interpreted as references to external supernaturals, actually are symbols of the structuring powers (or, as Jung called them, archetypes) of the unconscious. And it will be to these and the natural forces they represent—the forces and voices within you of the soul (Sila) of the universe—that you will return when you take that plunge, which is to befall you one day, sure as death.

And so, with that challenge before us, let us try to become acquainted with some of the tides and undertows of our inward sea. Let me tell you something of what I have recently heard about the wonders of the inward schizophrenic plunge.

The first experience is of a sense of splitting. The person sees the world going in two: one part of it moving away; himself in the other part. This is the beginning of the regressus, the crack-off and backward flow. He may see himself, for a time, in two roles. One is the role of the clown, the ghost, the witch, the queer one, the outsider. That is the outer role that he plays, making little of himself as the fool, a joke, the one kicked around, the patsy. Inside, however, he is the savior, and he knows it. He is the hero chosen for a destiny. Recently one such savior did me the honor of paying me three visits: a tall, beautiful young man with the beard and gentle eyes and manner of a Christ; LSD was his sacrament—LSD and sex. "I have seen my Father," he told me on the second occasion. "He is old now and has told me just to wait. I shall know when the time comes for me to take over."

The second stage has been described in many clinical accounts. It is of a terrific drop-off and regression, backward in time and biologically as well. Falling back into his own past, the psychotic becomes an infant, a fetus in the womb. One has the frightening experience of slipping back to animal consciousness, into animal forms, sub-animal forms, even plantlike. I think of the legend here of Daphne, the nymph who was turned into a laurel tree. Such an image, read in psychological terms, would be the image of a psychosis. Approached in love by the god Apollo, the virgin was terrified, cried for help to her father, the river-god Peneus, and he turned her into a tree.

"Show me the face you had before your father and mother were born!" We have had occasion before to refer to this meditation theme of the Japanese Zen masters. In the course of a schizophrenic retreat, the psychotic too may come to know the exaltation of a union with the universe, transcending personal bounds: the "oceanic feeling," Freud called it. Feelings arise then, too, of a new knowledge. Things that before had been mysterious are now fully understood. Ineffable realizations are experienced; and in fact, as we read about them, we can only be amazed. I have now read dozens of accounts; and they correspond, often amazingly, to the insights of the mystics and to the images of Hindu, Buddhist, Egyptian, and classical myth.

For example, a person who has never believed in, or even heard of, reincarnation will begin to feel that he has lived forever; that he has lived through many lifetimes, yet was never born and will never die. It is as though he had come to know himself as that Self (*atman*) of which we read in the *Bhagavad Gita:* "Never is it born, never does it die. . . . Unborn, eternal, permanent, and primeval, it is not slain when the body is slain." The patient (let us now call him that) has united what remains of his consciousness with the consciousness of all things, the rocks, the trees, the whole world of nature, out of which we all have come. He is in accord with that which has indeed existed forever: as we all are, actually, at root, and therein at peace—once again, as stated in the *Gita:* "When one completely withdraws the senses from their objects, like a tortoise drawing in its limbs, then is one's wisdom firmly fixed. In that serenity is surcease of all sorrow."

In short, my friends, what I find that I am saying is that our schizophrenic patient is actually experiencing inadvertently that same beatific ocean deep which the yogi and saint are ever striving

to enjoy: except that, whereas they are swimming in it, he is drowning.

There may come next, according to a number of accounts, the
sense of a terrific task ahead with dangers to be met and mastered;
but also a presentiment of invisible helpful presences that may
guide and help one through. These are the gods, the guardian dae-
mons or angels: innate powers of the psyche, fit to meet and to
master the torturing, swallowing, or shattering negative forces.
And if one has the courage to press on, there will be experienced,
finally, in a terrible rapture, a culminating overwhelming crisis—
or even a series of such culminations, more than can be borne.

These crises are mainly of four typical sorts, according to the
kinds of difficulty that will have conduced to the regressus in the
first place. For instance, a person who in childhood had been deprived of essential love, brought up in a home of little or no care,
but only authority, rigor, and commands, or in a house of tumult
and wrath, a drunken father raging about, or the like, will have
been seeking in his backward voyage a reorientation and centering
of his life in love. Accordingly, the culmination (when he will
have broken back to the start of his biography and even beyond,
to a sense of the erotic first impulse to life) will be a discovery of
a center in his own heart of tenderness and of love in which he
can rest. That will have been the aim and meaning of his entire
backward quest. And its realization will be represented through an
experience, one way or another, of some sort of visionary fulfillment of a "sacred union" with a wifely mothering (or simply
a mothering) presence.

Or if it had been a household in which the father had been nobody, a nothing, of no force in the home at all; where there had
been no sense of paternal authority, no one of masculine presence
who could be honored and respected, but only a clutter of domestic details and disordered feminine concerns, the quest will have
been for a decent father image, and that is what will have to be
found: some sort of symbolic realization of supernatural daughter-
hood or sonship to a father.

A third domestic situation of significant emotional deprivation is that of the child who feels itself to have been excluded from its family circle, treated as though not wanted; or with no family at all. In cases, for example, of a second marriage, where a second family has come along, a child of the first may feel and actually find itself excluded, thrown away, or left behind. The old fairy-tale theme of the wicked stepmother and stepsisters is relevant here. What such an excluded one will be striving for in his inward lonely journey will be the finding or the fashioning of a center— not a *family* center, but a *world* center—of which *he* will be the pivotal being. Dr. Perry told me of the case of a schizophrenic patient who was so completely and profoundly cut off that no one could establish any communication with him at all. One day, this poor mute person, in the doctor's presence, drew a crude circle, and then just placed the point of his pencil in the middle of it. Dr. Perry stooped and said to him, "You *are* in the center, aren't you! Aren't you!" And *that* message got through, initiating the course of a return.

There is a perfectly fascinating inside report of a schizophrenic breakdown in the next-to-last chapter of Dr. R. D. Laing's book *The Politics of Experience.*[6] This is an account given by a former Royal Navy commodore, now a sculptor, of a schizophrenic adventure of his own, at the culmination of which he experienced a fourth type of realization: a sense of sheer light, the sense of a terribly dangerous, overpowering light to be encountered and endured. His account suggests very strongly the Buddha-light described in the *Tibetan Book of the Dead,* which is supposed to be experienced immediately upon death, and which, if endured, yields release from rebirth but is for most too great to bear. The former Royal Navy man, a certain Mr. Jesse Watkins, thirty-eight years of age, had had no previous knowledge of Oriental philosophies or mythologies; yet, as the climax of his ten-day voyage approached, its imagery became all but indistinguishable from that of the Hindu and Buddhist faiths.

It all had begun with an alarming sense of time itself running backward. The gentleman, at home in the living room, had been listening inattentively to a popular tune on the radio when he began to have this uncanny experience. He got up and looked into a mirror to see what might be happening, and though the face that he saw there was familiar, it seemed to be of a stranger, not himself. Taken to an observation ward, he was put to bed and that night had the feeling that he had died, and that those in the ward around him had died too. He continued falling backward in time into a sort of animal landscape, where he wandered as a beast: a rhinoceros making rhinoceros sounds, afraid, yet aggressive and on guard. He felt, too, that he was a baby and could hear himself cry like a child. He was at once the observer and what he observed.

Given newspapers to read, he could make no headway because everything, every headline, opened out to widening associations. A letter from his wife gave the feeling that she was in a different world, which he would never again inhabit. And he felt that, where he was, he had tapped powers, powers inherent in us all. For example, a nasty cut on his finger, which he would not let the attendants treat, he actually healed in a single day by putting, as he declared, "a sort of intense attention on it." He found that by sitting up in bed and staring hard at noisy patients elsewhere in the ward, he could cause them to lie down and be still. He felt that he was more than he had ever imagined himself to be, that he had existed forever, in all forms of life, and was experiencing it all again; but also that he had now before him a great and terrible journey to accomplish, and this gave him a feeling of deep fear.

Now these great new powers that he was experiencing, both of control over his own body and of influence over others, are in India called the *siddhi*. They are recognized there (as they were experienced here, by this Western man) as powers latent in us all, inherent in all life, which the yogi releases in himself. We hear of them in Christian Science; also, in other types of "faith healing," praying people to health, and so forth. The miracles of shamans, saints, and saviors are, again, well-known examples. And as for the sense of an experience of identity with all being, all life, and of transformations into animal forms: consider the following chant of the legendary chief poet, Amairgen, of the first arriving Goidelic Celts, when their leading ship came to beach on the shores of Ireland:

> I am the wind that blows o'er the sea;
> I am the wave of the deep;
> I am the bull of seven battles;
> I am the eagle on the rock;
> I am a tear of the sun;
> I am the fairest of plants;
> I am a boar for courage;
> I am a salmon in the water;
> I am a lake in the plain;
> I am the word of knowledge;
> I am the head of the battle-dealing spear;
> I am the god who fashions fire [= thought] in the head.

We are thus on well-known mythic ground—strange and fluid though it may seem—as we follow in imagination the course of this ten-day inward journey. And its culminating passages too, though strange, will be curiously (in some secret way) familiar.

The voyager, as he tells, had a "particularly acute feeling" that the world he now was experiencing was established on three planes, with himself in the middle sphere, a plane of higher realizations above, and a sort of waiting-room plane beneath. Compare the cosmic image in the Bible, of God's heaven above, the earth beneath, and the waters beneath the earth. Or consider Dante's *Divine Comedy,* the temple towers of India and the Middle American Mayas, the ziggurats of old Sumer. Below are the Hells of suffering; aloft, the Heaven of light; and between, the mountain of ascending souls in stages of spiritual progress. According to Jesse Watkins, most of us are on the lowest level, waiting (*en attendant Godot,* one might say), as in a general waiting room; not yet in the middle room of struggle and quest at which he himself had arrived. He had feelings of invisible gods above, about, and all around, who were in charge and running things; and in the highest place, the highest job, was the highest god of all.

Moreover, what made it all so terrible was the knowledge that ultimately everybody would have to assume that job at the top. All those around him in the madhouse, who, like himself, had died and were in the middle, purgatorial stage, were—as he phrased it—"sort of awakening." (The meaning of the word *buddha,* let us recall, is "the awakened one.") Those all around him in the madhouse were on their ways—awakening—to assume in their own time that top position, and the one now up there was God. *God was a madman.* He was the one that was bearing it all: "this enormous load," as Watkins phrased it, "of having to be aware and governing and running things." "The journey is there and every single one of us," he reported, "has got to go through it, and you can't dodge it, and the purpose of everything and the whole of existence is to equip you to take another step, and another step, and another step, and so on. . . ."

Now is it not amazing to find such a set of Oriental themes set down in the log of the night-sea voyage of a British wartime naval officer, briefly mad? There is an early Buddhist fable of just such an end to a journey, preserved in a famous Hindu book of fables, the fable of "The Four Treasure-Seekers" in the *Panchatantra.* It is an account of four Brahmins, friends, who, having lost their fortunes, determined to set forth together to acquire wealth, and in the Avanti country (which is where the Buddha once lived and taught) they encountered a magician named Terror-Joy. This impressive fellow, when they had described to him their plight and begged for assistance, gave to each a magic quill with instructions to go north to the northern slope of the Himalayas, and wherever a quill dropped, he assured them, the owner of that quill would find his treasure.

Now the leader's quill dropped first, and they found the soil in that place to be all copper. "Look!" said he. "Take all you want!" But the others chose to continue, and so the leader, alone, gathered his copper and turned back. Where the quill of the second fell there was silver and its bearer was the second to return. That of the next revealed gold. "Don't you see the point?" said the fourth member of the party. "First copper, then silver, then gold. Beyond there will surely be gems." But the other held to the gold, and the fourth went on.

And so, as we read in the Indian text:

So this other went on alone. His limbs were scorched by the rays of the summer sun and his thoughts were confused by thirst as he wandered to and fro over the trails in the land of the fairies. At last, on a whirling platform, he saw a man with blood dripping down his body; for a wheel was whirling on his head. Then he made haste and said: "Sir, why do you stand thus with a wheel whirling on your head? In any case, tell me if there is water anywhere. I am mad with thirst."

The moment the Brahmin said this, the wheel left the other's head and settled on his own. "My very dear sir," said he, "what is the meaning of this?" "In the very same way," replied the other, "it settled on my head." "But," said the Brahmin, "when will it go away? It hurts terribly." And the fellow said: "When someone who holds in his hand a magic quill, such as you had, arrives and speaks as you did, then it will settle on his head." "Well," said the Brahmin, "how long have you been here?" The other asked: "Who is king in the world at present?" And on hearing the answer, "King Vinabatsa," he said: "When Rama was king, I was poverty-stricken, procured a magic quill, and came here, just like you. And I saw another man with a wheel on his head and put a question to him. The moment I asked the question (just like you), the wheel left his head and settled on mine. But I cannot reckon the centuries."

Then the wheel-bearer asked: "How, pray, did you get food while standing thus?" "My dear sir," said the fellow, "the god of wealth, fearful lest his treasures be stolen, prepared this terror, so that no magician might come so far. And if any should succeed in coming, he was to be freed from hunger and thirst, preserved from decrepitude and death, and was merely to endure the torture. So now permit me to say farewell. You have set me free from a sizable misery. I am going home." And he went.[7]

The old fable as here retold is presented as a warning to all of the danger of excessive greed. However, in its earlier form it had been a Mahayana Buddhist legend of the path to Bodhisattvahood, the immediate asking of the question having there been the sign of the spiritual voyager's selfless perfection of compassion. One is reminded of the figure of the maimed king of the medieval Christian legend of the Grail, and of the question there to be asked by the arriving innocent Grail Knight, who, upon asking it, will have healed the king and himself achieved the kingly role (see above, p. 164). One thinks also of the head crowned with thorns of the crucified Christ; and of a number of other figures: Prometheus, pinned to a crag of Caucasus, with an eagle tearing at his liver; Loki likewise fixed to a crag, and with the fiery venom of a cosmic serpent dripping forever on his head; or indeed Satan, as Dante saw him, at the center of the earth, as its pivot, corresponding in this position to his prototype, the Greek Hades (Roman Pluto), lord of both the underworld and of .wealth—who is exactly (in that marvelous way that we so often find when comparing mythic forms) the Occidental counterpart of India's earth-god Kubera, the very lord of wealth and of the painful turning wheel referred to in this fable.

In the case of our schizophrenic visionary, however, the role of the mad, terribly suffering god at the summit of the universe was felt to be too much for him to assume. For who, indeed, would be able both to face and to accept to himself willingly the whole impact of an experience of what life truly is—what the universe truly is—in the whole of its terrible joy? That perhaps would be the ultimate test of the perfection of one's compassion: to be able to affirm this world, just as it is, without reservation, while bearing all its terrible joy with rapture in oneself, and thereby madly willing it to all beings! In any case, Jesse Watkins, in his madness, knew that he had had enough.

"At times it was so devastating," he said, in speaking of his whole adventure, "that I'd be afraid of entering it again. . . . I was suddenly confronted with something so much greater than oneself, with so many more experiences, with so much awareness, so much that you couldn't take it. . . . I experienced it for a moment or two, but it was like a sudden blast of light, wind or whatever you like to put it as, against you; so that you feel that you're too naked and alone to be able to withstand it."

One morning he decided to let them give him no more sedatives and to come back, somehow, to his senses. He sat up on the edge of his bed, tightly clenched together his hands, and began repeating his own name. He kept on repeating it, over and over, and all of a sudden—just like that—he realized that it was all over, and so it was. The experiences were finished, and he was sane.

And here, I think we can say, is our clue to the method of the adventure, if one is ever to return home. It is this: *not* to identify one's *self* with *any* of the figures or powers experienced. The Indian yogi, striving for release, identifies himself with the Light and never returns. But no one with a will to the service of others and of life would permit himself such an escape. The ultimate aim of the quest, if one is to return, must be neither release nor ecstasy for oneself, but the wisdom and power to serve others. And there is a really great, as well as greatly celebrated, Occidental tale of such a round trip to the Region of Light in the *ten-year voyage* of Homer's Odysseus—who, like the Royal Navy Commodore Watkins, was a warrior returning from long battle years to domestic life, and required, therefore, to shift radically his psychological posture and center.

We all know the great story: Of how, having sailed with his twelve ships away from conquered Troy, Odysseus put into a Thracian port, Ismarus, sacked the city, slew its people, and—as he later reported—"took their wives and much substance," distributing these to his own men. Clearly, such a brute was not ready for domestic life; a complete change of character was required. And the gods, who are always alert to such things, saw to it that he should fall into competent hands.

First Zeus sent upon him a tempest that tore the sails of his ships to shreds and blew them for nine days, out of control, to the land of the Lotus Eaters—land of the hallucinogenic drug "forgetfulness," where, like Watkins in his madhouse, Odysseus and his freaked-out men were set floating on a sea of dream. Then follows the sequence of their mythological adventures, altogether different in kind from anything they had ever known.

There was, first, their encounter with the Cyclops and, after a costly release from his terrible cave, a period of elation, as they sailed on the winds of the god Aeolus; next, however, a dead calm and the toilsome ordeal of the twelve great ships reduced to rowing. They made it to land at the island of the cannibal Laestrygons, who sent eleven ships to the bottom, and the mighty Odysseus, up against forces now greater far than he could master, made away with a terrified crew in the one last hull remaining. Rowing wearily, still on a dead-calm sea, they advanced to what was to prove to be the crux of the entire night-sea adventure, the island of Circe of the Braided Locks, the nymph who turns men into swine.

This would be such a female as our already seriously humbled hero could not manhandle as mere booty. Her power surpassed his own. Fortunately for his fame, however, the protector and guide of souls beyond death to rebirth, the mystery-god Hermes, arrived just in time to protect him with both advice and a charm; so that, instead of being metamorphosed, the great mariner, so protected, was taken to Circe's bed, after which she directed him to the underworld and the shades down there of his ancestors. There he also met Tiresias, the blind prophetic sage in whom male and female knowledges are united. And when he had learned there all he could, he returned, much improved, to the formerly very dangerous nymph, who was now his teacher and guide.

Circe next directed him to the Island of the Sun, her own father, where, however—in the source-region of all light—his only remaining ship with its crew was shattered, and Odysseus, tossed alone into the sea, was carried by its irresistible tides right back to his daytime earthly wife (and life), Penelope . . . after an eight-year stop-off on the way with the middle-aged wifely nymph Calypso, and a brief pause, also, on the isle of pretty Nausicaa and her father, in whose night-sea craft he was finally carried in deep sleep home to his own sweet shore—now fully prepared for his life-to-come as a considerate spouse and father.

A significant feature of this great epic of the inward night-sea adventure is its representation of the voyager as never wishing to remain at any of its stations. In the land of the Lotus Eaters, those of his men who ate the flowery food had no desire ever to return home; but Odysseus dragged them weeping to his ships, bound them in the hulls, and rowed away. And even during his idyllic stay of eight years on the isle of Calypso, he would often be found on the beach alone, gazing homeward, out to sea.

Jesse Watkins too was able ultimately to distinguish himself in his worldly role from the madman in the asylum; and, like the turning point at the farthest reach of his classical prototype's course, where the last ship went to pieces at the Island of the Sun, so in this modern mariner's voyage, the turning point was reached at the brink of an experience of blasting light. Jesse Watkins, at that juncture, recognizing that he was not only a terrified madman about to experience annihilation, but also the sane man he once had been at home, from whose sphere of life he had become psychologically dissociated, sat (as we have heard) on his bed, clenched together his two hands, pronounced his daylight body's name, and returned to it, like a diver to the surface of the sea.

The usual and most appropriate mythological figure to symbolize such a return to life is "rebirth," rebirth to a new world; and that, exactly, was the figure that occurred to the mind of this self-rescued patient on experiencing spontaneous remission. "When I came out," he is reported to have told, "I suddenly felt that everything was so much more real than it had been before. The grass was greener, the sun was shining brighter, and people were more alive, I could see them clearer. I could see the bad things and the good things and all that. I was much more aware."

"Can we not see," remarks Dr. Laing in his commentary on the whole experience, "that this voyage is not what we need to be cured of, but that it is itself a natural way of healing our own appalling state of alienation called normality?"

Something much the same was the view, also, of both Dr. Perry and Dr. Silverman in the papers earlier mentioned; and, as I have most lately learned, the earliest documented proposal of this view was in a study published by C. G. Jung already in 1902, "On the Psychology and Pathology of So-called Occult Phenomena." [8]

In sum, then: The inward journeys of the mythological hero, the shaman, the mystic, and the schizophrenic are in principle the same; and when the return or remission occurs, it is experienced as a rebirth: the birth, that is to say, of a "twice-born" ego, no longer bound in by its daylight-world horizon. It is now known to be but the reflex of a larger self, its proper function being to carry the energies of an archetypal instinct system into fruitful play in a contemporary space-time daylight situation. One is now no longer afraid of nature; nor of nature's child, society—which is monstrous too, and in fact cannot be otherwise; it would otherwise not survive. The new ego is in accord with all this, in harmony, at peace; and, as those who have returned from the journey tell, life is then richer, stronger, and more joyous.

The whole problem, it would seem, is somehow to go through it, even time and again, without shipwreck: the answer being *not* that one should *not* be permitted to go crazy; but that one should have been taught something already of the scenery to be entered and powers likely to be met, given a formula of some kind by which to recognize, subdue them, and incorporate their energies. Siegfried, when he had slain Fafnir, took a taste of the dragon blood and immediately found, to his own surprise, that he understood the language of nature, both his own nature and nature without. He did not himself become a dragon, though he had derived from the dragon its powers—of which, however, he lost control when he returned to the world of general mankind.

There is always in the adventure great danger of what is known to psychology as "inflation," which is what overtakes the psychotic. He identifies himself either with the visionary object or with its witness, the visionary subject. The trick must be to become aware of it without becoming lost in it: to understand that we may all be saviors when functioning in relation to our friends or enemies: savior figures, but never The Savior. We may all be mothers and fathers, but are never The Mother, The Father. When a growing girl becomes aware of the pleasing effect that her blossoming womanhood is beginning to have upon others and takes the credit for this to her own ego, she has already gone a little crazy. She has misplaced her identification. What is causing all the excitement is not her own astonished little ego, but the wonderful new body that is growing up all around it. There is a Japanese saying I recall once having heard, of the five stages of man's growth. "At ten, an animal; at twenty, a lunatic; at thirty, a failure; at forty, a fraud; at fifty, a criminal." And at sixty, I would add (since by that time one will have gone through all this), one begins advising one's friends; and at seventy (realizing that everything said has been misunderstood) one keeps quiet and is taken for a sage. "At eighty," then said Confucius, "I knew my ground and stood firm."

In the spirit of all of which, let me now underscore the lesson of these purgatorial thoughts with the concluding words of that mad vision of Saint John which he beheld from his exile on the island of Patmos:

Then I saw a new heaven and a new earth; for the first heaven and the first earth had passed away, and the sea was no more. And I saw the holy city, new Jerusalem, coming down out of heaven from God, prepared as a bride adorned for her husband; and I heard a great voice from the throne saying, "Behold, the dwelling of God is with men. He will dwell with them, and they shall be his people, and God himself will be with them; he will wipe away every tear from their eyes, and death shall be no more, neither shall there be mourning nor crying nor pain any more, for the former things have passed away." . . . Then he showed me the river of the water of life, bright as crystal, flowing from the throne of God and of the Lamb through the middle of the street of the city; also, on either side of the river, the tree of life with its twelve kinds of fruit, yielding its fruit each month; and the leaves of the tree were for the healing of the nations.

XI

The Moon Walk—the Outward Journey

[1 9 7 0]

▣ Are we today turning mythology into fact? Let me introduce with a passage from Dante's *Divine Comedy* the truly wondrous topic of this chapter. It is of that moment of the poet's visionary journey where he takes off from the Earthly Paradise, to ascend to the moon, the first celestial stop of his spiritual flight to God's throne. He is addressing himself to the reader:

> O You who in a little boat, desirous to listen, have been following behind my craft which singing passes on, turn to see again your shores; put not out upon the deep; for haply, losing me, you would remain astray. The water which I take was never crossed. Minerva breathes, Apollo guides me, and the Muses nine point out to me the Bears.

That will set the mood. The breath of a goddess, Minerva, is to fill our sails, patroness of heroes; the naming of Apollo is a pleasant surprise; and we are to be guided by the Muses, teachers of all arts, pointing out to us the navigational stars. For although our voyage is to be outward, it is also to be inward, to the sources of all great acts, which are not out there, but in here, in us all, where the Muses dwell.

I remember when I was a very small boy my uncle one evening brought me down to Riverside Drive to see "a man," as he told me, "flying in an aeroplane [as they called them in those days] from Albany to New York." That was Glenn Curtis, 1910, in a sort of motorized box-kite he had built. There were people lined along the low wall at the westward margin of the city, watching, waiting, facing into the sunset. All the nearby rooftops, too, were crowded. Twilight fell. And then suddenly everybody was pointing, shouting, "There he comes!" And what I saw was like the shadow of a dark bird, soaring in the fading light some hundred feet above the river. Seventeen years later, the year I left Columbia, Lindbergh flew the Atlantic. And this year, on our television sets, we have seen two landings on the moon.

I want this chapter to be a celebration of the fabulous age in which we are living; also, of this country in which we are living; and of our incredible human race, which in the years just past broke free of its earth, to fly forth to the opening of the greatest adventure of the ages.

When I listen to some of my academic colleagues talk of their indifference to this epochal adventure, I am reminded of the anecdote of the little old lady who, when offered an opportunity to look at the moon through a telescope, commented, when she had done so, "Give me the moon as *God* made it!" The only really adequate public comment on the occasion of the first moon walk that I have found reported in the world press was the exclamation of an Italian poet, Giuseppe Ungaretti, published in the picture magazine *Epoca*. In its vivid issue of July 27, 1969, we see a photo of this white-haired old gentleman pointing in rapture to his television screen, and in the caption beneath are his thrilling words: *Questa è una notte diversa da ogni altra notte del mondo.*

For indeed that *was* "a different night from all other nights of the world"! Who will ever in his days forget the spell of the incredible hour, July 20, 1969, when our television sets brought directly into our living rooms the image of that strange craft up there and Neil Armstrong's booted foot coming down, feeling cau-

tiously its way—to leave on the soil of that soaring satellite of
earth the first impress ever of life? And then, as though immediately at home there, two astronauts in their space suits were to be
seen moving about in a dream-landscape, performing their assigned tasks, setting up the American flag, assembling pieces of
equipment, loping strangely but easily back and forth: their pictures brought to us, by the way, through two hundred and thirty-
eight thousand miles of empty space by that other modern miracle
(also now being taken for granted), the television set in our living
room. "All humanity," Buckminster Fuller once said, in prophecy of these transforming forces working now upon our senses, "is
about to be born in an entirely new relationship to the universe."

From the point of view of a student of mythology, the most important consequences of what Copernicus wrote of the universe in
1543 followed from his presentation there of an image controvert-
ing and refuting the obvious "facts" that everybody everywhere
could see. All mankind's theological as well as cosmological thinking, up to that time, had been based on concepts of the universe
visually confirmed from the point of view of earth. Also, man's
notion of himself and of nature, his poetry and his whole feeling
system, were derived from the sight of his earthbound eyes. The
sun rose eastward, passed above, leaning southward, and set blazing in the west. The Polynesian hero Maui had snared that sun to
slow it down, so that his mother could have time to finish her
cooking. Joshua stopped both the sun and the moon, to have time
to finish off a slaughter, while God, to assist, flung down from
heaven a hail of prodigious stones: "and there was no day like that
before it or after it, when Jehovah hearkened to the voice of a
man."

The moon was in ancient times regarded, and in parts of the
world still is regarded, as the Mansion of the Fathers, the residence of the souls of those who have passed away and are there
waiting to return for rebirth. For the moon itself, as we see it, dies
and is resurrected. Shedding its shadow, it is renewed, as life
sheds generations to be renewed in those to come. Whereas

against all this, which had been confirmed and reconfirmed in the scriptures, poetry, feelings, and visions of all ages, what Copernicus proposed was a universe no eye could see but only the mind imagine: a mathematical, totally invisible construction, of interest only to astronomers, unbeheld, unfelt by any others of this human race, whose sight and feelings were locked still to earth.

However, now, in our own day, four and one-quarter centuries later, with those pictures coming down to us from the point of view of the moon, we have all seen—and not only seen, but felt —that our visible world and the abstract construction of Copernicus correspond. That fabulous color photograph of our good earth rising as a glorious planet above a silent lunar landscape is something not to forget. Giuseppe Ungaretti published in that issue of *Epoca* the first verse of a new-world poetry in celebration of this moon-born revelation:

> *Che fai tu, Terra, in ciel?*
> *Dimmi, che fai, Silenziosa Terra?*

> What are you doing, Earth, in heaven?
> Tell me, what are you doing, Silent Earth?

All the old bindings are broken. Cosmological centers now are any- and everywhere. The earth is a heavenly body, most beautiful of all, and all poetry now is archaic that fails to match the wonder of this view.

In contrast, I recall the sense of embarrassment that I felt two Christmas Eves ago, the night of the first manned flight *around* the moon, when those three magnificent young men up there began reading to us, and sending down as their message to the world, the first chapter of the Book of Genesis: "In the beginning God created the heavens and the earth. And the earth was without form and void," and so on; all of which had nothing whatsoever to do with the world that they were themselves then actually viewing and exploring. I later asked a number of my friends what they had felt when they heard that coming down to them from the moon, and all, without exception, replied that they had found it wonderfully moving. How very strange! And how sad, I thought, that we should have had nothing in our own poetry to match the sense of that prodigious occasion! Nothing to match, or even to suggest, the marvel and the magnitude of this universe into which we then were moving! There was that same old childhood dream of some Babylonian-born Hebrew of the fourth century B.C., telling of the dawn of a world which those three men up there, even as they read, had refuted! How very disappointing! Better by far, it seemed to me, would have been those beautiful half-dozen lines from the opening of Dante's *Paradiso:*

> To the glory of Him that moves all things,
>   penetrates through the universe, and is resplendent
> in one part more, and in another less.

> In the heaven that most of his light receives
>   have I been, and I have seen things, to recount which,
>   descending, I neither know how nor have the power.

To predict what the imagery of the poetry of man's future is to be, is today, of course, impossible. However, those same three astronauts, when coming down, gave voice to a couple of suggestions. Having soared beyond thought into boundless space, circled many times the arid moon, and begun their long return: how welcome a sight, they said, was the beauty of their goal, this planet Earth, "like an oasis in the desert of infinite space!" Now *there* is a telling image: this earth, the one oasis in all space, an extraordinary kind of sacred grove, as it were, set apart for the rituals of life; and not simply one part or section of this earth, but the entire globe now a sanctuary, a set-apart Blessed Place. Moreover, we have all now seen for ourselves how very small is our heaven-born earth, and how perilous our position on the surface of its whirling, luminously beautiful orb.

A second thought that the astronauts, coming down, expressed was in reply to a question from Ground Control asking who was then doing the navigating. Their immediate answer was, "Newton!" Think of that! They were riding back securely on the mathematics of the miracle of Isaac Newton's brain.

This stunning answer brought to my mind the essential problem of knowledge considered by Immanuel Kant. How is it, he asks, that, standing in this place here, we can make mathematical calculations that we know will be valid in that place over there? Nobody knew how deep the dust on the surface of the moon was going to be, but the mathematicians knew exactly how to calculate the laws of the space through which the astronauts would fly, not only around our familiar earth, but also around the moon and through all those miles of unexplored space between. How is it, asked Kant, that mathematical judgments can be made *a priori* about space, and about relationships in space?

When you walk past a rippling mirror, you cannot predict what the dimensions of your passing reflection are going to be. Not so, however, in space. Through the whole of space there are no such transformations of the mathematics of dimension. When we saw on our television screens that parachuting spacecraft of the second moon flight descending from the sky to the very spot in the sea that had been programed for its splashdown, we all became eyewitness to the fact that, although the moon is over two hundred thousand miles away from us, a knowledge of the laws of the space through which it moves was already in our minds (or at least in Newton's mind) centuries before we got there. Also known beforehand was the fact that speeds out there could be timed according to earthly measure: that the distance covered in a minute out there would be the same as in a minute here. Which is to say, we had prior knowledge of those matters. And we know, also, that the same laws will apply when our spaceships get to Mars, to Jupiter, to Saturn, and even out beyond.

Space and time, as Kant already recognized, are the *"a priori* forms of sensibility," the antecedent preconditions of all experience and action whatsoever, implicitly known to our body and senses even before birth, as the field in which we are to function.

They are not simply "out there," as the planets are, to be learned about analytically, through separate observations. We carry their laws within us, and so have already wrapped our minds around the universe. "The world," wrote the poet Rilke, "is large, but in us it is deep as the sea." We carry the laws within us by which it is held in order. And we ourselves are no less mysterious. In searching out its wonders, we are learning simultaneously the wonder of ourselves. That moon flight as an outward journey was outward into ourselves. And I do not mean this poetically, but factually, historically. I mean that the actual fact of the making and the visual broadcasting of that trip has transformed, deepened, and extended human consciousness to a degree and in a manner that amount to the opening of a new spiritual era.

The first step of that booted foot onto the moon was very, very cautious. The second astronaut descended, and for a time the two moved about carefully, testing their own balances, the weights of their gear in the new environment. But then—by golly!—they were both suddenly jumping, hopping, loping about like kangaroos; and the two moon-walkers of the following voyage were giggling, laughing, enjoying themselves like a pair of lunatic kids— moonstruck! And I thought, "Well now, that lovely satellite has been out there circling our earth for some four billion years like a beautiful but lonesome woman trying to catch earth's eye. She has now at last caught it, and has caught thereby ourselves. And as always happens when a temptation of that kind has been responded to, a new life has opened, richer, more exciting and fulfilling, for both of us than was known, or even thought of or imagined, before." There are youngsters among us, even now, who will be *living* on that moon; others who will visit Mars. And their sons? What voyages are to be theirs?

I wonder how many of my readers saw that motion picture, *2001,* of the imagined space odyssey of a mighty spacecraft of the not very distant future, a future indeed that most of those watching the film would themselves live to see. The adventure opens with some entertaining views of a community of little manlike

apes a million or so years ago: a company of those apelike hominids known to science today as Australopithecines, snarling, fighting with each other, and generally behaving like any agglomera-
tion of simians. However, there was among them one who had in
his dawning soul the potentiality of something better; and that potential was evident in his sense of awe before the unknown, his
fascinated curiosity, with a desire to approach and to explore.
This, in the film, was suggested in a symbolic scene showing him
seated in wonder before a curious panel of stone standing mysteriously upright in the landscape. And while the others continued in
the usual way of ape-men, absorbed in their economic problems
(getting food for themselves), social enjoyments (searching for lice
in each other's hair), and political activities (variously fighting),
this particular one, apart and alone, contemplating the panel, presently reached out and cautiously felt it—rather as our astronaut's
foot first approached, then gently touched down on the moon. And
he was followed, then, by others, though not all; for indeed there
remain among us many still who are unmoved by what Goethe
called "the best part of man." These remain, even now, in the
condition of those prehuman apes who are concerned only with
economics, sociology, and politics, hurling bricks at each other
and licking then their own wounds.

Those are *not* the ones that are heading for the moon or even
noticing that the greatest steps in the progress of mankind have
been the products not of wound-licking, but of acts inspired by
awe. And in recognition of the continuity through all time of this
motivating principle in the evolution of our species, the authors of
this film of which I am speaking showed again symbolically that
same mysterious panel standing in a hidden quarter of the moon,
approached and touched there by space travelers; and then again,
floating free in most distant space, mysterious still—as it has always been and must forever remain.

One of the earliest signs of a separation of human from animal
consciousness may be seen in man's domestication of fire—which
I would like to relate to the symbolism of that slab. When this do-

mestication occurred, we do not know; but we do know that as early as 400,000 B.C. fires were being kindled and fostered in the caves of Peking Man. What for? That is something else that we do not know. It is clear that the hearths were not used for cooking. They may have been used for heat, or to keep dangerous animals away; more likely, though, for the fascination of the dancing flames. We have from all over the world innumerable myths of the capturing of fire; and in these it is usual to represent the adventure as undertaken not because anyone knew what the practical uses of fire would be, but because it was fascinating. People would dance around it, sit and watch it. Also, it is usual in these myths to represent the separation of mankind from the beasts as having followed upon that fundamental adventure.

Fire is revered generally as a deity to this day. The lighting of the household fire is in many cultures a ritual act. We hear of the holy Vestal Fire as the most honored goddess of Rome. The fascination of fire, like that of the symbolic panel in the film of which I have been telling, may be taken as the earliest sign in the records of our species of that openness to fascination and willingness to adventure for it at great risk which has been ever the essential mark of the uniquely human—as opposed to common animal— faculties of our species, and which is eminently represented in the adventure to which I am here giving praise.

I have discussed in earlier chapters some of the other orders of fascination by which the members of our species have been led to surpass themselves: the fascination felt by hunting tribes in the animal forms all about them, by planting tribes in the miracle of the planted seed, and by the old Sumerian priestly watchers of the skies in the passages of planets and circulation of stars. It is all so mysterious, so wonderfully strange! Nietzsche, it was, who called man "the sick animal," *das kranke Tier;* for we are open, undefined, in the patterning of our lives. Our nature is not like that of the other species, stereotyped to fixed ways. A lion has to be a lion all its life; a dog, to be a dog. But a human being can be an astronaut, a troglodyte, philosopher, mariner, tiller of the soil, or

sculptor. He can play and actualize in his life any one of any number of hugely differing destinies; and what he chooses to incarnate
in this way will be determined finally neither by reason nor even
by common sense, but by infusions of excitement: "visions that
fool him out of his limits," as the poet Robinson Jeffers called
them. "Humanity," Jeffers declares, "is the mold to break away
from, the crust to break through, the coal to break into fire, the
atom to be split." And what fools us out of our limits in this way?

> wild loves that leap over the walls of
> nature, the wild fence-vaulter science,
> Useless intelligence of far stars, dim knowledge
> of the spinning demons that make an atom.[1]

In the beginning, as it seems, it was the fascination of fire that
fooled man onward to a life style formerly unknown, where family
hearths would become the centers and revered sanctifiers of distinctly human circles of concern. Then no sooner was he separated
from the beasts than it was the animal and plant models of life
that impressed themselves on man's imagination, luring our human
species on to large mythological patternings both of the outward
social orders and of inward individual experiences of identity:
shamans living as wolves, ritualized covenants with the buffalo,
masked dancers, totem ancestors, and the rest. Or a whole community might govern itself according to plant laws and rites, sacrificing, dismembering, and interring its best and most vital members to increase the general good. "Truly, truly, I say unto you,"
we read in the John Gospel, in continuation of this image, "unless
a grain of wheat falls into the earth and dies, it remains alone; but
if it dies, it bears much fruit. He who loves his life shall lose it,
and he who hates his life in this world will keep it for eternal life"
(John 12:24–25). Or again, Christ's parable at the Last Supper of
himself as the True Vine: "As the branch cannot bear fruit by itself, unless it abides in the vine, neither can you, unless you abide
in me. I am the vine, you are the branches" (John 15:4–5).

As here expressed, the mythic imagery of the plant suggests an organic participation of the individual life in the larger life and body of the group, "fooling him out of his limits." Comparably, among hunting tribes with their rites based on mythologies of covenants with the animal world, a reciprocity is recognized that extends the bounds of concern of the human spirit to include much more than its own most immediate interests. The most exalting fascination that has ever, up to now, inspired human thought and life, however, was that which seized the priestly watchers of the night skies of Mesopotamia about 3500 B.C.: the perception of a cosmic order, mathematically definable, with which the structure of society should be brought to accord. For it was then that the hieratically ordered city-state came into being, which stands at the source, and for millenniums stood as the model, of all higher, literate civilization whatsoever. Not economics, in other words, but celestial mathematics were what inspired the religious forms, the arts, literatures, sciences, moral and social orders which in that period elevated mankind to the tasks of civilized life—again fooling us out of our limits, to achievements infinitely beyond any aims that mere economics, or even politics, could ever have inspired.

Today, as we all know, such thoughts and forms are of a crumbling past and the civilizations dependent on them in disarray and dissolution. Not only are societies no longer attuned to the courses of the planets; sociology and physics, politics and astronomy are no longer understood to be departments of a single science. Nor is the individual interpreted (in the democratic West, at least) as an inseparable subordinate part of the organism of a state. What we know today, if we know anything at all, is that every individual is unique and that the laws of his life will not be those of any other on this earth. We also know that if divinity is to be found anywhere, it will not be "out there," among or beyond the planets. Galileo showed that the same physical laws that govern the movements of bodies on earth apply aloft, to the celestial spheres; and our astronauts, as we have all now seen, have been transported by those earthly laws to the moon. They will soon be on Mars and

beyond. Furthermore, we know that the mathematics of those out-
ermost spaces will already have been computed here on earth by
human minds. There are no laws out there that are not right here;
no gods out there that are not right here, and not only here, but
within us, in our minds. So what happens now to those childhood
images of the ascent of Elijah, Assumption of the Virgin, Ascen-
sion of Christ—all bodily—into heaven?

What are you doing, Earth, in heaven?
Tell me, what are you doing, Silent Earth?

Our astronauts on the moon have pulled the moon to earth and
sent the earth soaring to heaven. From the deserts of Mars this
Mother Earth of ours will be again seen, higher, remoter, more
heavenly still; yet no nearer to any god than right now. And from
Jupiter, higher, farther; and so on; and so on: our planet ever
mounting, higher and higher, as our sons, grandsons, and their
great-great-grandsons proceed outward on the paths that we, in
these latest years, have just opened, searching, adventuring in a
space that is already present in our minds.

In other words, there has just now occurred a transformation of
the mythological field that is of a magnitude matched only by that
of the Old Sumerian sky-watch in the fourth millennium B.C., and
in fact, what is dissolving is the world not only of gods and men,
but of the state as well, which they, in that inspired time, brought
into being. I was greatly impressed, many years ago, by the works
of a man whom I still regard as having been the most acute student of mythologies of his generation: Leo Frobenius, who viewed
the entire history of mankind as a great and single organic process, comparable, in its stages of growth, maturation, and continuation toward senility, to the stages of any single lifetime. Very
much as the individual life begins in childhood and advances
through adolescence to maturity and old age, so likewise, the lifetime of our human race. Its childhood was of the long, long distant period of the primitive hunters, fishers, root-foragers, and
planters, living in immediate relationship with their animal and

plant neighbors. The second stage, which Frobenius termed the Monumental, commenced with the rise of the earliest agriculturally based, urban, and literate civilizations, each structured to accord with an imagined cosmic order, made known by' way of the movements and conditions of the planetary lights. For those lights were then supposed to be the residences of governing spirits; whereas, as just remarked, we now know them to be as material as ourselves. The laws of earth and of our own minds have been extended to incorporate what formerly were the ranges and the powers of the gods, now recognized as of ourselves. Hence, the whole imagined support of the Monumental Order has been withdrawn from "out there," found centered in ourselves, and a new world age projected, which is to be global, "materialistic" (as Frobenius termed it), comparable in spirit to the spirit of old age in its disillusioned wisdom and concern for the physical body, concentrating rather on fulfillments in the present than on any distant future. The residence of the spirit now is experienced as centered not in fire, in the animal and plant worlds, or aloft among the planets and beyond, but in men, right here on earth: the earth and its population, which our astronauts beheld and photographed rising above the moon into Heaven.

My friend Alan Watts in a lecture once proposed an amusing image to replace the old one (now no longer tenable) of man as a Heaven-sent stranger in this world, who, when the mortal coil of his body will have been cast away in death, is to soar in spirit to his proper source and home with God in Heaven. "The truth of the matter," Dr. Watts proposed to his audience, "is that you didn't come *into* this world at all. You came *out* of it, in just the same way that a leaf comes out of a tree or a baby from a womb. . . . Just as Jesus said that one doesn't gather figs from thistles or grapes from thorns, so also you don't gather people from a world that isn't peopling. Our world is peopling, just as the apple tree apples, and just as the vine grapes." We are a natural product of this earth, that is to say; and, as Dr. Watts observed in that same talk, if we are intelligent beings, it must be that we are the fruits of an intelligent earth, symptomatic of an intelligent energy system; for "one doesn't gather grapes from thorns." [2]

We may think of ourselves, then, as the functioning ears and eyes and mind of this earth, exactly as our own ears and eyes and minds are of our bodies. Our bodies are one with this earth, this wonderful "oasis in the desert of infinite space"; and the mathematics of that infinite space, which are the same as of Newton's mind—our mind, the earth's mind, the mind of the universe—come to flower and fruit in this beautiful oasis through ourselves.

Let us once more recall: when that protohuman troglodyte Sinanthropus, in his dismal cave, responded to the fascination of fire, it was to the apparition of a power that was already present and operative in his own body: heat, temperature, oxidation; as also in the volcanic earth, in Jupiter, and in the sun. When the masked dancers of the totemistic hunting tribes identified themselves with the holy powers recognized in the animals of their killing, it was again the apparition of an aspect of themselves that they were intuiting and honoring, which we all share with the beasts: instinctive intelligence in accord with the natural order of Mother Earth. Similarly, in relation to the plant world: there again, the apparition is of an aspect of ourselves, namely our nourishment and growth. Many mythologies, and not all of them primitive, represent mankind as having sprung plantlike from the earth—the earth "peopling"—or from trees. And we have the image of the "Second Adam," Christ crucified, as the fruit of the tree of life. There is also the Buddha's tree of wisdom; and Yggdrasil of the early Germans. All are trees revelatory of the wisdom of life, which is inherent already in the plantlike processes by which our bodies took shape in our mothers' wombs, to be born as creatures already prepared to breathe the world's air, to digest and assimilate the world's food through complex chemical processes, to see the world's sights and to think the world's thoughts according to mathematical principles that will be operative forever in the most distant reaches of space and of time.

I have noticed in the Orient that when the Buddhists build their temples they often choose a hilltop site with a great command of horizon. One experiences simultaneously in such places an expansion of view and diminution of oneself—with the sense, however, of an extension of oneself in spirit to the farthest reach. And I have noticed also, when flying—particularly over oceans—that the world of sheerly physical nature, of air and cloud and the marvels of light there experienced, is altogether congenial. Here on earth it is to the lovely vegetable nature-world that we respond; there aloft, to the sublimely spatial. People used to think, "How little is man in relation to the universe!" The shift from a geocentric to a heliocentric world view seemed to have removed man from the center—and the center seemed so important! Spiritually, however, the center is where sight is. Stand on a height and view the horizon. Stand on the moon and view the whole earth rising —even by way of television, in your parlor. And with each expansion of horizon, from the troglodytal cave to the Buddhist temple on the hilltop—and on now to the moon—there has been, as there must inevitably be, not only an expansion of consciousness, in keeping with ever-widening as well as deepening insights into the nature of Nature (which is of one nature with ourselves), but also an enrichment, refinement, and general melioration of the conditions of human physical life.

It is my whole present thesis, consequently, that we are at this moment participating in one of the very greatest leaps of the human spirit to a knowledge not only of outside nature but also of our own deep inward mystery that has ever been taken, or that ever will or ever can be taken. And what are we hearing, meanwhile, from those sociological geniuses that are, these days, swarming on our activated campuses? I saw the answer displayed the other day on a large poster in a bookstore up at Yale: a photograph of one of our astronauts on a desert of the moon, and the comment beneath him, "So what!"

But to return, finally, to the mythological, theological aspect of this moment: there was a prophetic medieval Italian abbot, Joachim of Floris, who in the early thirteenth century foresaw the

dissolution of the Christian Church and dawn of a terminal period
of earthly spiritual life, when the Holy Ghost, the Holy Spirit,
would speak directly to the human heart without ecclesiastical me-
diation. His view, like that of Frobenius, was of a sequence of historic stages, of which our own was to be the last; and of these he
counted four. The first was, of course, that immediately following
the Fall of man, before the opening of the main story, after which
there was to unfold the whole great drama of Redemption, each
stage under the inspiration of one Person of the Trinity. The first
was to be of the Father, the Laws of Moses and the People of Israel; the second of the Son, the New Testament and the Church;
and now finally (and here, of course, the teachings of this clergy-
man went apart from the others of his communion), a third age,
which he believed was about to commence, of the Holy Spirit, that
was to be of saints in meditation, when the Church, become
superfluous, would in time dissolve. It was thought by not a few
in Joachim's day that Saint Francis of Assisi might represent the
opening of the coming age of direct, penetecostal spirituality.
But as I look about today and observe what is happening to our
churches in this time of perhaps the greatest access of mystically
toned religious zeal our civilization has known since the close of
the Middle Ages, I am inclined to think that the years foreseen by
the good Father Joachim of Floris must have been our own.

For there is no divinely ordained authority any more that we
have to recognize. There is no anointed messenger of God's law.
In our world today all civil law is conventional. No divine authority is claimed for it: no Sinai; no Mount of Olives. Our laws are
enacted and altered by *human* determination, and within their secular jurisdiction each of us is free to seek his own destiny, his own
truth, to quest for this or for that and to find it through his own
doing. The mythologies, religions, philosophies, and modes of
thought that came into being six thousand years ago and out of
which all the monumental cultures both of the Occident and of the
Orient—of Europe, the Near and Middle East, the Far East, even
early America—derived their truths and lives, are dissolving from

around us, and we are left, each on his own to follow the star and spirit of his own life. And I can think of no more appropriate symbolic heroes for such a time than the figures of our splendid moon-men. Nor can I think of a more appropriate text on which to close this chapter's celebration of their doing than the following lines from Robinson Jeffers's *Roan Stallion:*

> The atoms bounds-breaking,
> Nucleus to sun, electrons to planets, with recognition
> Not praying, self-equaling, the whole to the whole, the micro-
> cosm
> Not entering nor accepting entrance, more equally, more ut-
> terly, more incredibly conjugate
> With the other extreme and greatness; passionately perceptive
> of identity. . . .[3]

The solar system and the atom, the two extreme extremes of scientific exploration, recognized as identical, yet distinct! Analogous must be our own identity with the All, of which we are the ears and eyes and mind.

The very great physicist Erwin Schrödinger has made the same metaphysical point in his startling and sublime little book, *My View of the World.*[4] "All of us living beings belong together," he there declares, "in as much as we are all in reality sides or aspects of one single being, which may perhaps in western terminology be called God while in the Upanishads its name is Brahman."

Evidently it is not science that has diminished man or divorced him from divinity. On the contrary, according to this scientist's view, which, remarkably, rejoins us to the ancients, we are to recognize in this whole universe a reflection magnified of our own most inward nature; so that we are indeed its ears, its eyes, its thinking, and its speech—or, in theological terms, God's ears, God's eyes, God's thinking, and God's Word; and, by the same token, participants here and now in an act of creation that is continuous in the whole infinitude of that space of our mind through which the planets fly, and our fellows of earth now among them.

XII

Envoy: No More Horizons

[1971]

What is, or what is to be, the new mythology?
Since myth is of the order of poetry, let us ask first a poet:
Walt Whitman, for example, in his *Leaves of Grass* (1855):

I have said that the soul is not more than the body,
And I have said that the body is not more than the soul,
And nothing, not God, is greater to one than one's-self is,
And whoever walks a furlong without sympathy walks to his
    own funeral, dressed in his shroud,
And I or you pocketless of a dime may purchase the pick of the
    earth,
And to glance with an eye or show a bean in its pod confounds
    the learning of all times,
And there is no trade or employment but the young man fol-
    lowing it may become a hero,
And there is no object so soft but it makes a hub for the
    wheeled universe,
And any man or woman shall stand cool and supercilious be-
    fore a million universes.

And I call to mankind, Be not curious about God,
For I who am curious about each am not curious about God,
No array of terms can say how much I am at peace about God
and about death.

I hear and behold God in every object, yet I understand God
not in the least,
Nor do I understand who there can be more wonderful than
myself.

Why should I wish to see God better than this day?
I see something of God each hour of the twenty-four, and each
moment then,
In the faces of men and women I see God, and in my own face
in the glass;
I find letters from God dropped in the street, and every one is
signed by God's name,
And I leave them where they are, for I know that others will
punctually come forever and ever.[1]

These lines of Whitman echo marvelously the sentiments of the
earliest of the Upanishads, the "Great Forest Book" (*Brihadaranyaka*) of about the eighth century B.C.

This that people say, "Worship this god! Worship that god!"
—one god after another! All this is his creation indeed! And he
himself is all the gods. . . . He is entered in the universe even
to our fingernail-tips, like a razor in a razor-case, or fire in firewood. Him those people see not, for as seen he is incomplete.
When breathing, he becomes "breath" by name; when speaking,
"voice"; when seeing, "the eye"; when hearing, "the ear"; when
thinking, "mind": these are but the names of his acts. Whoever
worships one or another of these—knows not; for he is incomplete as one or another of these.

One should worship with the thought that he is one's self, for
therein all these become one. This self is the footprint of that
All, for by it one knows the All—just as, verily, by following a

footprint one finds cattle that have been lost. . . . One should reverence the self alone as dear. And he who reverences the self alone as dear—what he holds dear, verily, will not perish. . . .

So whoever worships another divinity than his self, thinking, "He is one, I am another," knows not. He is like a sacrificial animal for the gods. And verily, indeed, as many animals would be of service to a man, so do people serve the gods. And if even one animal is taken away, it is not pleasant. What then if many? It is therefore not pleasing to the gods that men should know this.[2]

We hear the same, in a powerful style, even earlier, from the Egyptian *Book of the Dead,* in one of its chapters, "On Coming Forth by Day in the Underworld," as follows:

I am Yesterday, Today, and Tomorrow, and I have the power to be born a second time. I am the divine hidden Soul who created the gods and gives sepulchral meals to the denizens of the deep, the place of the dead, and heaven. . . . Hail, lord of the shrine that stands in the center of the earth. He is I, and I am he!

Indeed, do we not hear the same from Christ himself, as reported in the early Gnostic *Gospel According to Thomas?*

Whoever drinks from my mouth shall become as I am and I myself will become he, and the hidden things shall be revealed to him. . . . I am the All, the All came forth from me and the All attained to me. Cleave a piece of wood, I am there; lift up the stone and you will find me there.[3]

Or again, two more lines of Whitman:

I bequeath myself to the dirt to grow from the grass I love
If you want me again look for me under your bootsoles.[4]

Some fifteen years ago I had the experience of meeting in Bombay an extraordinarily interesting German Jesuit, the Reverend Father H. Heras by name, who presented me with the reprint of a

paper he had just published on the mystery of God the Father and
Son as reflected in Indian myth.[5] He was a marvelously open-
minded as well as substantial authority on Oriental religions, and
what he had done in this very learned paper was actually to interpret the ancient Indian god Shiva and his very popular son Gane-
sha as equivalent, in a way, to the Father and Son of the Christian
faith. If the Second Person of the Blessed Trinity is regarded in
his *eternal* aspect, as God, antecedent to history, supporting it,
and reflected (in some measure) in the "image of God" in us all, it
is then not difficult, even for a perfectly orthodox Christian, to
recognize the reflex of his own theology in the saints and gods of
alien worlds. For it is simply a fact—as I believe we have all
now got to concede—that mythologies and their deities are productions and projections of the psyche. What gods are there, what
gods have there ever been, that were not from man's imagination?
We know their histories: we know by what stages they developed.
Not only Freud and Jung, but all serious students of psychology
and of comparative religions today, have recognized and hold that
the forms of myth and the figures of myth are of the nature essentially of dream. Moreover, as my old friend Dr. Géza Róheim
used to say, just as there are no two ways of sleeping, so there are
no two ways of dreaming. Essentially the same mythological motifs are to be found throughout the world. There are myths and
legends of the Virgin Birth, of Incarnations, Deaths and Resurrec-
tions, Second Comings, Judgments, and the rest, in all the great
traditions. And since such images stem from the psyche, they
refer to the psyche. They tell us of its structure, its order and
its forces, in symbolic terms.

Therefore they cannot be interpreted properly as references,
originally, universally, essentially, and most meaningfully, to local
historical events or personages. The historical references, if they
have any meaning at all, must be secondary; as, for instance, in
Buddhist thinking, where the historical prince Gautama Shakyamuni is regarded as but one of many historical embodiments of
Buddha-consciousness; or in Hindu thought, where the incarna-

tions of Vishnu are innumerable. The difficulty faced today by Christian thinkers in this regard follows from their doctrine of the Nazarene as the *unique* historical incarnation of God; and in Judaism, likewise, there is the no less troublesome doctrine of a universal God whose eye is on but one Chosen People of all in his created world. The fruit of such ethnocentric historicism is poor spiritual fare today; and the increasing difficulties of our clergies in attracting gourmets to their banquets should be evidence enough to make them realize that there must be something no longer palatable about the dishes they are serving. These were good enough for our fathers, in the tight little worlds of the knowledge of their days, when each little civilization was a thing more or less to itself. But consider that picture of the planet Earth that was taken from the surface of the moon!

In earlier times, when the relevant social unit was the tribe, the religious sect, a nation, or even a civilization, it was possible for the local mythology in service to that unit to represent all those beyond its bounds as inferior, and its own local inflection of the universal human heritage of mythological imagery either as the one, the true and sanctified, or at least as the noblest and supreme. And it was in those times beneficial to the order of the group that its young should be trained to respond positively to their own system of tribal signals and negatively to all others, to reserve their love for at home and to project their hatreds outward. Today, however, we are the passengers, all, of this single spaceship Earth (as Buckminster Fuller once termed it), hurtling at a prodigious rate through the vast night of space, going nowhere. And are we to allow a hijacker aboard?

Nietzsche, nearly a century ago, already named our period the Age of Comparisons. There were formerly horizons within which people lived and thought and mythologized. There are now no more horizons. And with the dissolution of horizons we have experienced and are experiencing collisions, terrific collisions, not only of peoples but also of their mythologies. It is as when dividing panels are withdrawn from between chambers of very hot and very cold airs: there is a rush of these forces together. And so we are right now in an extremely perilous age of thunder, lightning, and hurricanes all around. I think it is improper to become hysterical about it, projecting hatred and blame. It is an inevitable, altogether natural thing that when energies that have never met before come into collision—each bearing its own pride—there should be turbulence. That is just what we are experiencing; and we are riding it: riding it to a new age, a new birth, a totally new condition of mankind—to which no one anywhere alive today can say that he has the key, the answer, the prophecy, to its dawn. Nor is there anyone to condemn here. ("Judge not, that you may not be judged!") What is occurring is completely natural, as are its pains, confusions, and mistakes.

And now, among the powers that are here being catapulted together, to collide and to explode, not the least important (it can be safely said) are the ancient mythological traditions, chiefly of India and the Far East, that are now entering in force into the fields of our European heritage, and vice versa, ideals of rational, progressive humanism and democracy that are now flooding into Asia. Add the general bearing of the knowledges of modern science on the archaic beliefs incorporated in *all* traditional systems, and I think we shall agree that there is a considerable sifting task to be resolved here, if anything of the wisdom-lore that has sustained our species to the present is to be retained and intelligently handed on to whatever times are to come.

I have thought about this problem a good deal and have come to the conclusion that when the symbolic forms in which wisdom-lore has been everywhere embodied are interpreted not as referring primarily to any supposed or even actual historical personages or events, but psychologically, properly "spiritually," as referring to the inward potentials of our species, there then appears through all something that can be properly termed a *philosophia perennis* of the human race, which, however, is lost to view when the texts are interpreted literally, as history, in the usual ways of harshly orthodox thought.

Dante in his philosophical work the *Convito* distinguishes between the literal, the allegorical, the moral, and the anagogical (or mystical) senses of any scriptural passage. Let us take, for example, such a statement as the following: *Christ Jesus rose from the dead*. The literal meaning is obvious: "A historical personage, Jesus by name, who has been identified as 'Christ' (the Messiah), rose alive from the dead." Allegorically, the normal Christian reading would be: "So likewise, we too are to rise from death to eternal life." And the moral lesson thereby: "Let our minds be turned from the contemplation of mortal things to abide in what is eternal." Since the anagogical or mystical reading, however, must refer to what is neither past nor future but transcendent of time and eternal, neither in this place nor in that, but everywhere, in all, now and forever, the fourth level of meaning would seem to be that in death—or in this world of death—is eternal life. The moral from that transcendental standpoint would then seem to have to be that the mind in beholding mortal things is to recognize the eternal; and the allegory: that in this very body which Saint Paul termed "the body of this death" (Romans 6:24) is our eternal life—not "to come," in any heavenly place, but here and now, on this earth, in the aspect of time.

That is the sense, also, of the saying of the poet William Blake: "If the doors of perception were cleansed every thing would appear to man as it is, infinite." And I think that I recognize the same sense in the lines of Whitman that I have just cited, as well as in those of the Indian Upanishad, the Egyptian *Book of the Dead,* and the Gnostic *Thomas Gospel*. "The symbols of the higher religions may at first sight seem to have little in common," wrote a Roman Catholic monk, the late Father Thomas Merton, in a brief but perspicacious article entitled "Symbolism: Communication or Communion?" [6] "But when one comes to a better understanding of those religions, and when one sees that the experiences which are the fulfillment of religious belief and practice are most clearly expressed in symbols, one may come to recognize that often the symbols of different religions may have more in common than have the abstractly formulated official doctrines."

"The true symbol," he states again, "does not merely point to something else. It contains in itself a structure which awakens our consciousness to a new awareness of the inner meaning of life and of reality itself. A true symbol takes us to the center of the circle, not to another point on the circumference. It is by symbolism that man enters affectively and consciously into contact with his own deepest self, with other men, and with God." " 'God is dead' . . . means, in fact, that symbols are dead." [7]

The poet and the mystic regard the imagery of a revelation as a fiction through which an insight into the depths of being—one's own being and being generally—is conveyed anagogically. Sectarian theologians, on the other hand, hold hard to the literal readings of their narratives, and these hold traditions apart. The lives of three incarnations, Jesus, Krishna, and Shakyamuni, will not be the same, yet as symbols pointing not to themselves, or to each other, but to the life beholding them, they are equivalent. To quote the monk Thomas Merton again: "One cannot apprehend a symbol unless one is able to awaken, in one's own being, the spiritual resonances which respond to the symbol not only as *sign* but as 'sacrament' and 'presence.' " "The symbol is an object pointing to a subject. We are summoned to a deeper spiritual awareness, far beyond the level of subject and object." [8]

Mythologies, in other words, mythologies and religions, are great poems and, when recognized as such, point infallibly through things and events to the ubiquity of a "presence" or "eternity" that is whole and entire in each. In this function all mythologies, all great poetries, and all mystic traditions are in accord; and where any such inspiriting vision remains effective in a civilization, every thing and every creature within its range is alive. The first condition, therefore, that any mythology must fulfill if it is to render life to modern lives is that of cleansing the doors of perception to the wonder, at once terrible and fascinating, of ourselves and of the universe of which we are the ears and eyes and the mind. Whereas theologians, reading their revelations counterclockwise, so to say, point to references in the past (in Merton's words: "to another point on the circumference") and Utopians offer revelations only promissory of some desired future, mythologies, having sprung from the psyche, point back to the psyche ("the center"): and anyone seriously turning within will, in fact, rediscover their references in himself.

Some weeks ago I received in the mail from the psychiatrist directing research at the Maryland Psychiatric Research Center in Baltimore, Dr. Stanislav Grof, the manuscript of an impressive work interpreting the results of his practice during the past fourteen years (first in Czechoslovakia and now in this country) of psycholytic therapy; that is to say, the treatment of nervous disorders, both neurotic and psychotic, with the aid of judiciously measured doses of LSD. And I have found so much of my thinking about mythic forms freshly illuminated by the findings here reported, that I am going to try in these last pages to render a suggestion of the types and depths of consciousness that Dr. Grof has fathomed in his searching of our inward sea. The title of the work, when it appears, will be *Agony and Ecstasy in Psychiatric Treatment* (Palo Alto: Science and Behavior Books, 1972).

Very briefly, the first order of induced experience that Dr. Grof reports upon, he has termed the "Aesthetic LSD Experience." In the main this corresponds to that which Aldous Huxley, in *The Doors of Perception,* described back in 1954, after he had swallowed and experienced the effects of four-tenths of a gram of mescalin. What is here experienced is such an astounding vivification, alteration and intensification, of all experiences of the senses that, as Huxley remarked, even a common garden chair in the sun is recognized as "inexpressibly wonderful, wonderful to the point, almost, of being terrifying." [9] Other, more profound effects may yield sensations of physical transformation, lightness, levitation, clairvoyance, or even the power to assume animal forms and the like, such as primitive shamans claim. In India such powers (called *siddhi*) are claimed by yogis, and are not supposed to have accrued to them from without, but to have arisen from within, awakened by their mystic training, being potential within us all. Aldous Huxley had a similar thought, which he formulated in Western terms, and of which I expect to have something to say a bit later on.

The second type of reaction, Dr. Grof has described as the "Psychodynamic LSD Experience," relating it to an extension of consciousness into what Jung termed the Personal Unconscious, and the activation there of those emotionally overloaded contents that are dealt with typically in a Freudian psychoanalysis. The grim tensions and terrified resistances to conscious scrutiny that are encountered on this level derive from various unconscious strains of moral, social, and prideful infantile ego-defenses, inappropriate to adulthood; and the mythological themes that in psychoanalytical literature have been professionally associated with the conflicts of these sessions—Oedipus complex, Electra complex, etc.—are not really (in their references here) mythological at all. They bear, in the context of these infantile biographical associations, no anagogical, transpersonal relevancy whatsoever, but are allegorical merely of childhood desires frustrated by actual or imagined parental prohibitions and threats. Furthermore, even when traditional mythological figures do appear in the fantasies of this Freudian stage, they will be allegorical merely of personal conflicts; most frequently, as Dr. Grof has observed, "the conflict between sexual feelings or activities and the religious taboos, as well as primitive fantasies about devils and hell or angels and heaven, related to narratives or threats and promises of adults." And it will be only when these personal "psychodynamic" materials will have been actively relived, along with their associated emotional, sensory, and ideational features, that the psychological "knot points" of the Personal Unconscious will have been sufficiently resolved for the deeper, inward, downward journey to proceed from personal-biographical to properly transpersonal (first biological, then metaphysical-mystical) realizations.

What Dr. Grof has observed is that, very much as patients during a Freudian psychoanalysis and in the "psychodynamic" stages

of a psycholytic treatment "relive" the basal fixations (and thereby
break the hold upon them) of their unconsciously rooted affect
and behavior patterns, so, in leaving this personal memory field .
behind, they begin to manifest both psychologically and physically
the symptomatology of a totally different order of relived experiences; those, namely, of the agony of actual birth: the moment
(indeed, the hours) of passive, helpless terror when the uterine
contractions suddenly began, and continued, and continued, and
continued; or the more active tortures of the second stage of de-
livery, when the cervix opened and propulsion through the birth
canal commenced—continuing with an unremitting intensification
of sheer fright and total agony, to a climax amounting practically
to an experience of annihilation; when suddenly, release, light!
the sharp pain of umbilical severance, suffocation until the bloodstream finds its new route to the lungs, and then, breath and breathing, on one's own! "The patients," states Dr. Grof, "spent hours in
agonizing pain, gasping for breath, with the color of their faces
changing from dead pale to dark purple. They were rolling on
the floor and discharging extreme tensions in muscular tremors,
twitches and complex twisting movements. The pulse rate was
frequently doubled, and it was threadlike; there was often nausea
with occasional vomiting and excessive sweating.

"Subjectively," he continues, "these experiences were of a transpersonal nature—they had a much broader framework than the
body and lifespan of a single individual. The experiencers were
identifying with many individuals or groups of individuals at the
same time; in the extreme the identification involved all suffering
mankind, past, present and future." "The phenomena observed
here," he states again, "are of a much more fundamental nature
and have different dimensions than those of the Freudian stage."
They are, in fact, of a mythological transpersonal order, not dis-
torted to refer (as in the Freudian field) to the accidents of an individual life, but opening outward, as well as inward, to what
James Joyce termed "the grave and constant in human sufferings."

For example, when reliving in the course of psycholytic treatment the nightmare of the first stage of the birth trauma—when the uterine contractions commence and the locked-in child, in sudden fright and pain, is awakened to a consciousness of itself in danger—the utterly terrified subject is overwhelmed by an acute experience of the very ground of being as anguish. Fantasies of inquisitorial torture come to mind, metaphysical anguish and existential despair: an identification with Christ crucified ("My God, my God, why hast thou forsaken me?"), Prometheus bound to the mountain crag, or Ixion to his whirling wheel. The mythic mode is of the Buddha's "All life is sorrowful": born in fear and pain, expiring in fear and pain, with little but fear and pain between. "Vanity of vanities, all is vanity." The question of "meaning" here becomes obsessive, and if the LSD session terminates on this note, there will generally remain a sense of life as loathsome, meaningless, a hateful, joyless inferno, with no way out either in space or in time, "no exit"—except possibly by suicide, which, if chosen, will be of the passive, quietly helpless kind, by drowning, an overdose of sleeping pills, or the like.

Passing to an intense reliving of the second stage of the birth trauma, on the other hand—that of the tortured struggle in the birth canal—the mood and the imagery become violent, not passive but active suffering being the dominant experience here, with elements of aggression and sadomasochistic passion: illusions of horrendous battles, struggles with prodigious monsters, overwhelming tides and waters, wrathful gods, rites of terrible sacrifice, sexual orgies, judgment scenes, and so on. The subject identifies himself simultaneously with both the victims and the aggressive forces of such conflicts, and as the intensity of the general agony mounts, it approaches and finally breaks beyond the pain threshold in an excruciating crisis of what Dr. Grof has aptly named "volcanic ecstasy." Here all extremes of pain and pleasure, joy and terror, murderous aggression and passionate love are united and transcended. The relevant mythic imagery is of religions reveling in suffering, guilt, and sacrifice: visions of the wrath of God, the universal Deluge, Sodom and Gomorrah, Moses and the Decalogue, Christ's Via Crucis, Bacchic orgies, terrible Aztec sacrifices, Shiva the Destroyer, Kali's gruesome dance of the Burning Ground, and the phallic rites of Cybele. Suicides in this Dionysian mood are of the violent type: blowing out one's brains, leaping from heights, before trains, etc. Or one is moved to meaningless murder. The subject is obsessed with feelings of aggressive tension mixed with anticipation of catastrophe; extremely irritable and with a tendency to provoke conflicts. The world is seen as full of threats and oppression. Carnivals and wild kicks, rough parties with promiscuous sex, alcoholic orgies and bacchanalian dances, violence of all kinds, vertiginous adventures and explosions mark the life styles struck with the ferocity of this stage of the birth experience. In the course of a therapeutic session a regression to this level may be carried to culmination in an utterly terrifying crisis of actual ego-death, complete annihilation on all levels, followed by a grandiose, expansive sense of release, rebirth, and redemption, with enormous feelings and experiences of decompression, expansion of space, and blinding, radiant light: visions of heavenly blue and gold, columned gigantic halls with crystal chandeliers, peacock-feather fantasies, rainbow spectrums, and the like. The subjects, feeling cleansed and purged, are moved now by an overwhelming love for all mankind, a new appreciation of the arts and of natural beauties, great zest for life, and a forgiving, wonderfully reconciled and expansive sense of God in his heaven and all right with the world.

    Dr. Grof has found (and this I find extremely interesting) that the differing imageries of the various world religions tend to appear and to support his patients variously during the successive stages of their sessions. In immediate association with the relived agonies of the birth trauma, the usual imagery brought to mind is of the Old and New Testaments, together with (occasionally) certain Greek, Egyptian, or other pagan counterparts. However, when the agony has been accomplished and the release experienced of "birth"—actually, a "second" or "spiritual" birth, released from the unconscious fears of the former, "once born" personal condition—the symbology radically changes. Instead of mainly Biblical, Greek, and Christian themes, the analogies now point rather toward the great Orient, chiefly India. "The source of these experiences," states Dr. Grof, "is obscure, and their resemblance to the Indian descriptions flabbergasting." He likens their tone to that of the timeless intrauterine state *before* the onset of delivery: a blissful, peaceful, contentless condition, with deep, positive feelings of joy, love, and accord, or even union with the Universe and/or God. Paradoxically, this ineffable state is at once contentless and all-containing, of nonbeing yet more than being, no ego and yet an extension of self that embraces the whole cosmos. And here I think of that passage in Aldous Huxley's *The Doors of Perception* where he describes the sense that he experienced in his first mescalin adventure of his mind opening to ranges of wonder such as he had never before even imagined.

> Reflecting on my experience [Huxley wrote], I find myself agreeing with the eminent Cambridge philosopher, Dr. C. D. Broad, "that we should do well to consider much more seriously than we have hitherto been inclined to do the type of theory which Bergson put forward in connection with memory and sense perception. The suggestion is that the function of the brain and nervous system and sense organs is in the main *eliminative* and not productive. Each person is at each moment capable of remembering all that has ever happened to him and of perceiving everything that is happening everywhere in the universe. The function of the brain and nervous system is to protect us from being overwhelmed and confused by this mass of largely useless and irrelevant knowledge, by shutting out most of what we should otherwise perceive or remember at any moment, and leaving only that very small and special selection which is likely to be practically useful."
>
> According to such a theory, each one of us is potentially Mind at Large. But in so far as we are animals, our business is at all costs to survive. To make biological survival possible,

Mind at Large has to be funneled through the reducing valve of
the brain and nervous system. What comes out at the other end
is a measly trickle of the kind of consciousness which will help
us to stay alive on the surface of this particular planet. . . .
Most people, most of the time, know only what comes through
the reducing valve and is consecrated as genuinely real by the
local language. Certain persons, however, seem to be born with
a kind of by-pass that circumvents the reducing valve. In others
temporary by-passes may be acquired either spontaneously, or
as the result of deliberate "spiritual exercises," or through hyp-
nosis, or by means of drugs. Through these permanent or temporary by-passes there flows, not indeed the perception "of everything that is happening everywhere in the universe" (for the
by-pass does not abolish the reducing valve, which still excludes
the total content of Mind at Large), but something more than,
and above all something different from, the carefully selected
utilitarian material which our narrowed, individual minds regard as a complete, or at least sufficient, picture of reality." [10]

Now it strikes me as evident through all this that the imagery of
mythology, stemming as it does from the psyche and reflecting
back to the same, represents in its various inflections various
stages or degrees of the opening of ego-consciousness toward the
prospect of what Aldous Huxley has here called Mind at Large.
Plato in the *Timaeus* (90 c-d) declares that "there is only one way
in which one being can serve another, and this is by giving him
his proper nourishment and motion: and the motions that are akin
to the divine principle within us are the thoughts and revolutions
of the universe." It is these, I would say, that are represented in
myth. As illustrated in the various mythologies of the peoples of
the world, however, the universals have been everywhere particu-
larized to the local sociopolitical context. As an old professor of
mine in Comparative Religions at the University of Munich used to
say: "In its subjective sense the religion of all mankind is one and
the same. In its objective sense, however, there are differing forms."

In the past, I think we can now say, the differing forms served the differing and often conflicting interests of the various societies, binding individuals to their local group horizons and ideals, whereas in the West today we have learned to recognize a distinction between the spheres and functions, on one hand, of society, practical survival, economic and political ends, and, on the other hand, sheerly psychological (or, as we used to say, spiritual) values. To return to the name, once more, of Dante: there is in the Fourth Treatise of the *Convito* a passage in which he discourses on the divinely ordained separation of state and Church, as symbolized historically in the joined yet separate histories of Rome and Jerusalem, the Empire and the Papacy. These are the two arms of God, not to be confused; and he rebukes the Papacy for its political interventions, the authority of the Church being properly "not of this world" but of Spirit—the relationship of which to the aims of this world is exactly that of Huxley's Mind at Large to the utilitarian ends of biological survival—which are all right and necessary too, but are not the same.

We live today—thank God!—in a secular state, governed by human beings (with all their inevitable faults) according to principles of law that are still developing and have originated not from Jerusalem but from Rome. The concept of the state, moreover, is yielding rapidly at this hour to the concept of the ecumene, i.e., the whole inhabited earth; and if nothing else unites us, the ecological crisis will. There is therefore neither any need any more, nor any possibility, for those locally binding, sociopolitically bounded, differing forms of religion "in its objective sense" which have held men separate in the past, giving to God the things that are Caesar's and to Caesar the things that are God's.

"God is an intelligible sphere whose center is everywhere and circumference nowhere." So we are told in a little twelfth-century book known as *The Book of the Twenty-four Philosophers*. Each of us—whoever and wherever he may be—is then the center, and within him, whether he knows it or not, is that Mind at Large, the laws of which are the laws not only of all minds but of all space as well. For, as I have already pointed out, we are the children of this beautiful planet that we have lately seen photographed from the moon. We were not delivered into it by some god, but have come forth from it. We are its eyes and mind, its seeing and its thinking. And the earth, together with its sun, this light around which it flies like a moth, came forth, we are told, from a nebula; and that nebula, in turn, from space. So that we are the mind, ultimately, of space. No wonder, then, if its laws and ours are the same! Likewise, our depths are the depths of space, whence all those gods sprang that men's minds in the past projected onto animals and plants, onto hills and streams, the planets in their courses, and their own peculiar social observances.

Our mythology now, therefore, is to be of infinite space and its light, which is without as well as within. Like moths, we are caught in the spell of its allure, flying to it outward, to the moon and beyond, and flying to it, also, inward. On our planet itself all dividing horizons have been shattered. We can no longer hold our loves at home and project our aggressions elsewhere; for on this spaceship Earth there is no "elsewhere" any more. And no mythology that continues to speak or to teach of "elsewheres" and "outsiders" meets the requirement of this hour.

And so, to return to our opening question: What is—or what is to be—the new mythology?

It is—and will forever be, as long as our human race exists— the old, everlasting, perennial mythology, in its "subjective sense," poetically renewed in terms neither of a remembered past nor of a projected future, but of now: addressed, that is to say, not to the flattery of "peoples," but to the waking of individuals in the knowledge of themselves, not simply as egos fighting for place on the surface of this beautiful planet, but equally as centers of Mind at Large—each in his own way at one with all, and with no horizons.

Reference Notes

II. The Emergence of Mankind

1. Carl Etter, *Ainu Folklore: Traditions and Culture of the Vanishing Aborigines of Japan* (Chicago: Wilcox and Follett, 1949), pp. 56–57.
2. George Bird Grinnell, *Blackfoot Lodge Tales* (New York: Charles Scribner's Sons, 1916), pp. 104–112. Joseph Campbell, *The Masks of God,* Vol. I, *Primitive Mythology* (New York: The Viking Press, 1959), pp. 282–286.
3. William Wyatt Gill, *Myths and Songs from the South Pacific* (London: Henry S. King and Company, 1876), pp. 77–79; cited in *The Masks of God,* Vol. I, pp. 198–199.

III. The Importance of Rites

1. Robinson Jeffers, *Roan Stallion, Tamar, and Other Poems* (New York: Horace Liveright, 1925), p. 232.

IV. The Separation of East and West

1. C. G. Jung, *Psychology and Alchemy, Collected Works,* Vol. 12 (Princeton: Princeton University Press, second ed., 1968), p. 222.
2. Shankaracharya, *Vivekachudamani* 293, 296, 307.

3. *Manavadharmashastra* 5. 147–151, 154 and 166.
4. *Grimnismol* 23.
5. Julius Oppert, "Die Daten der Genesis," *Königliche Gesellschaft der Wissenschaften zu Göttingen,* Nachrichten, No. 10 (May 1877), pp. 201–223.

V. The Confrontation of East and West in Religion

1. W. B. Yeats, *A Vision* (New York: The Macmillan Company; First Collier Books Edition, 1966), p. 300.
2. *The Collected Poems of W. B. Yeats* (New York: The Macmillan Company, 1956), pp. 184–185.
3. *Chhandogya Upanishad* 6.9–16.
4. *Brihadaranyaka Upanishad* 1.4.6 and 7, in part.
5. Daisetz T. Suzuki, "The Role of Nature in Zen Buddhism," in Olga Fröbe Kapteyn, ed., *Eranos-Jahrbuch 1953* (Zurich: Rhein-Verlag, 1954), p. 294.
6. Ibid., p. 319.
7. Ibid., pp. 298–299.
8. Ibid., p. 303.
9. Ibid., p. 308.
10. *Skanda Purana,* Vol. II, *Vishnukanda, Karttikamasa Mahatmya,* Ch. 17; cf. Heinrich Zimmer, *Myths and Symbols in Indian Art and Civilization,* Joseph Campbell, ed., Bollingen Series VI (New York: Pantheon Books, 1946), pp. 175 ff.

VI. The Inspiration of Oriental Art

1. Arthur Avalon (Sir John Woodroffe), *The Serpent Power* (Madras: Ganesh and Co., 1913, 1924, 1931, etc.), pp. 317–478.
2. Sermons and Collations, xcvi; translation by C. de B. Evans, from Franz Pfeiffer, *Meister Eckhart,* Vol. I (London: John M. Watkins, 1924, 1947), p. 240.
3. William Blake, *The Marriage of Heaven and Hell,* in Geoffrey Keynes, *Poetry and Prose of William Blake* (New York: Random House, 1927), p. 197.
4. Hajime Nakamura, "The Vitality of Religion in Asia," in *Cultural Freedom in Asia:* Proceedings of a Conference Held at Rangoon, Burma, Feb. 17–20, 1955, Convened by the Congress for Cultural Freedom (Rutland, Vt.: Charles E. Tuttle, 1956), p. 56.

5. J. Huizinga, *Homo Ludens: A Study of the Play-Element in Culture* (London: Routledge and Kegan Paul, 1949), pp. 34–35.
6. *Bhagavad Gita* 2:47 and 5:5.
7. From the Liao Chai Stories of P'u Sung-ling, translated by Rose Quong, in *Chinese Ghost and Love Stories* (New York: Pantheon Books, 1946), pp. 305 ff.

VII. Zen

1. *Kena Upanishad* 1.3.
2. Adapted from a translation by the Roshi Sokei-an, published in *The Cat's Yawn* (New York: First Zen Institute of America, 1947), p. 11.
3. Daisetz Teitaro Suzuki, *Essays in Zen Buddhism (Second Series)*, (London: Rider and Company, 1950), p. 87.
4. Adapted from ibid., p. 72.

VIII. The Mythology of Love

1. Wolfram von Eschenbach, *Parzival* XV, 740 (Karl Lachmann edition, Berlin and Leipzig, 6th ed., 1926), pp. 348–349.
2. There is an excellent translation by Helen M. Mustard and Charles E. Passage, published by Alfred A. Knopf and Random House, A Vintage Book, No. V-188.

IX. Mythologies of War and Peace

1. Josephus, *De Bello Judaico* 1.4. 1–6.
2. Translation by Dwight Goddard, *Laozus Tao and Wu Wei* (New York: Brentano's, 1919).
3. *Bhagavad Gita* 2.27, 30, 23.
4. Ibid. 2.31–32.

X. Schizophrenia—the Inward Journey

1. Vol. 96, Article 3, pp. 853–876, January 27, 1962.
2. Joseph Campbell, *The Hero with a Thousand Faces* (New York: Pantheon Books, 1949), p. 30.
3. Vol. 69, No. 1, February 1967.
4. *The Masks of God*, Vol. I, Chapters 6 and 8.
5. These accounts are from Knud Rasmussen, *Across Arctic Amer-*

ica (New York and London: G. P. Putnam's Sons, 1927), pp. 82–86, and H. Osterman, *The Alaskan Eskimos, as Described in the Posthumous Notes of Dr. Knud Rasmussen. Report of the Fifth Thule Expedition 1921–24.* Vol. X, No. 3 (Copenhagen: Nordisk Forlag, 1952), pp. 97–99.

6. (New York: Pantheon Books, 1967), Chapter 7, "A Ten-Day Voyage."
7. Translation by Arthur W. Ryder, *The Panchatantra* (Chicago: The University of Chicago Press, 1925), pp. 434–441.
8. *Collected Works,* Vol. I, pp. 3–92.

XI. The Moon Walk—the Outward Journey

1. Robinson Jeffers, "Roan Stallion," in op. cit., p. 20.
2. Alan Watts, "Western Mythology: Its Dissolution and Transformation," in Joseph Campbell, ed., *Myths, Dreams, and Religion* (New York: E. P. Dutton and Co., 1970), p. 20.
3. Ibid., p. 24.
4. (Cambridge: Cambridge University Press, 1964), p. 95.

XII. Envoy: No More Horizons

1. Walt Whitman, *Leaves of Grass,* Version of the First (1855) Edition, section 48, lines 1262–1280, edited with an Introduction by Malcolm Cowley (New York: The Viking Press, 1961), pp. 82–83.
2. *Brihadaranyaka Upanishad* 1.4.6–10, abridged.
3. *The Gospel According to Thomas* 99:28–30 and 95:24–28; translation by Guillaumont, Puech, Quispel, Till, and abd al Masih (New York: Harper & Row, 1959), pp. 55 and 43.
4. Whitman, op. cit., Section 52, lines 1329–1330; p. 86.
5. H. Heras, S.J., "The Problem of Ganapati," *Tamil Culture,* Vol. III, No. 2 (Tuticorn, April 1954).
6. Thomas Merton, "Symbolism: Communication or Communion?" in *New Directions 20* (New York: New Directions, 1968), pp. 11–12.
7. Ibid., pp. 1 and 2.
8. Ibid., pp. 1 and 11.
9. Aldous Huxley, *The Doors of Perception* (New York: Harper & Row, 1954), p. 54.
10. Ibid., pp. 22–24.

Index

FOR THE BEST IN PAPERBACKS, LOOK FOR THE

In every corner of the world, on every subject under the sun, Penguin represents quality and variety—the very best in publishing today.

For complete information about books available from Penguin—including Puffins, Penguin Classics, and Compass—and how to order them, write to us at the appropriate address below. Please note that for copyright reasons the selection of books varies from country to country.

In the United Kingdom: Please write to *Dept. EP, Penguin Books Ltd, Bath Road, Harmondsworth, West Drayton, Middlesex UB7 0DA.*

In the United States: Please write to *Penguin Putnam Inc., P.O. Box 12289 Dept. B, Newark, New Jersey 07101-5289* or call 1-800-788-6262.

In Canada: Please write to *Penguin Books Canada Ltd, 10 Alcorn Avenue, Suite 300, Toronto, Ontario M4V 3B2.*

In Australia: Please write to *Penguin Books Australia Ltd, P.O. Box 257, Ringwood, Victoria 3134.*

In New Zealand: Please write to *Penguin Books (NZ) Ltd, Private Bag 102902, North Shore Mail Centre, Auckland 10.*

In India: Please write to *Penguin Books India Pvt Ltd, 11 Panchsheel Shopping Centre, Panchsheel Park, New Delhi 110 017.*

In the Netherlands: Please write to *Penguin Books Netherlands bv, Postbus 3507, NL-1001 AH Amsterdam.*

In Germany: Please write to *Penguin Books Deutschland GmbH, Metzlerstrasse 26, 60594 Frankfurt am Main.*

In Spain: Please write to *Penguin Books S. A., Bravo Murillo 19, 1° B, 28015 Madrid.*

In Italy: Please write to *Penguin Italia s.r.l., Via Benedetto Croce 2, 20094 Corsico, Milano.*

In France: Please write to *Penguin France, Le Carré Wilson, 62 rue Benjamin Baillaud, 31500 Toulouse.*

In Japan: Please write to *Penguin Books Japan Ltd, Kaneko Building, 2-3-25 Koraku, Bunkyo-Ku, Tokyo 112.*

In South Africa: Please write to *Penguin Books South Africa (Pty) Ltd, Private Bag X14, Parkview, 2122 Johannesburg.*